CASES IN FINANCE
Second Edition

THE IRWIN SERIES IN FINANCE, INSURANCE AND REAL ESTATE

Stephen A. Ross
Sterling Professor of Economics and Finance
Yale University
Consulting Editor

FINANCIAL MANAGEMENT

Block and Hirt
Foundations of Financial Management
Eighth Edition

Brooks
PC FinGame: *The Financial Management Decision Game*
Version 2.0 - DOS and Windows

Bruner
Case Studies in Finance: *Managing for Corporate Value Creation*
Second Edition

Eun and Resnick
International Financial Management

Fruhan, Kester, Mason, Piper and Ruback
Case Problems in Finance
Tenth Edition

Helfert
Techniques of Financial Analysis: *A Modern Approach*
Ninth Edition

Higgins
Analysis for Financial Management
Fourth Edition

Levich
International Financial Markets

Nunnally and Plath
Cases in Finance
Second Edition

Ross, Westerfield and Jaffe
Corporate Finance
Fourth Edition

Ross, Westerfield and Jordan
Essentials of Corporate Finance

Ross, Westerfield and Jordan
Fundamentals of Corporate Finance
Third Edition

Stonehill and Eiteman
Finance: *An International Perspective*

White
Financial Analysis with an Electronic Calculator
Second Edition

INVESTMENTS

Bodie, Kane and Marcus
Essentials of Investments
Second Edition

Bodie, Kane and Marcus
Investments
Third Edition

Cohen, Zinbarg and Zeikel
Investment Analysis and Portfolio Management
Fifth Edition

Hirt and Block
Fundamentals of Investment Management
Fifth Edition

Lorie, Dodd and Kimpton
The Stock Market: *Theories and Evidence*
Second Edition

Morningstar, Inc. and Remaley
U.S. Equities OnFloppy
Annual Edition

Shimko
The Innovative Investor
Version 2.0 - Lotus and Excel

FINANCIAL INSTITUTIONS AND MARKETS

Flannery and Flood
Flannery and Flood's BankMaster: *A Financial Services Simulation*

Rose
Commercial Bank Management: *Producing and Selling Financial Services*
Third Edition

Rose
Money and Capital Markets: *Financial Institutions and Instruments in a Global Marketplace*
Sixth Edition

Rose and Kolari
Financial Institutions: *Understanding and Managing Financial Services*
Fifth Edition

Santomero and Babbel
Financial Markets, Instruments, and Institutions

Saunders
Financial Institutions Management: *A Modern Perspective*
Second Edition

REAL ESTATE

Berston
California Real Estate Principles
Seventh Edition

Berston
California Real Estate Practice
Sixth Edition

Brueggeman and Fisher
Real Estate Finance and Investments
Tenth Edition

Lusht
Real Estate Valuation: *Principles and Applications*

Smith and Corgel
Real Estate Perspectives: *An Introduction to Real Estate*
Second Edition

FINANCIAL PLANNING AND INSURANCE

Allen, Melone, Rosenbloom and VanDerhei
Pension Planning: *Pensions, Profit-Sharing, and Other Deferred Compensation Plans*
Eighth Edition

Crawford
Law and the Life Insurance Contract
Seventh Edition

Crawford
Life and Health Insurance Law
LOMA Edition

Hirsch
Casualty Claim Practice
Sixth Edition

Kapoor, Dlabay and Hughes
Personal Finance
Fourth Edition

Kellison
Theory of Interest
Second Edition

Skipper
International Risk and Insurance

CASES IN FINANCE
Second Edition

Bennie H. Nunnally, Jr.
and
D. Anthony Plath

University of North Carolina - Charlotte

Irwin
McGraw-Hill

Boston, Massachusetts   Burr Ridge, Illinois   Dubuque, Iowa
Madison, Wisconsin   New York, New York   San Francisco, California   St. Louis, Missouri

Irwin/McGraw-Hill

A Division of The **McGraw·Hill** *Companies*

Irwin Book Team

Publisher: *Michael W. Junior*
Sponsoring editor: *Gina Huck*
Editorial Coordinator: *Wendi Sweetland*
Marketing manager: *Katie Rose*
Project supervisor: *Maggie Rathke*
Production supervisor: *Pat Frederickson*

ISBN 0-256-15385-X

Printed in the United States of America

6 7 8 9 BKM BKM 0 9 8 7 6 5 4 3 2 1

To our parents and families, and to all the others who gave encouragement.

Preface

Why a Casebook?

The field of finance is exciting, sophisticated, and dynamic; and students should fully participate in this excitement. You are now preparing yourself to make competent decisions in a variety of business situations. Your focus of study must apply directly to the business decisions at hand and be relevant to the fast-paced financial world. In order to make sound financial decisions, you need to understand key financial management topics. The forty-eight cases in this book offer that opportunity, covering such topics as financial statement analysis, working capital management, capital budgeting, intermediate and long-term financing, risk management, valuation, and cost of capital and dividends. These cases are vehicles for you and your instructor to work together to keep this primary purpose of the study of finance plainly in view.

The purpose of this casebook is to reinforce and expand upon the theoretical material learned in the introductory undergraduate business finance course. Such reinforcement and expansion is accomplished not only by presenting relatively familiar material in a case format, but by the unique character of case study. First, today's student is absolutely correct in his or her insistence that business courses be relevant as well as firmly grounded in existing theory. Case study fulfills these requirements in a most efficient way. Since many of the cases in this book are based upon real company situations we have personally been involved with, you are able to see clearly how the theory of finance applies to the practical world.

Second, case study provides the opportunity for you to exchange ideas with your classmates and professor and serves as a tool to broaden and deepen your understanding of the material in question. This "learning by doing" environment adds an enjoyable and useful learning component to your education.

Who Should Use This Casebook ... and How It Should be Used

This book is intended primarily for use in conjunction with a standard introductory finance textbook or as the foundation for an introductory case course. The cases may be used as reinforcement of theory in an intermediate course as well. The flexibility of the case method and the varied nature of classroom environments are clear complements.

The cases are meant to generate discussion, focusing upon three elements: industry and company setting, the underlying finance theory, and the particular decision at hand. The first time you read a case you will become familiar with the broad issues. A closer second reading will reveal the detail necessary to address the problematic issues in each case. Finally, the questions at the end of each case will help you decide what action you might take to remedy the given dilemma. These questions vary in level of difficulty and ambiguity and are designed to help you learn through analysis and discussion.

Elements of the Casebook

This casebook has characteristics that make it a more pertinent and beneficial learning tool. Many of the case questions begin with the opportunity for you to examine compound growth data for sales and earnings for the given company. Completing this calculation can help clarify the importance of comparisons or benchmarks in economic analysis. Additional research or references are not necessary for the efficient handling of the cases. Often industry growth information is given as a part of the case narrative. In this way, the use and meaning of the benchmark is reinforced.

Additionally, the second edition contains many new features to enhance your learning experience.

- The number of cases have increased from 40 to 48, with 14 new cases to this edition -- providing a wider variety of coverage, especially in the areas of capital budgeting and cost of capital.
- More emphasis is placed on multinational situations. Specifically, "Clearline Filters," "Narodno Pivo dd," and "Carolina Furniture" address that aspect of finance.
- More emphasis is placed on ethical situations that may arise in the decision-making process. These concerns are addressed in "Specialty Chemicals, Inc.," "Retirement Planning," "Personality Associates," "Commercial Builders," and "Restore Inc."
- Cases include more background information for each individual company. Also, like the first edition, the new cases are based upon replicated company situations, which helps bring concepts to life.
- Select cases (14) have been updated to reflect the most current information.
- One case within each of the six sections is indicated as a "Challenge Case," which is designed to provide the opportunity for a more demanding quantitative approach to the elements of a particular section.

Quality Assurance

All of the cases have been class tested by our own students and in classrooms across the country. In fact, approximately 800 students and their professors have used the cases, providing us with valuable feedback.

It is important to you and to us that you use a dependable book that "works well." In addition to our attention to detail, the book has been proofread by accuracy checkers. These individuals bring to the text significant knowledge of finance, as well as an eye for detail and accuracy. This will be of great benefit to you as you work through the cases. Furthermore, we are confident that your experience with the book will be a satisfying one.

NOTE TO THE INSTRUCTOR

Teaching Notes

The Teaching Notes that accompany this casebook are for the purpose of facilitating the class discussion. The Notes begin with an outline of the learning objectives for the case. Such objectives relate directly to the administrative situation and the underlying theory reflected in the case, and the end-of-case questions. The Notes are clear and unambiguous. The Teaching Notes contain complete solutions to the questions presented in the casebook. In addition, each question is repeated preceding each solution.

Using the Casebook Data Disks

Each case that presents data in tabular form is represented by an electronic spreadsheet file contained on the data disks that accompany the casebook. These spreadsheet files are designed to operate on any IBM-compatible microcomputer platform that can run Excel. The spreadsheet files will function with any spreadsheet software package that is able to read Lotus files, including Quattro, and Quattro Pro.

Using the spreadsheet files is quite simple. Each file contains all of the data tables shown in the text for a given case, and the spreadsheets contain no special mathematical formulas or macro control sequences to confuse or distract students. The purpose of the spreadsheet templates is to provide students with a foundation for the construction of electronic models that address the questions and problems presented in the casebook, without forcing students to endure the tedium associated with data entry.

Irwin Custom Publishing

Everyone uses cases in a different way—for class discussion, team projects and presentations, or homework assignments. Therefore, a casebook needs to be flexible. IRWIN Custom Publishing provides you with this flexibility by allowing you to create a customized casebook specifically suited to your course needs. For your convenience, an IRWIN Custom Publishing order form is included in your complimentary copy of the casebook, as well as in the Teaching Notes. The order form provides detailed information on this flexible packaging option.

Acknowledgments

The development of a casebook is helped significantly by the viewpoint and assistance of others who are knowledgeable in the field. This book has benefitted from several persons who have given generously of their time, energy, and knowledge. Professors who have taught from, reviewed or checked the accuracy of the cases are:

Carroll D. Aby, Northwestern State University
Abdul Aziz, Humboldt State University
Curtis J. Bacon, Southern Oregon State College
Marvin E. Camburn, Illinois Benedictine College
Yashwand Dhatt, University of Southern Colorado
Cheri Etling, Wichita State University
Jon Ewert, College of Santa Fe
Elsie Fenic, Wright State University
Mohammed Ashraful Haque, Illinois College
Patricia Mathews, Mount Union College
Timothy Michaels, University of South Carolina - Columbia
Hersh Shefrin, Santa Clara University
Wonhi J. Synn, Elon College
Robert Sweeney, Wright State University.

Those who contributed cases to this collection are:

George W. Kester, Mark S. Bettner, and Elton "Skip" McGoun of Bucknell University; Michael D. Evans of Winthrop University; Edita K. Krajnovic of University of Ljubljana, Slovenia; Timothy B. Michael of the University of South Carolina - Columbia; A. Qayyam Khan of the University of Bridgeport; and John E. Baber of the University of North Carolina - Charlotte.

Our thanks to the editorial staff at Richard D. Irwin, specifically Wendi Sweetland and Gina Huck. We are extremely grateful to Bessie Truzy and J. Avery Love for word processing assistance. All errors remain solely our responsibility.

Contents

V. _Financial Structure, The Cost of Capital, and Dividend Policy_

VI. _Other Topics in Financial Management_

*= Challenge Cases

PART I

FINANCIAL ANALYSIS, PLANNING, AND STRATEGY

Case 1

Financial Ratio Analysis

Triple A Office Mart

Susan Burke, president of Triple A Office Mart, studied her notes for the afternoon meeting with the bank's commercial loan committee. The profitable company, organized in 1978, sold a complete line of office equipment, furniture, and supplies. Two stores operated in two adjoining states in the southwestern United States. Budgetary control of the two stores was centralized in the store and office complex which operated in the larger of the two cities. In preparation for the meeting, Burke wondered about the type of information the bank might have with which to make a decision on her loan. She was also concerned about how the bank would view a profitable company that needed to borrow funds.

The stores had operated profitably since their inception. Triple A was organized by Burke and a college roommate, Virginia Best, one year after their graduation. Best left the company after only three years to participate in an overseas venture. Her interest was sold to Burke at that time.

With the advent of the personal computer, a major component of company sales, and a general trend in the economy toward specialty stores, Triple A had experienced excellent growth in revenue and earnings. Table 1 illustrates a portion of the firm's sales and earnings history. Table 2 provides balance sheets for selected years.

The firm had issued no common stock or long-term debt in the recent past. In fact, the second store was opened in 1992 without any additional long-term financing. In the case of the new store, however, there was an increase in inventory and bank borrowing. The company's financial staff wondered if this were a normal state of affairs for an expansion situation. Triple A had traditionally handled its credits well, and the stockholders were generally satisfied with the firm's return on equity. (Stock was offered to the public for the first time in 1980).

The primary benefit to the company was the strong local economy. Although it was primarily a service economy, it supported Triple A almost perfectly. A nearby college of business administration, which published an economic report and forecast concerning the local economy, stated that since 1990 the growth of the local GNP had been in the range of 8–10 percent. Susan Burke had, as a long-range plan, every intention of participating in the region's growth and of contributing to it through the efficient operation of her firm.

In recent months during early 1996, there had been cause for concern on the part of company management. Prices from suppliers had risen and the firm's financial managers wondered about the effect of this upon profitability and the general operation of the business. The suppliers to the firm were varied, since the firm carried a wide range of office equipment and supplies. As a result, it was not possible to develop a strong and mutually supportive relationship with any one supplier. In general, the company had to deal with the vagaries of the economy.

Foremost in Burke's thinking was to maintain a sensible payout ratio for the equity investors, one which reflected the operational reality of the company. Firms that were similar in product line and sales pattern to Triple A paid a dividend which amounted to 30–60 percent of earnings. Growth in sales volume beyond the nominal growth in the economy usually came about as a result of market share being taken away from competitors. Triple A's management intended to survive in the region in which they operated. The relatively stable payout ratio which the company had maintained for several years seemed appropriate given revenue growth.

In preparation for her meeting with the bank, Susan Burke had concerns about the financial condition of her firm and whether there was a trend in the financial statements that might cause the bank to become wary of Triple A as a continuing customer. For example, Susan wondered whether the firm's inventory level had increased at a rate that was harmful to the firm's liquidity position. It was important to convince the bank that the firm was well run and that all aspects of its operation indicated managerial consistency and skill.

TABLE 1

Triple A Office Mart
Income Statement (selected years)

	1993	1994	1995	1996
Sales	$3,800,000	$4,180,000	$4,850,000	$6,000,000
Cost of goods sold	(2,460,000)	(2,975,000)	(3,200,000)	(4,180,000)
Gross profit	$1,340,000	$1,205,000	$1,650,000	$1,820,000
Selling, admin. and				
depreciation expenses	($684,000)	($820,000)	($898,408)	($1,015,467)
Interest	(30,780)	(30,780)	(42,372)	(35,313)
Profit before tax	$625,220	$354,220	$709,220	$769,220
Taxes	(187,566)	(106,266)	(212,766)	(230,766)
Net income	$437,654	$247,954	$496,454	$538,454

TABLE 2				
Triple A Office Mart				
Balance Sheet				
	1993	1994	1995	1996
Cash	$295,000	$326,040	$378,300	$468,000
Accounts receivable	11,400	12,540	20,700	18,000
Inventory	950,000	1,028,595	1,559,407	1,735,207
Total current assets	1,256,400	1,367,175	1,958,407	2,221,207
Property, plant, equip. (net)	450,000	501,600	501,600	503,000
Total assets	$1,706,400	$1,868,775	$2,460,007	$2,724,207
Accounts payable	$152,000	$167,200	$190,000	$300,000
Notes payable - bank	----	----	289,776	113,326
Accrued wages & taxes	114,000	125,000	145,500	180,000
Total current liabilities	266,000	292,200	625,276	593,326
Long-term debt	342,200	342,000	342,000	342,000
Common stock				
(120,000 shares)	600,000	600,000	600,000	600,000
Retained earnings	498,200	634,575	892,731	1,188,881
Total liabilities and equity	$1,706,400	$1,868,775	$2,460,007	$2,724,207

QUESTIONS

1. Calculate the compound average annual growth rate in sales and profit after tax for Triple A.

2. What are Triple A's earnings per share and dividends per share for each year shown in Tables 1 and 2?

3. Calculate some financial ratios for the company for the last three years shown. (Include profit margin, receivables collection period, current ratio, quick ratio, inventory turnover.) What has been the compound growth in inventory, and total current assets?

4. Comment on the trend of the financial ratios.

5. Is Triple A a good short-term borrowing client for the bank?

6. If the typical firm in the industry in which Triple A operates has a debt ratio of 52 percent, and a compound annual growth in gross profit of 8 percent, what advice would you give Triple A concerning its debt ratio?

7. If the company's compound sales growth slowed to half its present rate, what would be the likely effect upon external financing needs? What is the desired effect upon inventory if such a change occurs?

8. For a company such as Triple A, comment on the importance of inventory control and accounts receivable collection policy.

9. Why is there a difference between the company's sales growth and its profit growth? Specifically, how is the difference likely to influence borrowing needs? To what is the difference due? How should Triple A address this difference? Comment upon the firm's payout ratio relative to its sales growth. Is it appropriate? Why or why not?

10. Based upon the information provided in the case and upon your ratio analysis only, will the bank likely recommend more long-term borrowing for the firm or provide short-term funding?

Case 2

The Du Pont Method of Financial Analysis

Airline Profitability Analysis[*]

In March 1989, Robert Williams, a security analyst with Smith, Jones, and Brown Investment Company, was reviewing the 1988 financial statements for six commercial airlines (code names A, B, C, D, E, and F) the firm was considering for investment. Williams was asked to analyze comparatively the profitability of the airlines and to summarize his results for a forthcoming meeting with his manager. The most recent income statement and balance sheet data for each of the six airlines are shown in Table 1. Other selected financial data are shown in Table 2.

In his college finance course, Williams had been introduced to an especially revealing and useful method of evaluating a firm's profitability—the Du Pont method—which expresses the rate of return on assets (ROA) by multiplying the profit margin by the total asset turnover:

$$ROA = [\text{Net Income} \div \text{Sales}] \ x \ [\text{Sales} \div \text{Assets}] = \text{Margin} \ x \ \text{Turnover}.$$

The return on a firm's assets depends upon not only the profit per dollar of sales (margin), but also the sales per dollar of asset investment (turnover). Some firms such as grocery stores have low margins, but high turnover. Other firms, such as jewelry stores, have low turnover, but high profit margins. Even within the same industry, the combinations of margin and turnover may be different. For example, consider a discount jewelry chain (low margin, high turnover) versus an upscale jewelry store (high margin, low turnover). Firms that cut prices are often attempting to offset the resulting lower margins with higher turnover, thus increasing their ROAs.

He had also learned that the Du Pont equation can be expanded to obtain the rate of return on common equity (ROE):

$$
\begin{aligned}
ROE \ &= [\text{Net Income} \div \text{Sales}] \ x \ [\text{Sales} \div \text{Assets}] \ x \ [\text{Assets} \div \text{Common Equity}] \\
&= \text{Margin} \ x \ \text{Turnover} \ x \ \text{Leverage} \\
&= \text{ROA} \ x \ \text{Leverage}
\end{aligned}
$$

[*] This case was prepared by Mark S. Bettner and George W. Kester, both of Bucknell University, whose cooperation is acknowledged with appreciation.

If a company uses 100 percent equity financing, its ROE would be equal to its ROA since its total assets would be equal to its common equity. In this case, the firm uses no debt financing and the leverage multiplier (total assets divided by common equity) would be equal to 1.0. However, if less than 100 percent equity financing is used, the leverage multiplier would be greater than 1.0 and ROE would exceed ROA. Note that both positive and negative ROAs are magnified by the leverage that results from the use of debt. Of course, the ROEs can be calculated directly by dividing net income by common equity. However, the Du Pont method is more revealing by showing how profit margin, turnover, and leverage interact to determine ROE.

Williams had learned that the Du Pont method is useful for evaluating a firm's ROA over time as well as in relation to other firms in the same industry. Thus, he wondered if it could be useful for analyzing the six airlines.

Williams realized that a picture is worth a thousand words, or, in the case of financial analysis, a thousand numbers. Figure 1 shows a graphic depiction of the Du Pont method. This chart illustrates the determinants of a firm's profitability and the effects that various policies and decisions are likely to have on a firm's ROE.

For example, the effects of improving asset turnover can be easily traced through the chart to the likely impact on ROE, thus highlighting the importance of effective cash, receivables, and inventory management, and the efficient utilization of fixed assets. Similarly, the effect of improved profitability through greater expense control can be traced through the chart.

Williams was aware, however, that changes in one variable may affect one or more of the other variables included in the chart. For example, tighter control of receivables may result in additional expenses, as well as a decline in sales. Or an increase in fixed assets to expand capacity, which initially reduces asset turnover, may increase a firm's expected sales and profits.

As an aid to understanding the determinants of airline profitability, Williams adapted the Du Pont chart to the airline industry. The result is shown in Figure 2. In addition to relating ROE to profit margin, turnover, and leverage, the Du Pont chart shown in Figure 2 shows the determinants of revenue for airlines.

Revenue for an airline is determined by traffic and yield. Traffic, or revenue passenger-miles, refers to the number of miles passengers actually fly on the airline's route system. Yield refers to the revenue received per passenger-mile. An airline's traffic is in turn determined by its capacity and load factor. Capacity, or available seat-miles, refers to the number of miles passengers would
fly on the airline's route system if all seats were filled for all flights. Load factor measures the percentage of capacity actually utilized (traffic divided by capacity).

An airline's efficiency is often measured by expressing operating expenses as unit costs (per available seat-mile).

TABLE 1						
The Du Pont Method						
Airline Financial Statements						
Fiscal Year Ended 1988						
($ millions)						
Income Statement:	**A**	**B**	**C**	**D**	**E**	**F**
Revenue	$8,824.3	$814.4	$6,915.4	$860.4	$8,981.7	$5,707.0
Operating expenses	(8,017.8)	(743.9)	(6,418.3)	(774.4)	(8,316.8)	(5,273.4)
Operating profit	$806.5	$70.5	$497.1	$86.0	$664.9	$433.6
Nonoperating income	$143.3	$10.7	$56.3	$19.3	$538.2	($40.9)
Interest expense	(209.1)	(18.8)	(97.5)	(19.9)	(214.3)	(123.2)
Profit before tax	$740.7	$62.4	$455.9	$85.4	$988.8	$269.5
Income taxes	$263.9)	($24.9)	($149.0)	($27.4)	($388.9)	($104.5)
Net profit before nonrecurring items	$476.8	$37.5	$306.9	$58.0	$599.9	$165.0
Nonrecurring income	$0.0	$0.0	$0.0	$0.0	$524.4	$0.0
Net profit	$476.8	$37.5	$306.9	$58.0	$1,124.3	$165.0
Balance Sheet:						
Cash	$54.9	$8.2	$822.8	$210.0	$1,086.8	$78.0
Marketable securities	1,231.7	40.3	0.0	0.0	45.8	0.0
Accounts receivable	833.6	52.5	644.5	37.0	743.0	381.1
Other current assets	524.6	43.2	183.9	18.0	274.3	362.4
Total current assets	$2,644.8	$144.2	$1,651.2	$265.0	$2,149.9	$821.5
Net fixed assets	$6,312.3	$483.7	$3,566.2	$1,036.0	$3,941.3	$3,163.3
Other assets	835.1	102.3	530.9	7.4	609.5	1,364.1
Total assets	$9,792.2	$730.2	$5,748.3	$1,308.4	$6,700.7	$5,348.9
Notes payable	$78.6	$0.0	$16.2	$0.0	$446.2	$0.0
Accounts payable	710.4	81.6	558.6	35.3	495.1	371.1
Accrued expenses	1,072.0	38.4	118.3	76.2	1,074.9	433.4
Current maturities	134.6	7.0	20.3	10.0	85.4	85.7
Other current liabilities	800.0	47.2	678.5	31.4	767.5	318.9
Total current liabilities	$2,795.6	$174.2	$1,391.9	$152.9	$2,869.1	$1,209.1
Long-term debt	$1,206.5	$130.9	$563.1	$369.5	$1,648.9	$1,332.9
Capital leases	1,543.0	40.2	166.4	0.0	411.3	0.0
Other liabilities	949.1	78.4	1,418.1	218.6	542.8	737.4
Total liabilities	$6,494.2	$423.7	$3,549.5	$741.0	$5,472.1	$3,279.4
Preferred stock	$150.0	$0.0	$0.0	$0.0	$2.5	$0.0
Common equity	3,148.0	306.5	2,208.8	567.4	1,226.1	2,069.5
Total liabilities & equity	$9,792.2	$730.2	$5,748.3	$1,308.4	$6,700.7	$5,348.9

Source: *Compact Disclosure* (Bethesda, Maryland: Disclosure), various issues.

TABLE 2

The Du Pont Method
Other Selected Financial Data
Fiscal Year 1988
($ millions)

	A	B	C	D	E	F
Operating margin*	15.4%	12.9%	12.3%	17.7%	13.2%	11.6%
Load factor	63.5%	54.4%	57.1%	57.7%	67.9%	61.3%
Price-to-earnings ratio	5.6	7.8	7.5	9.4	9.4	9.2

Notes: * Operating margin is computed by dividing operating income before depreciation and amortization by revenue.

Source: *Ratings and Reports, Value Line Investment Survey*, September 25, 1992, pp. 251-264.

NOTE:

For preparation of this case, students are encouraged to conduct research on the background, trends, and problems of the airline industry.

QUESTIONS

1. What is the Du Pont method? That is, how does it differ from the more familiar ratio analysis?

2. Using the Du Pont method, calculate the profit margin, asset turnover, return on assets (ROA), and return on equity (ROE) for each of the six airlines.

3. Evaluate the results in terms of the determinants of ROE.

4. Robert Williams wondered if an airline's revenue could be increased simply by increasing its yield (price per passenger-mile). Using Figure 2 as a frame of reference, what do you think?

5. Does the Du Pont method seem relevant for the airline industry? Why or why not?

6.   How are financial ratios assessed? That is, how is the information gained from financial ratio analysis evaluated in order to provide the most useful information?

7.   In terms of a time frame, is there a probable minimum number of years or periods which would maximize the usefulness of ratio analysis, particularly the Du Pont method?

Case 3

Time Value of Money Analysis

Retirement Planning, Inc.

Mike Abbott, president of Retirement Planning, Inc., was delighted to receive a call from John Jordan. John had been referred by Joe Jones, a local CPA. John was interested in planning for retirement. He had saved consistently over the years and participated in a company-sponsored retirement plan, John was not sure how comfortable he would be during his retirement years. Mike and John agreed to meet the following Monday to review John's finances. It was agreed that John's wife, Mary, would also attend the meeting.

Mike's firm specializes in personal financial planning. The firm has developed a great deal of expertise in helping individuals develop comprehensive strategies for retirement. This area has proven to be very lucrative with the growing public awareness of the need to begin planning and saving for retirement as soon as possible.

The objective of the initial client meeting was to obtain background information, explain the services offered by the firm, and discuss the fees for those services. During this meeting, Mike learned that John and Mary were both 62 years old. John is currently the vice president of marketing for EFC, Inc., a midsized manufacturing company. He has been with the company for 22 years. Mary is a homemaker.

Mike asked John and Mary to describe their retirement objective. John said, "I'd like to retire in three years at age 65 and be comfortable. We want to be able to travel and spend time with our grandchildren. We also want to be able to spend a great deal of time on the golf course." It was obvious to Mike that John and Mary had not fully formulated their retirement goals. This was a common occurrence; most clients Mike met with did not have a clear retirement objective established.

To plan effectively for retirement, the following factors must be quantified:

- Target retirement age.
- Desired retirement income.
- Estimated life expectancy.
- Expected rate of inflation over the planning period.

John and Mary had established their target retirement age but did not have a specific income goal in mind. Moreover, they were unsure how to address this question. Mike suggested that they review their current spending patterns.

By reviewing their checkbook register for the prior 12 months, John and Mary were able to document how much they spent for food, clothing, travel, entertainment, and other

This case was prepared by Michael D. Evans, Winthrop University, whose cooperation is acknowledged with appreciation.

household expenses.

They noted that they now spend $50,000 per year to maintain their present lifestyle. Some changes in spending would be expected at retirement. For example, job-related expenses (i.e., clothing, commuting, lunches, and payroll taxes) would decrease. However, travel and entertainment expenses would increase. It was decided that they would need $60,000 (pre-tax) per year in today's dollars at retirement. John's current income is $90,000 per year. Mike learned that both John and Mary are in good health. In fact, their family histories indicate that they could expect to live to age 85.

The Jordans' assets are shown in Table 1. An investment account was established at ABC Securities 10 years ago. John and Mary relied heavily on the recommendations made by their broker, I. M. Slick. They believe their investments have performed adequately, but they don't really have a basis for comparison. Previously, their investment experience had been limited to investing in certificates of deposit.

John also participates in the company's 401(k) plan. This deferred compensation plan allows John to contribute up to 15 percent of his salary before-tax. The company matches the first 3 percent John contributes. The annual addition to John's 401(k) account is expected to be $9,000, which will be invested in a diversified portfolio of mutual funds. The expected return for this portfolio is 8 percent.

In addition, the Jordans each have an Individual Retirement Account at ABC Securities. The monies are invested in zero-coupon bonds which mature at John's retirement date. The bonds were priced to yield 8 percent annually.

Mike was pleased to see that the Jordans have no debt other than the current balance on credit cards. Credit card debt is paid in full monthly so that finance charges are avoided.

Finally, at age 65, John will begin receiving $22,000 per year in social security benefits. Mary will also qualify for social security based on John's earnings record. Her annual benefit will be $12,000.

Now that Mike has gathered all the necessary information, his challenge is to determine if the Jordans can achieve their retirement income goal of $60,000 in today's dollars. Mike wanted to be sure that he presented a comprehensive assessment of the Jordans' situation.

TABLE 1
John and Mary Jordan *Investment Assets* *July 31, 1995*

Account at ABC Securities	$ 160,000
John's 401(k)	86,000
John's IRA	22,300
Mary's IRA	11,000
Total Investment Assets	$ 279,300

QUESTIONS

1. What are the key variables in retirement planning?

2. How much in annual income will the Jordans require at retirement in three years if inflation averages 4 percent per year?

3. Assume that John will retire July 31, 1998. The Jordans will require the annual income computed in question 2 over their life expectancy. Draw a time line to show the required income stream. Assume the income stream will remain constant over the years (i.e., there will be no inflation). How would you describe this income stream? The payments will be received at the beginning of each year.

4. How much capital would the Jordans require at John's retirement to generate their desired income stream? Assume an 8 percent discount rate. How would the amount be affected if from the year 2006 forward the discount rate is assumed to be 6 percent? Discuss the difference between the two amounts.

5. What are the sources of the Jordans' retirement income?

6. What will the value of the Jordans' investment portfolio at ABC Securities grow to on July 31, 1998, if the expected rate of return is 8 percent annually, or 4 percent semi-annually?

7. What will be the value of the Individual Retirement Accounts on July 31, 1998, if they grow 8 percent annually, or 4 percent semi-annually? What is the effective annual rate at 4 percent semi-annual compounding?

8. What will the 401(k) grow to on July 31, 1998, assuming an 8 percent annual return. Remember to take into account the annual additions made at the end of each year.

9. What is the lump-sum equivalent of the social security benefits the Jordans will receive? Ignore cost-of-living increases. Assume benefits will be paid annually; the first payment will occur on August 1, 1998. It is expected that 20 annual payments will be made. (Compute the present value using an 8 percent discount rate.)

10. Will the Jordans be able to achieve their retirement income objective? (Discuss the effect of changes in the discount rate over the period August 1, 1998 - August 17, 1998).

11. What alternatives would the Jordans have if retirement projections indicated that they could not meet their income objective?

12. The Jordans' broker, I. M. Slick, has recommended that they sell the zero-coupon bonds in their IRAs and invest the proceeds in a real estate limited partnership. This venture offers the opportunity for a 15 percent annual return. But, it also carries substantial risk. I. M. Slick will receive a commission of 8 percent of the monies invested in the partnership. Do you think this is an appropriate investment recommendation for Mr. Slick to make? Why or why not? Should the Jordans sell the bonds and invest in the partnership? Why or why not?

Case 4

Interest Rate Forecasting and Financial Strategy

Babes-N-Toyland

Wally Ligenfelt, Vice President for Economic Planning at Babes-N-Toyland, absolutely *hated* January. After the Christmas selling season ended, sales at Babes-N-Toyland—an upscale retail chain of toy and infant supply stores—plummeted. In addition, January meant that it was time for him to begin preparing the annual forecast of macroeconomic conditions for use by the firm's strategic planners. As a five-year veteran of Babes-N-Toyland's management team, Wally realized he needed to get this report finished in a hurry, because the marketing department would soon be calling to request his assistance in forecasting sales and inventory levels for the coming year.

      Before turning to the day's work, Wally glanced through his stack of Monday-morning mail in hopes of finding something to cheer him up. What he found, however, caused him to roll up his sleeves, forget about his routine plans for the day, and plunge into his work. It was the following memo from his boss, Abigail Fortenbury, the President of Babes-N-Toyland:

EXHIBIT 1

Babes-N-Toyland Internal Correspondence
Personal and Confidential
(Do not duplicate)

To: W. Ligenfelt, Economic Planning

From: A. Fortenbury, President

Date: January 7, 1993

Subject: Corporate Strategy Changes

As you know, Babes-N-Toyland just concluded a banner year. After our largest national rival, Child World Inc., closed its doors forever last year, and Lionel Corporation entered Chapter 11 bankruptcy protection, our market share advanced to 20 percent of the $15 billion toy market. While this is indeed good news for our entire organization, we face some new, potentially devastating challenges in the year ahead.

Reviewing the monthly profit-and-loss figures I just received from Bill Sheckland in Accounting, I see that our operating margin has fallen from its customary 14 percent to a little over 10 percent. The entry of discount merchants into our major market area—particularly Wal-Mart, Kmart, and Target Stores—forced many of our retail outlets to reduce transaction prices during the holiday selling season. Because we compete head-to-head with these retail giants in practically all of our prime geographic locations, we must take drastic action in the coming year to defend our market share.

Over the holidays, I met with Brad Hinkle and several other members of the Board of Directors to discuss this threat. Based on our discussions, we plan to implement several strategic changes at Babes-N-Toyland in the coming year, including:

1.   **Broadening our product line.**

2.   **Refurbishing our domestic retail outlets.**

3.   **Expanding our base of retail stores in Europe and Asia.**

4.   **Reducing our corporate headquarters staff.**

EXHIBIT 1
(continued)

Page 2

In order to prepare for a special meeting of the Board on Monday, January 19, I need the following information from your office:

1. Yield curve data and analysis, showing the trends in interest rates over the last few years along with an explanation of these trends.

2. Information concerning the stability of current prices, and the rate of inflation that we will likely face over the next several years.

3. Your analysis regarding debt issuance by Babes-N-Toyland. Specifically, is the timing right for our organization to undertake significant capital projects financed with debt?

The Board realizes we need a quick response to the competitive threat I outlined above. They will probably suggest that we float a rather large bond issue to fund these changes. Based on my preliminary discussions with our underwriters, I think we can currently issue 3-year bonds priced to yield 6.4 percent per annum; 5-year bonds priced to yield 7.3 percent; and 10-year bonds priced to yield 8.4 percent. Before I begin serious negotiations with the underwriters, however, I want our in-house analysis team to give me a thorough overview of current credit conditions in the debt market.

Please call my secretary and set up a meeting with me on Thursday, January 14. Bring the information I requested above to our meeting, and be prepared to answer some of my questions as I prepare for the Board meeting on the 19th.

With little more than a week to prepare his report, Wally quickly got to work. He called the economic data shown in Table 1 up on his computer, and used this information to prepare a quick estimate of the market risk premia shown in Table 2. As he began working, he couldn't stop thinking about Item #4 in Fortenbury's list of pending changes. *Administrative staff reductions*—why, that could mean *his* position, and *his* department! Wally knew it was high time to demonstrate his value at Babes-N-Toyland by responding to his boss' request with timely information and insightful analysis.

TABLE 1			
Treasury Security Yields			
Maturity	August 1991	August 1992	November 1992
3 months	5.33%	3.13%	3.20%
6 months	5.39	3.21	3.43
1 year	5.78	3.47	3.80
2 years	6.43	4.19	4.65
3 years	6.80	4.72	5.23
4 years	7.23	4.86	5.72
5 years	7.43	5.60	6.12
6 years	7.51	5.87	6.34
7 years	7.74	6.12	6.56
8 years	7.79	6.32	6.87
9 years	7.86	6.47	6.95
10 years	7.90	6.59	7.18
30 years	8.14	7.39	7.53

Source: *Federal Reserve Bulletin*, various issues.

TABLE 2				
Babes-N-Toyland, Inc.				
Risk Premia Information for Fixed Income Securities				
December 27, 1992				
			Default Risk Premia:		
Maturity	Maturity Risk Premia	Liquidity Risk Premia	AAA-Rated Bonds	B-Rated Bonds	C-Rated Bonds
3 months	0.0%	0.0%	0.9%	1.8%	3.1%
6 months	0.0	0.0	0.9	1.8	3.1
1 year	0.0	0.0	0.9	1.8	3.1
2 years	0.2	0.0	0.9	1.8	3.1
3 years	0.3	0.1	0.9	1.8	3.1
4 years	0.5	0.1	0.9	1.8	3.1
5 years	0.6	0.2	0.9	1.8	3.1
6 years	0.7	0.2	0.9	1.8	3.1
7 years	0.7	0.3	0.9	1.8	3.1
8 years	0.7	0.3	0.9	1.8	3.1
9 years	0.8	0.3	0.9	1.8	3.1
10 years	0.8	0.4	0.9	1.8	3.1

QUESTIONS

1. Using the data provided in Table 1, construct the yield curves for August 1991, August 1992, and November 1992.

2. Evaluate the change in the shape of the yield curve between (a) August 1991 and August 1992, and (b) August 1992 and November 1992 using expectations theory and market segmentation theory.

3. Calculate the one-year forward rates of interest implied by the November 1992 yield curve over the period 1993–2002.

4. Using the one-year forward rates obtained in Question 3, calculate the expected annual inflation rate in each of the next ten years, and use this information to obtain the average rate of price appreciation expected over the 1993–2002 period. In your calculations, assume a strict expectations theory approach to nominal interest rate construction, where:

$$k_{nominal} = k_{real} + \text{Expected Inflation Premium.}$$

5. Examine the information provided in Table 2. Do these data lead you to believe that the annual inflation rates you calculated in Question 4 might be incorrect? Why or why not?

6. Using the data provided in Tables 1 and 2, prepare a revised estimate of (a) the one-year forward interest rates implied by the November 1992 yield curve over the 1993–2002 period; and (b) the expected annual inflation rate in each of these years.

7. How would the yield curve for (a) an AAA-rated firm, (b) a B-rated firm, and (c) a C-rated firm, differ from the Treasury security yield curve you constructed in Question 1? Plot the individual yield curves for each of these risky securities to demonstrate your answer.

8. In Question 1 you constructed a series of yield curves using Treasury security yields, while in Question 7 you constructed yield curves using the term structure of interest rates for various classes of risky debt. In most cases, financial analysts prefer the former approach to yield curve construction. Why is it better to construct the yield curve using the term structure of returns drawn from Treasury securities rather than risky corporate bonds?

9. Can you use the information provided in the case to estimate Babes-N-Toyland's bond rating? If so, identify this rating, and explain how you obtained it.

10. If Babes-N-Toyland issues 10-year corporate bonds to fund its expansion plans and these bonds are priced to sell at par in the market, what is the semi-annual coupon payment that the firm must offer its bondholders?

11. Based on your answers to Questions 1 through 10, is now a good time for Babes-N-Toyland to issue a large quantity of long-term debt securities? Why or why not?

Case 5

Financial Forecasting with Pro Forma Statements

Pop's Recycling Company

In April 1991, the owner and manager of Pop's Recycling Company, J. R. Vann, approached the Crewe National Bank (CNB) concerning a loan. This visit to the bank was the second for Vann in the last eighteen months. An unusual occurrence, he thought, for a highly profitable firm. The company (a recycler of metal, glass, and paper) was in the midst of a healthy increase in sales. Operations were begun in 1980, and the firm had shown a profit each year since 1982.

The company was founded in 1980 by J. R. Vann in response to the growing usage of recycled material in the manufacture of paper products, as well as metal and glass products. The primary raw material was scrap, which was hauled in by scrap collectors of various size. While paper and glass were recycled by the company, the business consisted mainly of the processing of scrap metal.

There had been considerable consolidation in the metal recycling business during the past decade. In fact, J. R. Vann, known as Pop to nearly everyone, started Pop's Recycling Company against the advice of certain business associates. Their primary concern was the apparent falloff in the availability of scrap metal. As a result of that trend, some of the small brokers or recycling yards had either gone out of business or had been bought by larger recycling yards such as Pop's. That meant the larger, more well-established yards were getting stronger, which in turn meant that a new entrant into the business faced an uphill climb. J. R. Vann, however, was convinced that he could make a strong showing in the business. He had become familiar with the business, over the years, through prior employment in the steel industry. As a result of that conviction, his entire savings and a sizable loan from a local insurance company launched Pop's Recycling Company.

The processing of the steel taken in from its "across the scale" purchase of scrap metal consisted of shredding or shearing the metal. Shredding was used to process such metal as junk cars, the primary source of scrap, and shearing was used to process steel bars and other structural type steel. The company took in approximately 30,000 tons of metal which required shredding and about 15,000 tons of metal which needed to be sheared.

The processed metal was shipped to foundries across the United States for use in a variety of applications. In fact, the company was such an important supplier of metal to specific foundries, it had become necessary to keep a certain level of inventory on hand in order to ensure that the demand could be met without delay. The sales forecast for Pop's for 1992 was $14,500,000.

The recycling companies which had survived the "shake-out" of the 1980s, as it had become known throughout the economy, meant to stay very loyal and dependable relative to their customer base. Accordingly, a good relationship with the foundries was a must. At the level of Pop's, this meant keeping a steady supply of scrap metal throughout the year. That goal created a need for cash. Further, machinery had to be kept in good working order and suppliers expected to be paid within the 30-day limit, which had become standard in the business. Of the approximately sixty competitors on the east coast of the United States, twenty were in the mid-Atlantic region and considered direct competitors of Pop's. Thus, a well-managed balance sheet was essential. In that regard, industry averages for certain items are shown as Table 3. Of special concern were the company's payables and inventory levels. Mr. Vann believed that a reasonable level in these areas would permit him to maintain a solid relationship with his suppliers and his customers. Vann believed that his long term debt would be constant, that is, would remain at its present level. In addition, he hoped to move the profit nearer to the industry average level, or beyond.

The loan which Mr. Vann sought from CNB was for the purpose of increasing the company's stock of scrap metal. In recent months, a large portion of railroad track and rolling stock was being dismantled at certain points in the immediate region, and an unusually large supply of steel had become available. These "bulges" in the incoming supply of scrap metal were a typical occurrence. It provided the recycling companies an opportunity to build up their backlog of steel and other metals. Such a supply would be used to feed the emerging and successful new, smaller steel companies in the United States. (The cold-roll production process used by foundries had given some hope to the once flagging steel industry).

In order to properly manage the situation, Vann considered a loan of $200,000 to be adequate for his short-term needs. The financial statements which follow illustrate certain aspects of the company's operating history.

The bank's loan officer, Cheryl Fries, wanted to make the correct and appropriate decision. Pop's Recycling had a long-standing reputation as a well-run company. In addition, her informal grapevine indicated that Vann handled his credits well. If the analysis of the company's financial statements bore out these impressions, the bank would have gained another solid commercial customer. The essential questions which Fries wanted to answer related to the necessity of the loan, the size of the loan, and if it were actually needed. She began an analysis of the company's needs based upon the audited financial statements shown as Tables 1 and 2.

TABLE 1
Pop's Recycling Company
Income Statement Data

	1987	1988	1989	1990	1991
Sales	$8,200,000	$8,700,000	$9,500,000	$11,000,000	$12,000,000
Profit after tax	$410,000	440,000	332,000	330,000	336,000

TABLE 2

Pop's Recycling Company
Balance Sheet

	1987	1988	1989	1990	1991
Cash	$290,100	$239,266	$229,500	$215,500	$205,100
Accounts receivable	418,200	488,070	532,950	425,000	634,742
Inventory	964,500	1,171,036	1,489,525	2,598,693	3,220,087
Total current assets	$1,672,800	$1,898,372	$2,251,975	$3,239,193	$4,059,929
Fixed assets, net	2,509,200	2,786,061	3,150,513	3,138,540	3,452,383
Total assets	$4,182,000	$4,684,433	$5,402,488	$6,377,733	$7,512,312
Accounts payable	$385,020	$408,476	$647,869	$1,140,650	$1,550,175
Accrued wages and taxes	510,480	541,098	581,400	610,470	673,130
Notes payable - bank	150,000	78,000	75,000	75,000	75,000
Total current liabilities	$1,045,500	$1,027,574	$1,304,269	$1,826,120	$2,298,305
Long-term debt	$585,480	665,839	775,200	775,200	1,101,600
Owners' equity	1,020,408	1,020,408	1,020,408	1,143,801	1,143,795
Earned surplus	1,530,612	1,970,612	2,302,611	2,632,612	2,968,612
Total liabilities and equity	$4,182,000	$4,684,433	$5,402,488	$6,377,733	$7,512,312

TABLE 3

Pop's Recycling Company
Selected Operating Data for Major Recyclers, 1991

Profit margin on sales	5 Percent
Total debt-to-total assets	25 Percent
Inventory-to-sales	28 Percent
Accounts payable as a percent of sales	10 Percent
Current ratio	1.80:1

QUESTIONS

1. Develop some additional financial data which will further illustrate the company's condition.

2. Calculate the compound growth rate in sales and earnings for the company.

3. Determine the amount of external borrowing needed by the company, if any.

4. Discuss the company's debt ratio relative to the industry averages.

5. What is the consequence to the bank and to the company of staying within the industry average for the inventory/sales ratio and the accounts payable/sales ratio? Discuss also the relevance of the profit margin to your analysis.

6. If the bank has a philosophy of lending to businesses which have good potential as long-term customers, does Pop's fit into this category? Why or why not?

7. From your answers to Questions 1 and 6, comment further upon Pop's ratios relative to the industry data from Table 3. Specifically, do the ratios calculated in Question 1 seem relevant for the bank's decision? Why or why not?

8. Are there any long-term financing implications of pro forma analysis?

9. If Pop's is a successful business, are there any reasons given in the case as to why this may be so? If there are, what are they?

10. How should the bank proceed?

Case 6

Cash Budgeting

Personal Computers, Inc.[*]

Personal Computers, Incorporated, (PCI) was founded in 1986 by Steve Wilson, an industrial engineer and former procurement agent for a large, international chemical producer. From humble beginnings in a two-car garage, by the end of 1993 PCI had grown into a dominant regional competitor with hundreds of business and professional customers.

Wilson originally got the idea for PCI after building home computers for several friends and business associates. Using standard components, Wilson would assemble and test the computers in his garage after work and on weekends. Gradually developing a network of personal references and reliable suppliers, he left his full-time job to start Personal Computers, Inc., in late 1986.

Microcomputers, it turned out, were easy to build-to-order. Each consisted of several large components: a case unit (with an integrated power supply), a motherboard (containing the computer's microprocessor and memory circuitry), floppy and fixed disk drives with separate controller circuits, a video card and monitor, and a keyboard. Customer decisions were centered around the speed and memory capacity of the motherboard circuits, the speed and storage capacity of the fixed disk drive, and the display resolution or clarity of the monitor and the video card subsystem.

In 1986, the microcomputer industry was still in its infancy. The user (retail) market was dominated by four or five large, national manufacturers, each with its own established and exclusive distribution channel. Though off-brand components were available from mail-order parts distributors, the average user (or potential user) lacked the knowledge and skill necessary to acquire and assemble reliable computers from quality parts. Wilson created PCI to capitalize on his ability to spot good prices and well-made components.

The first few years of success for PCI was derived mostly from its ability to obtain quality microcomputer parts from the West Coast. Wilson's experience as a purchasing agent was a definite asset, and this was evident several months after the start of the business. After attending a local business trade show for two days in early 1987, PCI had hard orders equal to four months of steady production. Wilson had set prices fully a third lower than his other local competitors, and he promised a quality product as well. This price advantage carried PCI through the end of 1989.

In mid-1988, one of PCI's largest customers decided to install a local area network (LAN) which would allow all of the individual computers in the company to share the same information, software, and laser printers. Though PCI had not been involved in network software or hardware up to that point, Wilson thought that computer networking would be a likely area for growth as the market for business computers matured. PCI accepted the challenge, at the urgent request of the client, and gained a great deal of practical experience by

[*]This case was prepared by Timothy B. Michael, The University of North Carolina at Charlotte, whose cooperation is acknowledged with appreciation.

designing, installing, servicing, and expanding the network. Within two years, PCI had hired another network specialist. The firm began to shift its focus away from individual computers and toward integrated networks for small- to medium-sized businesses.

By late 1993, PCI was acknowledged to be one of the best specialty network shops in the region. Wilson, as technical manager, had hired a total of three network engineers and a full-time computer technician. Assembly was done by up to ten part-time technicians, mostly local college students. The office staff included a business manager, an accounts payable/receivable clerk, and a receptionist. PCI also had two salespeople, though approximately half of the firm's dollar sales was still generated through referrals and repeat customers.

While Wilson was a competent manager of PCI's technical matters, he shared the planning function with his business manager, Mike Thompson. Thompson had received a bachelor's degree in business finance and management information systems from a local university a few years earlier, and had shown that his knowledge of the computer systems and software industry was quite extensive. After his arrival in 1992, Thompson automated the office at PCI and eventually increased productivity in the face of greater sales and order volumes. In late 1993, having completed the most important of his operational streamlining projects, Thompson turned his attention toward forecasting operations for the next full year, 1994.

In late November 1993, Mike worked with the sales staff to develop a reasonable estimate of 1994 sales. PCI's total sales had been growing at about 25 percent per year, but the firm had begun to concentrate more on selling networking software and expertise rather than just quality computers. It was expected that total sales in 1994 would grow by 15 percent over 1993 sales. After allowing for seasonal variations, Thompson produced an estimate of 1994 sales in dollars, by month. These figures are shown in Table 1, along with 1993 monthly sales for comparison.

By combining these figures with other information, Thompson intended to draft a cash budget for 1994, by month. To forecast monthly collections, the office clerk generated a list of customer invoices which had been paid during the month of November 1993. Mike thought that a pattern of monthly collections could be seen by examining the dollar amounts and the original dates of the sales invoices. A summary of this information is given in Table 2.

Though PCI had stated credit terms of 1/5, net 30, it granted credit to slightly less than half of its customers. Credit customers rarely took the discount, and though some paid late, defaults were extremely rare. Having service agreements with clients also helped remind them to pay PCI's invoices. Mike felt that the pattern of collections in November would be close to what he could expect for each month in 1994.

To estimate future cash payments, Thompson would need to analyze the relationship between PCI's cost of goods sold and total sales. In the past, the cost of goods sold had amounted to approximately 60 percent of monthly sales in dollars. Computer component purchases averaged 59 percent of the cost of goods sold, with direct labor and overhead each amounting to another 25 and 16 percent, respectively. Direct labor, overhead, and roughly half of the component purchases were paid for in the month incurred, but half of the component purchases were paid for in the following month. PCI had found several suppliers that would grant the firm credit terms, usually with payment due in less than twenty days. As was common in the computer industry, some suppliers still demanded a company check for payment upon delivery.

Salaries for 1994 were expected to total $221,000, and payroll taxes were expected to be $18,000. Office expenses, which included utilities, telephone service, office supplies, and lease payments on a photocopier, were estimated at $32,500 for the year. PCI leased five vehicles, two cars for the salespeople and three delivery vans, and the cost of insurance and lease payments for these totaled approximately $30,000 per year. Cash payments for all of these expenses would be spread evenly throughout the year. Rent was a different matter.

PCI had negotiated a five-year lease for a 2,950 square foot space in a new business park. The location was classified as "mixed use," with approximately half of the floor space outfitted for retail use (or computer assembly, in this case) and the other half divided into offices. PCI's rental agreement stipulated that the firm was to pay a fixed amount per square foot per year and an additional amount based on the firm's quarterly sales, known as percentage rent or overage. PCI paid $10 per square foot per year fixed rent, but this amount was divided into twelve equal monthly payments. The percentage rent agreement required PCI to pay 1 percent of quarterly sales, and these payments were usually made in the months following the close of each calendar quarter: January, April, July, and October. The next scheduled overage payment was to be made in January, 1994.

PCI's sales staff received a 3 percent commission on any sales which directly resulted from their effort. In the recent past, approximately half of all sales had been from past clients or contacts generated by the technical staff, and half had been primarily due to the work of the sales staff. Commissions were usually paid during the month following the original sale.

In addition to sales commissions, all salaried employees expected to receive a 5 percent cash bonus for "exceptional performance," based on their annual salary, in June and December.

Thompson had already calculated the firm's expected tax liability for the coming year, and determined that PCI would need to make estimated tax payments totaling $42,000. One-fourth of this amount would have to be paid in April, July, and October, with the final payment to be made in January 1995. The firm had an estimated tax payment of $9,000 due in January, 1994.

Finally, PCI was planning to make several large cash investments over the next twelve months. In February, the firm would update and extend its existing computer network by purchasing $42,500 worth of new computer equipment and laser printers. A site license for an emerging network software program would have to be purchased in June at a cost of $26,000. In September, Wilson planned to acquire exclusive regional distribution rights to another network operating system, and this would cost approximately $35,000.

At present, it was estimated that PCI would have approximately $15,000 in its transactions account on December 31, 1993. Mike generally liked to maintain an account balance of at least $10,000 at all times. This was the smallest amount that would allow him to sleep comfortably at night.

As Thompson pondered the data he had collected, he reflected on his relationship with the firm's bankers. Though PCI had not needed to use short-term borrowing in the recent past, Mike was certain that he could obtain funds on short notice, provided that he could show the bank a comprehensive and realistic cash budget. First, he would have to determine exactly how much cash would be needed and when, and then he could use the cash budget to illustrate how excess cash in later months could be used to repay any necessary previous borrowing. In addition, a budget would show the timing and amount of any cash available for investment in short-term, liquid securities which could be sold when cash was later needed to fund operations or special projects.

TABLE 1		
Personal Computers, Inc. *Dollar Sales per Month*		
Month	**1993**	**Forecasted for 1994**
January	$101,200	$116,400
February	102,400	116,400
March	94,700	110,200
April	115,900	133,800
May	126,800	145,500
June	111,300	128,000
July	71,000	81,400
August	70,800	81,400
September	101,200	116,400
October	116,300	133,800
November	126,500	145,500
December	75,900	87,300
Total Sales	$1,284,000	$1,396,100

TABLE 2	
Personal Computers, Inc. *Collections Summary for November 1993*	
Month of Invoice	**Amount**
September	$5,060
October	58,150
November	56,925
Total collected	$120,135

QUESTIONS

1. Develop a worksheet which shows expected monthly cash collections for January through December 1994.

2. Develop a worksheet which shows expected monthly cash payments for January through December 1994.

3. Using the worksheets calculated in Questions 1 and 2, create a cash budget which clearly shows the following items:

     a. The cash on hand at the beginning of each month.

     b. The total cash on hand after net cash from (used by) operations has been calculated for each month.

     c. The new borrowing required in any month.

     d. Any cumulative amount borrowed, less repayment, in each month.

     e. The ending balance for each month.

     f. The amount of cash available for short-term investment (if any) in each month.

Assume that PCI will use excess cash (as it becomes available) to repay any outstanding (cumulative) borrowing from prior months.

4. After developing his cash budget, Mike discussed PCI's borrowing needs with his local branch calling officer. The banker outlined three types of short-term borrowing arrangements:

     a. A revolving credit agreement:

     The bank would guarantee the availability of a certain amount of funds over a one-year period in exchange for a commitment fee (to be paid on the unused amount of the line of credit). The interest paid on any money borrowed would be variable and based on the prime rate, and rates could change monthly.

     b. A line of credit:

     The bank would authorize (but not guarantee) loans up to a certain amount during the year. Again, the interest paid would be based on the prime rate, and could change monthly. In addition, an average compensating balance of approximately $5,000 would have to be held in PCI's transaction (checking) account during the course of the year.

     c. A one-year term loan:

     PCI could obtain a loan large enough to cover the amount needed during the year. This loan would pay interest at a fixed rate, but the interest on the loan would be determined at creation, and PCI would be responsible for the entire interest amount, regardless of when it repaid the principal.

From Mike Thompson's perspective, what should be the most important characteristics of any short-term borrowing arrangement? Which of these alternatives would best meet PCI's needs? .

5. PCI will have some excess cash to invest during 1994. Discuss the nature of short-term, liquid investments (marketable securities) which may be available to PCI. What investments, if any, would be most appropriate for Thompson to use in anticipation of a need for these funds later in the year?

6. Use a computer spreadsheet program to create the collections worksheet, payments worksheet, and cash budget from Questions 1, 2, and 3, above.

7. Suppose a monthly cash budget proves to be inadequate for forecasting PCI's borrowing needs. What information would be needed to calculate a cash budget on a weekly or biweekly basis?

8. A cash budget is just one tool for monitoring the financial position of a firm. What other information or accounting reports could Mike use to track the day-to-day status of PCI?

9. Suppose PCI continues to change its product mix from the building and selling of computers to the selling of network expertise. In general, for each dollar of sales revenue, the relative cost of raw materials (disks and manuals) for network software is lower than the relative cost of computer components, but the cost of the specialized labor and overhead is much higher. How will this change in focus influence PCI's cash needs over the next several years?

10. Mike Thompson made many assumptions when forecasting PCI's 1994 operations. How could sensitivity analysis be used to better model the cash situation of the firm for the new year?

Case 7

Financial Forecasting and Planning

Personality Associates

In 1982, Personality Associates was founded by Carl Myers to provide "complete psychological counseling for the family." Myers, who had earned a PhD in clinical psychology in 1978, believed that psychological counseling needed to take a more open and family-oriented approach toward the general public. Gone were the days of the aloof and arcane counselor, a generic title used by many, who simply stroked his chin and listened. Myers' idea was to offer family counseling with a well-qualified professional staff in a modern, relaxed setting. They offered a variety of counseling formats, from individual and family therapy to small group seminars, and interpersonal communication skill development.

The location was a tree-lined, pleasant street in a mixed commercial and residential area of a city in North Carolina. The location was ideal and seemed to reflect the image that Myers hoped to portray.

The business began with an infusion of money from Myers and two associates whom he knew from graduate school. Almost from the beginning the business was successful. It appeared that one's reputation in the world of clinical psychology developed directly from the word-of-mouth endorsement. Myers, before he began Personality Associates, had taught in an adjunct capacity at a nearby university. The members of the psychology department and the staff of the school's counseling center immediately recognized Myers' talents as a sensitive and skillful practitioner. It followed then that referrals would be made by the faculty members and others at the university. As a result, the number of individuals who experienced the benefits of Personality Associates increased at a steady rate. Revenue for 1995 was $1.6 million. The staff was made up of eight full-time and part-time licensed psychologists and counselors.

The business was incorporated in 1985 by Myers and two other partners with a total capitalization of $200,000. The initial capitalization was contributed equally by the three partners. This was based upon their original contribution to the partnership and was maintained until the date of incorporation. Tables 1 and 2 provide the most recent income statement and balance sheet. The financial statements shown as Tables 1 and 2 reflect the state of the business up to the present. In the minds of Myers and his associates, the future held both great opportunities and challenges.

The building that housed Personality Associates was owned by the corporation, free and clear. The substantial profit after-tax (retained earnings) earned since the company's inception had been used to completely amortize the mortgage. That situation had left the company essentially debt free and solely owned by Myers and two of his associates—the original investors.

It had become increasingly clear over the past 15–20 years that the public was willing to accept the "for-profit" medical care facility. In the public view, such an organization, as part of a chain, provided services in locations often not directly served by the more regionally focused municipal facilities. As a result of that trend Personality Associates was poised to expand.

Regardless of the apparent economic feasibility of expansion, there were matters of ethics and quality control that concerned Myers. In short, what was the nature of the conflict, if any, between the for-profit aspect of the business and the great need to provide carefully monitored, high-quality professional service? Myers wanted to make sure that the internal mechanisms traditionally used in the business to assure quality would be maintained. In addition to certain state licensing requirements, many such operations used peer monitoring and evaluation to ensure conformity to accepted rules of conduct and the providing of high-quality service.

Myers was very interested in discussing his concerns about peer-monitoring and all such quality-control issues with his business associates. He was particularly concerned that he not appear to distrust his associates. For example, what type of mechanism would he need to review matters of quality-control while not limiting the professional skills of his associates? His associates were, after all, individuals who were highly skilled, but each had his or her own way of relating to clients. The need for quality control was certain to become more important as the business expanded.

Revenue for the company was expected to increase by a compound annual rate of 15 percent over the next five years or so. The projections were based upon revenue growth over the past several years and, more important, on the backlog of clients that the company now had. The owner/managers began to think about and discuss the possibility of building a new facility in a rapidly growing suburb of the city in which they now operated.

One concern that Myers had was the reliability of the projected increase in revenue. A friend of his who taught finance and economics courses cautioned him concerning taking too narrow a view of the forecasting process. The suggestion was to consider alternative forecasting techniques when looking at the relatively long-term future. Time series analysis and analysts' forecasts were two recommendations for added breadth in the firm's forecasting efforts. Myers wondered what added information those tools would bring to the decisions that needed to be made. Indeed, he also wondered exactly what the recommended forecasting techniques were.

In addition to the foregoing concern, the issue of forecasting cash needs for a closely held firm versus a publicly held firm was also raised. In other words, did the fact that Personality Associates did not have access to the capital markets have an effect on the firm's ability to raise funds? Moreover, did the closely held nature of the firm influence the level of cash needed? These and other issues were of great concern to Myers and his associates as they began the process of taking the next logical step in the firm's growth cycle.

Myers and his associates also wondered about the firm's potential growth, relative to maintaining ownership control of the firm. While strong revenue and profit growth were desirable, there was a desire, perhaps a need, among the owners to maintain control of the business. Myers planned to enlist the help of a local accounting firm in resolving the issue of expansion versus control. He hoped that the firm would provide detailed projections of the balance sheet and income statement for the next several years. Myers knew that such a projection would warrant such financial detail as a cash flow statement as well as a more thorough breakdown of the current assets. The overarching question for Myers concerning ownership control versus growth was that of maintaining high-quality service in the face of expansion. Were the two compatible?

Before such a project was begun, however, several important matters had to be resolved. Among these were the following:

(1)   How should the projected need for approximately $150,000 to refurbish the interior of the present facility be acquired? The present facility had once been a small hotel, and Personality Associates had converted it to an efficient office. What was once the lobby served as a reception area/waiting room, and there were rooms on the ground floor and on the top (second) floor which had become the private counseling areas. In any case, the question of the level of short-term borrowing needed was important as well as its effect upon the balance sheet if any future borrowing were needed.

(2)   Friends of Myers in the construction business had told him that the land and the necessary building in the suburban area would cost approximately $850,000. Myers' projections indicated $400,000 in revenue for the first year of operation for the new facility. Given the need for approximately $1,000,000, — the $150,000 for refurbishing and the expansion funds — the questions of timing and the maturity structure of the funds became most urgent. In the past the annual profit after-tax had been set aside to service the mortgage loan. At present, however, the plans called for the expansion to be completed by the end of 1999. Would there have to be external financing to augment the profits retained in the business?

TABLE 1 **Personality Associates** *Income Statement* *December 31, 1995*	
Revenue	$1,600,000
Total expenses*	(1,120,000)
Profit before tax	480,000
Taxes (35%)	(168,000)
Profit after tax	$312,000

Note: *   Total expenses include salaries and benefits for the full-time staff and three part-time therapists. The profit after-tax figure is added to retained earnings each period, in total. Total costs will increase by $100,000 when the new facility becomes operational.

TABLE 2	
Personality Associates *Balance Sheet* *December 31, 1995*	
Current assets*	$290,000
Fixed assets, net	1,250,000
Total assets	$1,540,000
Current liabilities	$10,000
Long-term debt	30,000
Owner's equity	200,000
Surplus	1,300,000
Total liabilities and equity	$1,540,000

Note: * Consists entirely of cash.

QUESTIONS

1.   What are some of the considerations necessary for a firm when projecting distant cash flows?

2.   Is the projection of distant cash flows likely to differ for a closely held firm versus a publicly held firm? If so, how will it differ?

3.   What are some elements (major characteristics and advantages, if any) of time series forecasting?

4.   Prepare financial information for the company in order to illustrate the financial position in the year before the expansion is complete and the year after the completed expansion.

5.   Assume the profit after tax for the next three years is available for investment on a short-term basis at 8-percent interest. What will be the amount of external financing needed by the firm at the end of 1998 if the need projected at present is $1,000,000? (Current liabilities should not exceed 1 percent of total assets).

6.   The company's owners wish to retain majority control in the business, now and in the future. Does the projected financing permit this?

7. Discuss the proposed expansion in the following contexts. Is expansion feasible for the company? Are there likely any ethical issues related to operating a chain of therapy centers?

8. How should the company manage the ethical issue of a chain of counseling centers relative to the public? Relative to the bankers? Are sound ethical practices sometimes inconsistent with strong profitability?

9. How should the owner/managers deal with the question of growth versus maintaining control of the business?

10. What managerial/financial problems will likely occur with expansion?

11. Generally, what are some reasonable sources of expansion funds for the type of expansion planned by Personality Associates?

12. Based upon the data and information in the case, should the company pursue the proposed expansion?

13. Are there likely to be quality control problems with the expanded operation? If so, how should these be minimized?

Case 8

Financial Forecasting and Corporate Strategy

Rapid Fire Batteries, Inc.

At one point early in her career, Allison Miller thought that the demise of the domestic automobile industry represented the end of the world. As a young mechanical engineering graduate from a prestigious midwestern university, Allison eagerly accepted employment with a large domestic auto manufacturer soon after leaving college in 1981. Over the next few years, she enjoyed an attractive, upwardly-mobile lifestyle and a series of impressive promotions. By late 1984, Allison managed a department of junior engineers working to refine fuel injection technology for her employer's entire product line. In early 1985, Allison believed that her position and reputation in the auto industry provided almost complete job security for the next several years.

Then the bottom fell out. In mid-1985, Allison's employer faced a major drop in sales. The firm decided to reduce manufacturing overhead and channel its remaining cash flow into new product development efforts initiated in 1982. Allison's department was consolidated with three other engineering units, and her management position with the firm was eliminated. While Allison negotiated a substantial severance payment from the firm, her promising career appeared to be in shambles.

For several months following her dismissal, Allison tried in vain to find work with another manufacturing firm. Given her age and experience, however, she never seemed to be the candidate that employers had in mind. She was either too young to supervise other engineers, or she was too well-qualified for a staff engineering position. By the end of 1985, with her severance nest egg and personal savings nearly exhausted, Allison was desperate.

But Allison was determined to make a comeback in the automobile industry. Given her technical training and prior work experience, she realized that the next generation of automobiles would require more powerful and more compact batteries to power the added electronic components they would carry. In early 1986, Allison assembled a business plan for a start-up company to manufacture a newly designed auto battery. Using the last of her personal savings and a substantial loan from her parents, Allison hired an accountant and an attorney to help her polish the business plan, while she single-handedly designed the new battery and applied for a patent on her work.

Allison's idea turned out to be a hit in the marketplace. Using her contacts in the auto industry, she was able to convince a few equipment suppliers to the big three domestic automobile manufacturers that her product was superior to existing auto batteries. They agreed to purchase a small number of batteries from Allison's start-up company, if she could arrange the financing and guarantee production of 5,000 new batteries within a six-month period. Now that Allison had customers waiting in line, a brand new patent from the government, a resume showing technical and managerial work experience, and a solid business plan, she easily convinced a New York venture capitalist to finance her dream. In 1987, Rapid Fire Batteries,

Inc. opened for business with Allison as president and chief executive officer.

During its first several years of operation, Rapid Fire sold batteries exclusively to component suppliers serving the domestic auto manufacturing industry. While the firm produced its entire output from a small, suburban factory near Detroit, its products were branded to carry only the vehicle manufacturer's name. By 1991, Allison grew tired of selling products under another firm's identity. She was anxious to promote the Rapid Fire name, and eager to distance her company from the cyclical nature of the domestic automobile industry. She decided to change Rapid Fire's corporate strategy and become an independent producer of aftermarket, replacement batteries selling to local auto parts retailers.

Tables 1 and 2 provide Rapid Fire's sales and income history for the first three years following Allison's revision of the firm's business strategy. At first, sales came slowly and profit margins were somewhat thin, but as Allison's product established a reputation within the Detroit auto parts market, orders began to accelerate. In 1993, Rapid Fire sold 100,000 batteries, earning a respectable $264,000 on sales of $4.5 million.

Now, however, Allison wanted to revise her business plan for a second time. She hoped to expand Rapid Fire beyond the metropolitan Detroit market and achieve national distribution through large auto parts chain stores by the year 2000. In order to meet this goal, Allison realized she must broaden Rapid Fire's product line to compete effectively against other well-known battery brands like the Sears' Diehard. At year-end 1993, Allison's firm manufactured a single product, the Rapid Fire Advantage battery, and offered a modest four-year warranty on this product. Other national brands carried a full, unlimited mileage, unlimited life warranty for original purchasers. Allison knew Rapid Fire must match these terms to gain business from any national auto parts retailers. But how?

Given Rapid Fire's modest origins and limited financial resources, the firm could hardly afford the significant warranty claims liability that a full warranty would require. Rapid Fire's product performance tests, shown in Table 3, demonstrate that the firm faced little risk in offering a four-year warranty, but the firm's financial exposure would change dramatically with the introduction of an unlimited warranty. Five years after production, 30 percent of all Advantage batteries would fail. By the sixth year following production, another 40 percent would fail; and by the seventh year after production, virtually all Advantage batteries still in service would fail. Allison realized that these failure rates were typical for all automobile batteries, and she also knew that other battery manufacturers simply increased their selling prices to cover expected future warranty claims.

After several weeks of research, Allison prepared Tables 4 and 5. Table 4 represents her best estimate of how many Rapid Fire customers would keep their batteries for more than four years beyond the original purchase date, thus qualifying for a warranty claim. Notice that virtually all original purchasers of Rapid Fire batteries plan to sell the vehicles containing a replacement battery within seven years of the battery's initial purchase. Table 5 provides information allowing Allison to forecast Rapid Fire's manufacturing costs and output prices over the next few years. Using these two tables, Allison decided to conduct a bold experiment. Rapid Fire would introduce a new product, the Rapid Fire Supreme battery, in early 1994. This battery would be functionally and mechanically identical to the Rapid Fire Advantage, except the Supreme would offer a full, lifetime warranty to its original purchaser. Regardless of the failed battery's age, Rapid Fire would replace it free of charge with a new battery if the original retail customer had registered his purchase within thirty days of the original sale.

Because Rapid Fire had no prior experience offering an unlimited warranty product, Allison realized that permanent introduction of the Supreme battery might cannibalize sales from the popular Rapid Fire Advantage. Even worse, this new product might bankrupt the company with excessive warranty claims if she failed to price the new battery correctly. As a safety measure, Allison decided to offer the Supreme only in 1994, and promote it as a special, limited time offer. Rapid fire could then evaluate its warranty claims experience from 1994 sales between 1995 and 2001, and use the 1994 sales experience to gain additional information before announcing a full, unlimited warranty on its entire product line in 2002.

Allison now faced a second business dilemma. How should Rapid Fire price the Supreme battery to cover the firm's expected future warranty claims, return an adequate profit margin on sales, and offer her customers a good value in comparison with other similar products on the market? Allison realized that auto parts retailers could purchase batteries from her competitors that carried an unlimited warranty for $40 to $60. She also knew that Rapid Fire's after-tax cost of capital was approximately 14 percent, and she planned to invest all funds the firm received in connection with future warranty claims back into the business at this rate of return. Allison wanted to preserve Rapid Fire's 1993 profit margins following the introduction of the Supreme, and she estimated that added promotional expenses associated with the new product introduction would reach $150,000. Finally, Allison believed that Rapid Fire could sell 40,000 Supreme batteries in 1994 within the suburban Detroit auto parts market.

TABLE 1 **Rapid Fire Batteries, Inc.** *Corporate Sales History*			
	1991	**1992**	**1993**
Units sold (Advantage battery)	20,000	50,000	100,000
Average net selling price (per battery)	$43	$43	$45

TABLE 2			
Rapid Fire Batteries, Inc.			
Statement of Revenue and Expense			
December 31, 199x			
	1991	**1992**	**1993**
Net sales revenue	$860,000	$2,150,000	$4,500,000
Cost of goods sold:			
Direct materials	(270,000)	(675,000)	(1,400,000)
Direct labor	(173,400)	(433,500)	(900,000)
Manufacturing overhead	(96,600)	(241,500)	(500,000)
Cost of goods sold	($540,000)	($1,350,000)	($2,800,000)
Gross profit	$320,000	$800,000	$1,700,000
Selling expense	($96,000)	($160,000)	($425,000)
Administrative expense	(64,000)	(80,000)	(153,000)
General expense	(16,000)	(40,000)	(68,000)
Depreciation	(64,000)	(240,000)	(425,000)
Total operating costs	($240,000)	($520,000)	($1,071,000)
Net operating income	$80,000	$280,000	$629,000
Interest expense	(32,000)	(98,000)	(189,000)
Earnings before taxes	$48,000	$182,000	$440,000
Income taxes (40%)	(19,200)	(72,800)	(176,000)
Earnings after tax	$28,800	$109,200	$264,000

TABLE 3							
Rapid Fire Batteries, Inc.							
Product Performance Test Results							
Projected Failure Rates for the Advantage Battery							
	Age of Battery (in years)						
	1	2	3	4	5	6	7
Product Failure Rate	0%	0%	0%	0%	30%	40%	30%

TABLE 4
Rapid Fire Batteries, Inc.
Warranty Retention Forecast for the Supreme Battery

Proportion of Supreme customer base retaining warranty coverage:		
5 years after original purchase	6 years after original purchase	7 years after original purchase
60%	50%	30%

TABLE 5
Rapid Fire Batteries, Inc.
Inflation Forecast: 1994 through 2001

Year	Producer Price Index	Consumer Price Index
1994	2%	3%
1995	4	2
1996	3	4
1997	3	3
1998	3	3
1999	3	3
2000	3	3
2001	3	3
Average annual inflation rate	3%	3%

QUESTIONS

1. Historically, how much has it cost Rapid Fire to produce each Advantage battery? Prepare a per-unit statement of revenue and expense for the firm covering the 1991–93 period to answer this question.

2. How much will it cost Rapid Fire to produce each Advantage battery over the course of the next ten years?

3. In developing a forecast of the total cost to produce the new Supreme battery in 1994, does your forecast of unit cost for the Advantage battery offer any useful information? Why or why not?

4.   Given the product performance data shown in Table 3 and the warranty retention forecast shown in Table 4, how many warranty claims can Rapid Fire expect to receive in 1999, 2000, and 2001 from its sales of the Supreme battery?

5.   In developing the total cost of warranty claims for the Supreme battery, is it necessary to consider potential claims <u>before</u> 1999? Is it necessary to consider potential claims <u>after</u> 2001? Why or why not?

6.   Given your answers to Questions 4 and 5, what is the total cost of warranty claims that Rapid Fire will experience in 1999, 2000, and 2001?

7.   How can Rapid Fire incorporate the projected cost of future warranty claims from 1994 sales of its Supreme battery within the pricing framework of this product?

8.   What is the wholesale price at which Rapid Fire should offer the Supreme battery to its customers?

9.   Given your answer to Question 8, should Rapid Fire proceed with its plans to introduce the Supreme battery in 1994? In formulating your answer to this question, consider the *qualitative*, as well as *quantitative*, information provided by the case, and your personal knowledge of the market for automobile batteries. In particular, consider:

         a.   Rapid Fire's size and market share in the replacement battery market.

         b.   The price elasticity of demand for automobile batteries.

         c.   Rapid Fire's ability to reduce its selling price in order to capture market share in the replacement battery market.

10.   Review the pricing analysis you prepared for Rapid Fire, Inc., especially the information contained in your answers to Questions 1 and 7. As you examine these data, does it seem that an important piece of information necessary to price the Supreme battery is missing? Pay particular attention to the unit sales volume and production cost figures at Rapid Fire over the 1991–93 period, and think about the total cost to manufacture the Supreme battery. Can you see any reason to revise your pricing analysis in a significant way?

PART II

WORKING CAPITAL MANAGEMENT

Case 9

Accounts Receivable Policy

Bison Tool Corporation*

In March 1980, Karen Woodward was reviewing the credit policy of Bison Tool Corporation. She was concerned about the increased cost of carrying the company's accounts receivable. The prime interest rate had recently increased to an all-time high of 16 percent. She noticed that the company's receivables' collections had become slower, resulting in a need to increase its short-term borrowings.

Bison Tool Corporation manufactured a diverse line of small hand tools, including screwdrivers, pliers, hacksaws and blades, and wrenches. Its product lines were marketed through an established distribution system of 4,000 retail hardware stores located throughout the United States. Its headquarters and manufacturing facilities were located along the Susquehanna River in the rolling hills of central Pennsylvania.

The company's sales in 1979 were approximately $150 million. Its annual sales growth of 8 percent exceeded the industry growth rate of 6 percent per year, and its profit margins were nearly double those of other hand tool manufacturers.

The company offered credit terms of "net 30" to its customers, a common practice in the industry. Even though many of its customers were small, thinly capitalized hardware stores, Bison Tool Corporation's credit standards and collection policies were somewhat liberal. Nonetheless, its average collection period had historically been about 40 days and its bad debt losses were low, averaging 2 percent of annual sales.

During the past year, there had been a significant slowdown in the company's receivables' collections. The average collection period had increased to 60 days. A recent aging of the company's receivables is shown in Table 1. Because of this trend, as well as the high cost of carrying receivables, Woodward was reviewing the company's credit policy and wondering about ways to reduce the firm's investment in receivables. In particular, she wondered if the company should begin offering a cash discount for early payment. She recognized that the management of accounts receivable involved a trade-off between costs and benefits. Changes in credit policy should be made only when the marginal returns of doing so would exceed the related marginal costs.

She decided to evaluate the effects of offering a cash discount for payment within a 10-day discount period. She was unsure of the most appropriate discount percentage; however, 2 percent was an industry practice. She was also unsure of the number of customers that would take advantage of the discount. Given the nature of the company's customers, she did not believe that more than 50 percent would be able to take advantage of the discount. She decided to assume that the remaining customers would continue to stretch their trade credit. Thus, the

* This case was prepared by George W. Kester, Bucknell University, whose cooperation is acknowledged with appreciation.

average collection period from these customers would continue at the current level of 60 days' sales. She did not believe that the change in credit terms would have a noticeable effect on the company's sales. Because of the adverse economic environment, however, she estimated that the company's bad debt losses would increase to 3 percent of sales.

Bison Tool Corporation's variable expenses, including direct labor, materials, supplies, packaging, freight, and sales commissions, were approximately 75 percent of sales. The company's other expenses—including indirect labor, overhead, salaries, rent, depreciation, property taxes, and insurance—were expected to remain fixed during the foreseeable future.

The company's short-term borrowing requirements were met through an unsecured line of credit with its local bank. The interest rate charged on borrowing under the line of credit floated with the bank's prime interest rate. The company was charged prime plus 2 percent. The average prime interest rate was forecast to be 15 percent during the next 12 months. Almost all of the company's sales were on credit. Total sales during 1980 were forecast to be $160 million.

TABLE 1

Bison Tool Corporation
Receivables Aging Schedule
February 28, 1980

Age (days)	Amount	Percent
0 - 30	$10,235,140	40.2%
31 - 60	7,352,710	28.9
60 - 90	4,833,020	19.0
Over 90	3,027,651	11.9
	$25,448,521	100.0%

QUESTIONS:

1. As Karen Woodward, evaluate the marginal costs and benefits of offering a cash discount as a means of speeding up the company's receivables' collections. What is your recommendation? (Hint: A computerized spreadsheet will be quite helpful in your analysis.)

2. What if interest rates decline in future years? How would this affect your recommendation?

3. What else might Woodward do to speed up the company's receivables' collections?

4. Do the case data and information provide any insight into possible reasons for the slowdown in accounts receivable collections?

5. Why will some customers continue to "stretch" their trade credit? Are there incentives that Bison might offer to prevent this practice? If so, what might they be?

6. What are the primary elements of a firm's credit policy? Is Bison Tool Company focusing on the appropriate element of its credit policy revision?

7. Are there any other steps that may be taken to speed up collection? Consider your answer to Question 1?

8. Compare the information in Table 1 with the average collection period. What is the similarity of the information that each provides?

9. What if interest rates rise further? What would be the probable effect upon Woodward's decision?

Case 10

Pledging Accounts Receivable versus Factoring

Aero-Strip, Inc.

Many business managers look forward to new federal regulations and restrictive government legislation the same way that college students look forward to final exams. In both cases, it takes hard work and sacrifice to prepare for the inevitable; there are usually a few surprises along the way leading to even more hard work and sacrifice; and in the end, failure to make the grade can ruin any chances for success. In spite of these pressures, most students run in to at least one obnoxious classmate who seems especially well-prepared for the rigors of exam week–and even relishes the opportunity to demonstrate his knowledge on the most dreaded final exam. If you've ever known a student that fits this description, then you know Howard McGrath.

Howard is an eternal optimist, a fast-talker, and a born entrepreneur. He financed his college education selling student magazine subscriptions in his dormitory, and many fellow dorm residents purchased magazines from Howard just to shut him up and get him out of their rooms. After college, Howard drifted through a series of industrial sales positions and enjoyed modest success in business, but he never seemed to find his true calling in life. That was before the passage of the Clean Air Act of 1990.

How, you might ask, did an industrial salesman find his life's work in a piece of environmental legislation? It's a fair question.

Many managers viewed the Clean Air Act's mandated reductions in toxic emissions as an unnecessary and unwelcome intrusion in the private sector. Howard, on the other hand, saw a new business opportunity. As an industrial sales representative working in the aerospace coatings industry, Howard sold airplane paint. He knew that airplanes require frequent paint jobs, and he also knew that stripping the old paint from just one Boeing 727 produced 70,000 gallons of polluted water, 175 pounds of solid hazardous waste, and 10,000 pounds of toxic air emissions.

To comply with the Clean Air Act, Howard's commercial aviation customers–mainly small- and medium-sized air charter companies–needed to find a quick way to repaint fleet aircraft that would generate far less environmental waste. Teaming up with mechanical engineer Steve Fuller, an old college acquaintance Howard had met while selling magazines in the dorm, Howard developed an automated process that used bursts of high-intensity light to remove old aircraft paint. Following paint removal, Steve invented a process to blast the remaining dirt and grime from the airframe using ice crystals, and then vacuum the liquid residue from the shop floor. Using the new aero-strip process, Howard and Steve could reduce waste products from a 727 refinishing job to five pounds of solid material; the time needed to complete the job fell from 48 to 14 hours; and the cost of aircraft refinishing was cut in half.

Opening for business in late 1990, Howard and Steve quickly attracted many commercial aviation clients. They specialized in serving small- and medium-sized charter companies, because their small stripping plant lacked the space to accommodate the huge volume of business from any of the major airlines. As a growing business, Howard and Steve faced a variety of financial problems. Aero-Strip, Inc. always seemed to be strapped for cash. While the firm enjoyed healthy profit margins on its individual sales, these funds were always reinvested back into the business as soon as they came through the door. Moreover, many of the receivables owed to the firm came through the door late, as Aero-Strip's commercial clients stretched their accounts payable to the maximum. In spite of these problems, Howard and Steve never considered hiring a full-time credit manager, because the firm's outside accountant and attorney were usually able to handle routine financial matters on a contract basis.

This arrangement worked reasonably well during Aero-Strip's first few years of operation, but by 1993 the firm's cash shortage and receivables management problems reached the critical point. Howard knew he needed to borrow to finance future business expansion, but Aero-Strip lacked the solid credit rating necessary for an unsecured loan. His banker offered to extend accounts receivable financing at prime-plus-three, payable in advance on a discount basis. The bank required a discount from face value of 20 percent on all up-to-date receivables pledged as collateral against the loan, and a deep 50 percent discount on pledged receivables that were one-to-thirty days late. Delinquencies stretching beyond 30 days were unacceptable to the bank as collateral. Under the terms of this financing package, the bank would reserve the right to reject all new invoices it felt were of poor credit quality. Even worse, the bank insisted that Howard hire a full-time credit manager at $25,000 per year before it would approve the accounts receivable financing arrangement.

Shopping for more favorable credit terms, Howard located a factoring company that would purchase Aero-Strip's new receivables and extend credit for the duration of the firm's average collection period. Based on a thorough evaluation of the business, the factor concluded that it would approve 80 percent of Aero-Strip's new invoices for purchase, charge a 2 percent commission against all invoices submitted for purchase, and require a factor's reserve equal to 10 percent on all approved invoices, The factor would require an annual interest rate equal to prime-plus-two, payable in the form of simple interest on a nondiscount basis. Unfortunately, the factor refused to advance funds against existing accounts receivable, because most Aero-Strip customers were small businesses with limited credit histories, and the credit quality of many outstanding invoices was somewhat questionable.

For Howard, the moment of truth had arrived. The prime lending rate stood at 6 percent, and the business desperately needed to borrow $100,000 in cold, hard cash within the next ninety days. Reviewing the information shown in Tables 1 through 3, Howard noted that 85 percent of Aero-Strip's net sales represented credit sales, and the firm's stated credit terms were 2/10, net 30. Howard realized that these terms were standard in Aero-Strip's industry; and thinking about his competitors, Howard remembered that these firms typically operated with a 50 percent debt ratio, a times-interest-earned ratio equal to 2.3, and an average collection period of 32 days. While the percentage of uncollectible receivables usually ran around 5 percent among Aero-Strip's competitors, Howard's close association with his customers had limited Aero-Strip's receivables' write-off to just over 1 percent in recent years.

Nevertheless, Howard felt that his best customers often took advantage of him by paying scant attention to the firm's credit policy. Perhaps by selling receivables to a factor, he could instill greater payment discipline in his customers. After all, Aero-Strip's competitors showed an average collection period of around thirty days, and Howard believed that his customers could use a little payment discipline. At the same time, Aero-Strip needed cash quickly, and the factoring arrangement might provide too little, too late. After pondering these issues for several days, Howard still couldn't decide which financing alternative was a better choice for Aero-Strip.

TABLE 1

Aero-Strip, Inc.
Accounts Receivable Ledger
December 31, 1993

Customer	Invoice Date	Amount
Ace Aviation, Inc.	12/20/93	$7,296
	11/04/93	3,689
Express Shuttle	12/17/93	$4,291
	12/03/93	14,263
	11/10/93	1,132
	10/06/93	6,608
Lomax Charters	12/20/93	$1,986
	12/07/93	511
	11/08/93	5,429
Miller Aerial Surveying	12/28/93	$2,000
	12/22/93	1,870
	12/07/93	9,251
	11/26/93	5,792
	11/18/93	7,843
	11/12/93	8,792
	11/05/93	7,323
	09/07/93	2,071
Pointers Aviation, Inc.	12/17/93	$2,557
	12/03/93	5,975
	10/12/93	3,392

Estimated Uncollectible Accounts

Age of Account	Estimated Uncollectible Percentage
0 - 15 days	0.0%
15 - 30 days	0.5
31 - 60 days	2.0
61 - 90 days	5.0
Beyond 90 days	30.0

TABLE 2

Aero-Strip, Inc.
Statement of Revenue and Expense
January 1, 1993 - December 31, 1993

Net sales revenue	$705,882
Less:　Cost of goods sold	(367,624)
Gross profit	$338,258
Less:　Operating expenses	(176,470)
Net operating income	$161,788
Less:　Interest expense	(112,739)
Earnings before taxes	$49,049
Less:　Taxes	(18,721)
Net income	$30,328

TABLE 3

Aero-Strip, Inc.
Balance Sheet
December 31, 1993

Cash	$27,000
Accounts receivable (net)	100,000
Inventory	848,071
Total current assets	$975,071
Net fixed assets	$1,139,929
Total assets	$2,115,000
Accounts payable	$277,821
Notes payable - bank	187,458
Accrued wages and taxes	34,721
Total current liabilities	$500,000
Long-term debt	$989,000
Total liabilities	$1,489,000
Common stock	$419,392
Retained earnings	206,608
Total liabilities and equity	$2,115,000

QUESTIONS

1. Develop an aging schedule of accounts receivable for Aero-Strip, Inc.

2. Evaluate the credit quality of Aero-Strip's accounts receivable portfolio. Does the firm have a problem with its credit policy? If so, how severe is this problem?

3. Should Aero-Strip prepare an aging schedule of accounts receivable on a regular basis. If so, what information can the firm gain from this report? If not, why is this information not necessary to the firm?

4. Given Aero-Strip's current receivables portfolio, how much total financing will the pledging arrangement provide over the next ninety days?

5. If Aero-Strip decides to sell its new invoices to the factor, how much total financing will the factoring arrangement provide over the next ninety days?

6. What is the effective annual interest rate (i.e., APR) associated with (a) pledging accounts receivable, and (b) factoring accounts receivable?

7. Suppose that you represent the commercial bank working with Aero-Strip to arrange a loan secured by the firm's accounts receivable. How would you sell the pledging arrangement to Aero-Strip's managers? In particular, what are the advantages associated with the pledging arrangement, and what disadvantages does the firm face in factoring its receivables? How would you try to convince Aero-Strip that pledging accounts receivable is superior to factoring?

8. Suppose that you represent the factor, and you are working with Aero-Strip to arrange the sale of its accounts receivable portfolio to your firm. How would you sell the factoring arrangement to Aero-Strip? In particular, what are the advantages associated with factoring accounts receivable, and what disadvantages does Aero-Strip face in pledging its receivables to the bank? How would you try to convince the firm that selling its accounts receivable to your employer is superior to the pledging alternative?

9. What are the total annual dollar costs of (a) pledging, and (b) factoring? In Question 6, you determined the effective <u>percentage</u> costs of pledging and factoring. Are these <u>percentage</u> costs consistent with the <u>dollar</u> costs you obtained in this question? Why or why not?

10.   Based on your answers to Questions 1 through 9, which financing alternative–factoring or pledging–should Aero-Strip select? Why?

11.   After a detailed analysis of Aero-Strip's receivables portfolio, suppose the factor denies 30 percent of Aero-Strip's new receivables submitted to the firm for purchase. How would this change affect the relative attractiveness of factoring? In particular, how would the effective percentage cost of factoring change? How would the total dollar cost of factoring change? How would this change alter Aero-Strip's current financing plans?

12.   Given the 30 percent denial rate described in Question 11, what should Aero-Strip do? Make sure to review the firm's current financial position, as well as its current cash needs, in formulating your answer.

Case 11

Working Capital Policy

Ohio Rubber Works, Inc.

Ohio Rubber Works, Inc. was established in the period immediately following World War II. Its major customer base in those years was the automobile industry. Because the company was located in northwest Ohio, shipment of its finished products to the automobile assembly plants located in Ohio and Michigan was accomplished with relative ease. The company was incorporated in 1947 and had undergone the gradual reshaping through acquisitions and mergers that has characterized so many U.S. firms up to the present. By 1993, the company's customer base was much more varied than it had been during the early years.

The products now being made by Ohio Rubber Works, Inc. consisted mainly of industrial hoses and belting (pulleys and conveyer belts) for a variety of industrial uses, from automobile manufacturing to mining. While a substantial amount of the company's output was sold to various intermediaries (wholesalers, jobbers, and the like), a significant amount of revenue was generated by special order materials, especially from the airline industry and the military. As a result of that situation and the general nature of its business, the company was very interested in maintaining control of all aspects of its financial situation. Especially important were the monitoring and control of the firm's working capital.

Such control included the relationship between short-term and long-term financing and the effect of each upon the return on stockholder's equity. The company's financial managers were determined to see that the company survived the downsizing, reshaping, and general changes in the manufacturing climate so prevalent in recent years within the United States. Careful attention to the balance sheet, as the company's controller had put it, was considered very important.

The company's controller, Carol Henning, had recently begun a review of the firm's working capital policy. At present, the firm's financial structure appears as shown in Table 1.

The current interest rate on short-term borrowing is 6 percent. The company's long-term debt has a nine percent interest rate. The firm is in the thirty-five percent tax bracket (federal, state and local taxes). Sales for 1993 were $70 million. The 1993 profit margin was 7.65 percent. Henning knew from published industry data that firms in similar lines of business, with similar customer bases, had a return on equity one to three percentage points higher than Ohio Rubber Works.

Henning wondered whether the firm's working capital policy was overly conservative. Would a more aggressive policy increase the firm's already strong return on common equity? At present the firm's current assets were financed with long-term debt. Henning was very interested in the effect upon ROE of financing the fluctuating or temporary portion of current assets with short-term debt. In addition, she wanted to add 40 percent of the permanent current assets to those financed short-term. The objective was to examine the effect of this change in policy upon the return to the common stockholders and, if the change was positive, to present the plan to the company's finance committee. The finance committee was made up of Henning, the corporate treasurer, the vice president of finance, and the controller from the firm's two operating divisions.

In considering working capital changes relative to financing, Henning reflected upon the actual movement of certain working capital items within the firm. In a situation such as that of Ohio Rubber Works, inventory control was a major concern. The varied product lines and customer types highlighted the need for attention to the effect of inventory upon working capital management. Of particular interest to firms in this situation is the ratio of inventory to sales, relative to the desired ratio. The major aspect of that consideration was maintaining the desired ratio as the business cycle ebbed and flowed in its usual pattern.

The sales for Ohio Rubber Works over the past 10 years had been steadily growing. The reverses in sales and earnings during this upward trend had been slight, and the desired ratio of inventory to sales had been well maintained. In addition, Henning, as she examined historical data for the company, observed a reasonably consistent cash conversion cycle—one which was not only consistent in terms of trend, but in terms of industry comparisons as well. Industry data were obtained from a variety of published sources, including trade journals. Ohio Rubber Works typically had an inventory conversion period of 42 days. As was typical in the industry, the firm's average collection period for receivables was 45 days. The firm usually operated on a 60-day accounts payable cycle, also standard in the industry.

TABLE 1

Ohio Rubber Works, Inc.
Balance Sheet
Year-End 1993
($000s)

Current assets*	$16,000	Current liabilities	$3,500
Fixed assets, net	$24,000	Long-term debt	$14,000
		Common equity	$22,500
Total assets	$40,000	Total liabilities and capital	$40,000

Note: * Twenty percent of financed current assets are considered temporary, that is, they fluctuate with the level of sales.

QUESTIONS

1. Calculate the return on equity (ROE) for the company under the present policy and the proposed policy. Which one yields the higher ROE? (Assume that a present interest of 9 percent is paid on the total amount of long-term debt. That is, the total amount of current assets currently financed with borrowed funds is $14.0 million. Any new financing pattern will total that same amount. Assume also that the change from long-term debt to short-term debt, for a portion of total debt, is "frictionless," which means there are no penalties or fees attached to retirement of a portion of the long-term debt).

2.   Comment upon your findings in Question 1. Consider increased or decreased risk related to the change in policy, and also relative to the change in ROE. Should Henning recommend the change in policy?

3.   If the yield curve for 1994 is projected to be steeper than 1993, would this change your answer to Question 2? If so, how would it change your answer? In answering the question, comment upon the meaning of a steeper or less steep yield curve.

4.   In interpreting information concerning the yield curve, what are reasonable long-term and short-term "proxies" for yield curve data?

5.   How would a move toward more sales to the "special" category of customer be likely to influence management's thinking concerning short-term versus long-term financing?

6.   What advantage does the company seem to have concerning the relationship between inventory and sales? That is, what has likely caused the inventory-to-sales ratio to remain at a desired level in recent time?

7.   Within a reasonable range, what is your estimate of the percent of inventory to total assets of the typical U.S. manufacturing firm? Discuss this in relationship to Henning's concern about inventory as a component of working capital.

8.   What are the elements of a firm's cash conversion cycle? How do these elements interrelate to provide information concerning the ability of a firm to pay its debts? What is the cash conversion cycle for Ohio Rubber Works? What are the implications of a longer conversion cycle?

9.   If a downturn in the company's sales should occur, what adjustments would management want to make quickly and accurately, relative to working capital?

10.   Does the company's finance committee seem to be adequately staffed? Why or why not?

PART III

CAPITAL BUDGETING

Case 12

Basic Evaluation of Cash Flows

B. J. Plastic Molding Company

The B. J. Plastic Molding Company was founded in 1975 by George Crawford. The company supplied extruded and molded plastic to commercial construction contractors in the mid-Atlantic/Sunbelt region, basically the area reaching from Maryland to Florida. The company was named for Crawford's two grandchildren, Brenda and Jeffrey. The two cousins were both four years old at the time of the company's founding; but now in 1995 at age 24, they found themselves in the enviable positions of controller, Brenda, and general manager, Jeffrey, of the growing company.

Sales revenue for B. J had increased from $150,000 in 1975 to $12.2 million for 1995. Selected revenue and profit data are presented in Table 1. The company's profits had maintained a steady rate of increase over the period. As with most well-run businesses, however, there were changes in the external (industry) environment that could become opportunities for the company.

The staff with which the two young managers worked willingly accepted their placement into very responsible positions in the company. This was due in part to the employees' dedication to George Crawford, now partially retired but still closely involved in the day-to-day operations of the business. Beyond that, however, the two young people had proven themselves over several summers on the job while they were college students. Their summer duties had ranged from work in the storage and shipping department to jobs in the accounting department.

Over the period 1975–1995, the region in which the company operated had experienced economic fortunes somewhat better than the country as a whole. As one indication of the region's fiscal health, a banking publication showed the region's banks leading the national average in core deposit growth, return on equity, and asset growth for the first half of the decade of the 1990s. Such a report was verified by data on the output of goods and services for the region.

One of the primary components and indicators of the region's economic vitality was the commercial building industry. In Georgia, North Carolina, and Virginia, the construction industry was especially healthy. As George Crawford often remarked to his grandchildren, "those buildings may be glass, steel, and brick on the outside, but there is a lot of plastic and vinyl on the inside."

Indeed, B. J. Plastic Molding Company had developed a reputation for manufacturing and fabricating a wide-range of plastic products. In addition, the company managed to operate with the highest regard for the natural environment, its workforce was efficient, and employee turnover was low.

In early 1995, company management determined that the sales growth could be increased by at least 50 percent if a range of manufacturing efficiencies could be implemented. In fact, it was the responsibility of Brenda and Jeffrey, in the summer before their last year in college, to do an analysis of all the economic variables related to the company's future prospects. Both Jeffrey and Brenda had majored in business in college and had concentrated in finance and economics. As a result of that background, both were usually willing to "put numbers on their ideas" when an opportunity was being discussed.

The pair took that open-ended assignment and refined it to illustrate an assessment of the region, the industry, and the company. Tables 2 and 3 provide the essence of their findings. Based upon this information and their overall knowledge of operating trends in the industry, company management decided upon a modest expansion program.

Under consideration was an increase in capacity for the company's primary product. That product was bulk sheet and strip molding sold to the building industry for final shaping and fabrication. B. J. bought its raw plastic (material not colored or shaped in any way) from three manufacturers. The product was then molded or extruded to meet the needs of builders and various subcontractors. B. J. shipped directly to these endusers. B. J. was considered by industry analysts as slightly above average in terms of sales growth.

The molds and extruders were placed in a layout long thought to be optimal. The company, several years earlier, had brought in a consultant who specialized in operations research/industrial engineering to verify the efficiency of the shop floor layout. In any case, the machinery could be replaced individually, as new technology, wear and tear, or other factors rendered an item obsolete or unserviceable.

The machine under consideration for replacement was an X2-A extruder. The X2 now in use was fully depreciated and would be sold as scrap. Its replacement, the X2-A, was a faster, more efficient machine. Certain economic data concerning the productivity of the X2-A are presented in Table 4. The machine's cost would be $42,000, including shipping and installation. The salvage value of the X2-A is its estimated market value five years hence. The cost of funds for long-term investment is 10-14 percent after tax, based upon estimates of capital costs prepared by the two young managers. Such costs reflected the required yields on the company's mix of debt and equity.

The young analysts knew that capital expenditure analysis was not done in a vacuum. There were several areas of concern that they expressed relative to the proposed purchase of the X2-A. The firm's capital structure was a particularly interesting aspect of the overall health of the firm. Specifically, they wondered if a move toward more debt financing would alter the discount rate used in the capital budgeting analysis. (They accepted the fact that risk was relatively invariant across the modest list of past and potential capital expenditures.) The X2-A extruder was not significantly more or less risky than any other of the company's capital expenditures. There was also a concern about the choice of depreciation methods used. That is, how would straight-line depreciation be likely to alter the outcome of the analysis for the X2-A. Related to the question of cash flow, Brenda and Jeffrey wanted to make it clear to those involved in the analysis that 12 percent was the discount rate to be used. That was based upon a more specific calculation of the firm's cost of capital.

TABLE 1

B. J. Plastic Molding Company
Selected Income Statement Data
($000s)

	1989	1990	1991	1992	1993	1994	1995
Sales revenue	$6,900	$7,500	$8,200	$9,000	$10,200	$11,400	$12,200
Net income after tax	552	638	738	765	928	980	1,073

TABLE 2

Regional Commercial Building Activity:
1993 to 2001

New office space[*]	18%
Population growth	4
New business start-ups	12
Increase in industry demand	14

Notes: * In terms of square feet.

             Percentages refer to compound average annual growth.

TABLE 3

B. J. Plastic Molding Company
Balance Sheet
December 30, 1995
($000s)

Assets		Liabilities and Equity	
Cash	$500	Accounts payable	$800
Accounts receivable	112	Accrued wages and taxes	200
Inventory	588	Notes payable (bank)	875
Total current assets	$1,200	Total current liabilities	$1,875
Land	$3,475	Mortgage debt	3,150
Buildings*	4,150	Total liabilities	$5,025
Equipment*	6,175		
Total fixed assets	$13,800	Common stock	$2,500
		Retained earnings	7,475
		Total equity	$9,975
Total assets	$15,000	Total liabilities and equity	$15,000

Note: * Buildings and equipment are net of depreciation.

TABLE 4

B. J. Plastic Molding Company
Incremental Data for the X2-A Extruder

	1997	1998	1999	2000	2001	2002
Net income after tax	$3,000	$3,500	$3,600	$3,600	$3,600	-----
Depreciation expense*	8,400	13,440	7,980	5,040	4,620	$2,520

Note: * Based on ACRS depreciation.

QUESTIONS

1.   Should the X2-A machine be *considered* for purchase by the company? Why or why not?

2.   What are some relevant pieces of information necessary for the decision to purchase or not purchase the machine?

3.   Evaluate the economic feasibility of the X2-A.

12-4

4.   Should the company purchase the machine? Why or why not?

5.   If the company had a list of potential capital expenditures would the X2-A likely be on that list?

6.   What factors permit an independent project's inclusion in the firm's capital budget?

7.   What part does capital structure play in the capital budgeting process?

8.   Cite as many steps or sequences as you can of the capital budgeting process in the typical manufacturing firm. Would the process differ significantly for a nonmanufacturing firm?

9.   What is the economic rationale for use of the NPV or IRR in capital budgeting?

10. In capital budgeting analysis, is one discounted cash flow method, NPV/IRR, preferable?

11. What effect would straight-line depreciation have upon the NPV of the X2-A? (Answer this question without any calculations.)

12. In capital budgeting analysis, how, in your opinion, should risk be defined?

Case 13

Net Present Value, IRR,
and the Payback Period

Infomercial Entertainment, Inc.

In the good ol' days—before cable TV, fax machines, and multimedia personal computers—the phrase, "... and now a word from our sponsor ..." usually meant just that. Television commercials were confined to thirty- and sixty-second messages, grouped together to occupy only two or three minutes of viewing time. Occasionally, if you stayed up late enough sitting in front of the tube, you'd see thirty-minute segments on riveting topics like "How to Turn $10 Into $10 Million by Investing in Real Estate That Nobody Wants." Since few people—except for a few former savings and loan executives—managed to stay awake through these half-hour programs, the shows attracted little interest.

The era of the infomercial, those thirty-minute paid video advertisements devoted to selling a particular idea or product, didn't really begin until after the 1992 presidential campaign. Following Ross Perot's unsuccessful bid for public office, however, things started looking up for this new marketing venue. If Perot could use the half-hour segments on late-night TV to capture 19 percent of the popular vote, surely other advertisers could use the infomercial as a way to communicate their message to a sleepy, yet receptive, audience.

Indeed, in the wake of the election, many Fortune-500 corporations selling consumer products were eager to take the plunge and go head-to-head with Letterman on late-night TV. Unfortunately, obtaining exclusive airtime and marketing rights in multiple television markets on the same night was a distribution nightmare. Traditional advertising agencies that purchased large blocks of television time bought it during prime viewing hours. In contrast, late-night time was sold by individual stations to local advertisers on a spot basis. Consequently, nationwide distribution of corporate infomercials could be almost impossible.

Fortunately, the free enterprise system specializes in impossible situations. In late 1992, sensing a new business opportunity, Infomercial Entertainment, Inc. (IEI) was chartered to corral local late-night television time, and serve as a contract distribution agent for corporate clients seeking to air thirty-minute infomercials throughout the United States. While IEI originally set out to be a distribution agent for late-night TV time, the firm soon realized that many medium-sized corporate advertisers lacked the production and duplication equipment necessary to produce multiple copies of their infomercial messages.

Sensing a new opportunity to expand their business, IEI's management team sought to provide video production and duplication services for their customers. Through the careful purchase of used video equipment from a bankrupt motion picture studio in 1993, IEI could acquire the necessary electronics and video hardware for $200,000, plus a $25,000 charge for installation and delivery of the equipment. This equipment would be depreciated according to the MACRS schedule for five-year property shown in Table 1.

IEI's managers believed they could mass-produce infomercial videos and offer them to corporate clients for $10 each. In 1993 the firm forecast total volume of 5,000 infomercial videos, and estimated the materials cost of production at 50 percent of the net sales price. Labor and overhead expenses would amount to an additional 12 percent of the unit selling price. The firm expected sales to grow at a constant 5 percent annually over the next ten years, at which time the newly acquired video equipment would be worn-out. Finally, IEI would require an additional investment in working capital totaling $10,000 to support the initial sales increase promised by the Infomercial project.

While IEI was interested in expanding its production operations, the firm also realized that acquisition of the video equipment would give it the added opportunity and capacity to produce corporate training videos for commercial clients. IEI's managers believed they could produce 875 different training films in 1993, and that clients would order, on average, five copies of each film. The firm believed that demand for its training videos would grow at 7 percent annually over the next 10 years. Each training video would carry a net price of $8 per copy, production and materials costs would total 43 percent of this selling price, and overhead expenses would average 10 percent of the unit selling price. IEI would require an additional $5,000 investment in working capital to support the Training Video project.

After a ten-year service life, IEI could sell its video equipment for a nominal $20,000. The firm's after-tax weighted average cost of capital is 10 percent, and the video production projects—including both infomercials and training films—are considered to be only slightly more risky than the firm's current business ventures. IEI's marginal tax rate is 35 percent, and the firm's financial statement forecast shows that production costs and overhead expenses will maintain a constant relationship with sales over the next 10 years.

TABLE 1	
MACRS Recovery Allowance Percentages: Five-Year Property	
Ownership Year	**Recovery Percentage**
1	20%
2	32
3	19
4	12
5	11
6	6
	100%

QUESTIONS

1.   What are the annual net cash flows associated with (a) the Infomercial project, (b) the Training Video project, and (c) the Combined project (i.e., the combination of the Infomercial and Training Video projects)?

2. Use the undiscounted payback method to rank-order the three capital budgeting alternatives facing IEI. Based on this ranking, should the firm pursue (a) the Infomercial project, (b) the Training Video project, or (c) the Combined project? Why? In your answer, assume that IEI's longest acceptable payback period is 4 years.

3. Examine the payback periods you obtained for (a) the Infomercial project, and (b) the Training Video project. Notice that when the analyst rounds the payback period for these projects to the nearest year, it is impossible to rank-order them. Why is this the case? Can you think of a method involving the undiscounted payback technique that might permit a more precise determination of these projects' payback periods? If so, describe this method, and use it to rank-order the three investment alternatives facing IEI.

4. Review your answer to Question 3. In order to incorporate fractional-year time periods within the payback framework, you made an important assumption about the timing of cash flows associated with each of these three projects. What is this assumption, and why is it dangerous to make such an assumption in most capital budgeting circumstances?

5. Now use the net present value methodology to evaluate the three capital budgeting alternatives facing IEI. Based on this evaluation, should the firm pursue (a) the Infomercial project, (b) the Training Video project, or (c) the Combined project? Why?

6. As a final evaluation of the three capital budgeting alternatives facing IEI, use the internal rate of return methodology to rank-order these projects. Based on this evaluation, should the firm pursue (a) the Infomercial project, (b) the Training Video project, or (c) the Combined project? Why?

7. Given your knowledge of the shortcomings of the IRR methodology, is it accurate to use this method to evaluate the project alternatives facing IEI? Be sure to provide the necessary evidence to support your answer.

8. Review your answers to Questions 2, 5, and 6. Compare the manner in which (1) the undiscounted payback method, (b) the net present value method, and (c) the IRR method rank-ordered the three investment alternatives facing IEI. Based on this comparison, does any particular method of capital project evaluation seem superior to the other two? Why or why not? In *general* terms, is it possible to suggest that any of the three methods is superior to the other two? Why or why not?

9.   The case reports that both the Infomercial project and the Training Video project are considered slightly more risky than IEI's current business ventures. Suppose that this was <u>not</u> the case, and that the Training Video project exhibits substantially greater uncertainty than either the Infomercial project or IEI's other business ventures. Describe how you would incorporate this change within the framework of the capital budgeting analysis using (a) the net present value procedure, and (b) the IRR procedure.

10.   Given the information provided in Question 9 and your response to this question, use the NPV and IRR methods to reevaluate (a) the Infomercial project, (b) the Training Video project, and (c) the Combined project. How does the NPV of each project change when the risk level of the Training Video project is substantially greater than the riskiness of the Infomercial project? How does the IRR change in this circumstance? Based on your revised capital budgeting analysis, which project should IEI select? Why?

Case 14

The Replacement Decision in Capital Budgeting

Restore Incorporated

Restore Incorporated was organized in 1975 by Ted Schadler and his son, Bob. The company restored classic and antique cars in terms of both body and engine work. The company was located in a large southeastern U.S. city and drew customers from at least a 300-mile radius. Restore had 10 employees. Ted and Bob occasionally worked on the shop floor, but they served primarily as president and controller, respectively.

The company began as an extension of Ted Schadler's hobby, fixing up old cars for himself and his friends. As the hobby grew, a shop was acquired, and soon there was more work than could be handled by one person. It soon became necessary for Schadler to decide whether he would pursue the business full-time to earn a living, doing something he really enjoyed.

As the business grew and Schadler's reputation as a reliable, expert restorer became known, the usual need for controls and attention to financial matters became evident. It was that set of circumstances that presented an opportunity for Bob Schadler, a recent graduate of a highly reputable university accounting program, to join the company as controller.

Initially, Bob and his dad performed a great many of the tasks on the shop floor — Bob had picked up knowledge of engine repair while still a youngster. Customers liked the idea that Bob, after finishing a job on cylinder walls, would coat them with petroleum jelly before inserting the pistons —"just to ensure no initial friction"— he would say. This individual attention brought in new customers at a steady rate. The business soon began to hire and train additional help, and Ted and Bob gave an increasing amount of time to the managerial end of the business. By 1995, the annual revenue was $5 million.

Accompanying the steady growth in revenue experienced by the company was an increasing need to maintain a strong rate of profitability. Two families and, in a great sense, an entire community, saw Restore Incorporated as a major income-producing asset. As a result of the attention to financial details, a knowledge of value creation, and the building of economic worth, capital budgeting was handled in an efficient manner.

As an example, a decision now faced the company that would require careful consideration of certain data and information that had come to the attention of the Schadlers. At a trade show that dealt with auto body work machinery, Bob Schadler had observed a machine that would press dents from the car's sheet metal. The machine was known as a "universal" because it also had attachments for sanding and for spraying heavy coatings such as primer necessary as a base for the final body paint. It appeared that the machine, if purchased, would provide significant labor savings for the company. It was necessary to investigate the actual efficiency of the machine before a decision to purchase could be made. To that end, Bob Schadler decided to talk to his cost accountant and a manufacturer's representative.

In a setting in which internal investments (capital budgeting) are handled efficiently, the usual sources of ideas for such expenditures are: the sales and marketing staff, the company's cost accountants, research and development personnel, and the engineering or production staff. In a company such as Restore, wherein the management structure is very economical, usually the cost accountant, the top company management, and a representative from the manufacturer formed major expenditure decisions.

The information from the meeting related directly to the economic effect the machine would have upon the firm. The machine, an Automaster 1, was priced at $60,000 and had a useful life of approximately eight years. Restore's cost accountant, Barbara Bome, outlined the economic effect of the machine upon the company in Table 1.

The Automaster I would have a salvage value as follows:

Probability	Estimate
0.30	$5,000
0.20	7,000
0.50	6,500

The foregoing data were constructed by Bome and the manufacturer's represen.ative for the machine. There would also be an increase in working capital at the time of purchase of the new machine. This would amount to $2,000 and was for the purpose of adding extra paint, primer, and other materials that would allow sufficient practice time on the new machine.

The machine to be replaced was purchased two years earlier and was being depreciated to a zero salvage value. Bome reminded Bob Schadler that the present machine had originally cost $24,000. Its 10-year useful life was depreciated using the straight-line method. Bome also reported that the original machine could be sold for $15,000. It appeared that smaller body shops, do-it-yourselfers and others, provided a reasonably good secondary market for auto body finishing equipment. The firm's combined federal, state, and local marginal tax rate was 30 percent.

In a small but well-run company such as Restore Incorporated, the reliability of internal economic information was an extremely important matter, as it would be in any for-profit business. In the case of Restore with its "small-shop" approach to doing business, there were no checks and double-checks through several layers of management to ensure that a potential investment met the strategic and economic needs of the firm.

This situation was perhaps less important due to the relatively few capital expenditure projects that were necessary. On the other hand, before the company's money was spent, close consultation between Bome and Bob Schadler was very important. The background for such discussion was always the trade and accounting data organized by Bome and the revenue or customer projections contributed by Bob. It was by necessity an objective and rigorous analysis, with the elder Schadler often playing the roll of devil's advocate by asking hard questions.

In terms of the Automaster 1, however, there was an aspect of the business for which the potential purchase had far-reaching implications for the small firm. In the city in which Restore Incorporated operated, there was an unusual shortage of reliable labor. To a large extent, the work done by the company was labor intensive. By necessity, there was a lot of hand buffing, polishing, and engine overhauls, all of which required patient labor. Any machinery purchased was as an assist to that labor. The Automaster 1 would most likely replace two of the lesser skilled persons, whose primary duties were to perform the initial sanding of a car's finish as a preparation for painting.

Normally in a tight labor market the exchange of human labor for machine labor would be desirable. In this case there appeared to be a clear and immediate economic justification for such a move, as Table 1 indicates. However, there was an ethical question that deeply concerned the Schadlers.

Within the geographical area served by the company, a steady and reliable pool of labor had been provided by a city and county business-sponsored job training program. In effect, the program operated as follows: An alliance of city and county leaders (city council members, county commissioners, members of the clergy) had teamed up with influential corporate executives and other business leaders to mentor youth heretofore believed unemployable. The youths' problems had been brought on by minor brushes with the law, truancy, poor educational attainment and aspirations, and the like. Significant sums of money and great amounts of time had been directed toward not only locating employment for such persons, but toward providing ongoing support as they sought to establish themselves as wage earners. In other words, after an individual was selected for the program and overseen by a permanent staff of two full-time persons (all other staff served on a volunteer basis), regular classes and meetings were required to strengthen skills, and commitment, and to monitor progress. The purpose of the classes and meetings was to bolster basic skills such as oral and written communication, to increase understanding the basics of the U.S. economic system, and to promote discussion of problems encountered at work. The program had been in place for 12 years, and the model had been replicated in several other cities around the country.

The program provided the bulk of the labor used by Restore Incorporated. In addition, Ted Schadler had become a very forceful spokesperson for the program and had helped to recruit many of his business colleagues into it. Of course, there are ebbs and flows in any employment situation. That is, occasionally employees are let go due solely to the changing needs of the job market—this was normal and expected. It was, however, never an easy step to take for a strong advocate of such a useful and mutually beneficial arrangement. Also, several academic studies done over the years, which focused upon the jobs program relative to the geographical area, had concluded that rather far-reaching benefits accrued to the area because of the program. Those benefits were listed as a steadily increasing standard of living as measured by rises in disposable income. The higher standard of living attracted additional businesses to the area, reduced the high school dropout rate, and lowered the crime rate. The data made available to the county's business leaders by a local bank forecast economic growth in the range of 10–15 percent annually for the foreseeable future.

Thus it was against the foregoing background that the Schadlers considered whether to invest in the Automaster 1, which had immediate apparent economic benefits. Additionally, they were very concerned about the ethical question, in their minds at least, concerning their advocacy of the jobs program while preparing to reduce their labor force by approximately 20 percent. Tables 2 and 3 illustrate the firm's balance sheet and certain revenue and income projections, respectively.

TABLE 1	
Restore Incorporated	
Economic Data for Automaster 1	
Gross cost (including shipping)	$60,000
Increased (incremental) annual revenue	$12,000

TABLE 2

Restore Incorporated
Balance Sheet
December 31, 1995
($000s)

Current assets	$75	Current liabilities	$30
Land	$ 800	Debt (mortgage)	$1,200
Buildings (net)	800	Equity	400
Equipment (net)	1,000	Surplus	1,045
Total fixed assets	$2,600	Total long-term capital	$2,645
Total assets	$2,675	Total liabilities & capital*	$2,675

Note: *   The discount factor used in capital budgeting calculations is 8 percent; this is based upon the average cost of funds to the company.

TABLE 3

Restore Incorporated
Projected Revenue and Income
($000s)

	1996	1997	1998	1999
Revenue	$6,000	$6,900	$7,866	$8,445
Earnings after tax	440	464	538	652

QUESTIONS

1. Comment upon the company's "process" for assessing capital budgeting ideas.

2. Calculate compound growth rates for the company's projected revenue and earnings.

3. Evaluate the cash flows for the purchase of the Automaster 1 and the replacement of the original machine.

4. Is there an economic justification for the replacement? Please explain your answer.

5. Should the original machine be replaced?

6. Comment upon the ethical and other aspects of the company's potential reduction of its workforce.

7. What additional economic information would be useful in the replacement decision?

8. Assess the Schadler's concern over the ethics question.

9. Discuss the probability estimate of the new machine's salvage value. Is it reasonable that the manufacturer would be involved in this process?

10. Consider the company's size (sales and assets) and its line of business—will unforeseen obsolescence of the Automaster I affect the potential replacement of this machine?

Case 15

Sensitivity Analysis and the Cost of Capital

Kirby Industries

The management of Kirby Industries was intent upon a refinement of its capital budgeting practices. The company, which operated in several lines of business through three business units, had what it considered a typical capital budgeting process; that is, the corporate controller's staff distributed a capital budgeting manual to the operating divisions. The manual included the officially approved guidelines for asset expansion within the firm.

The company has existed since the 1950s, although its form and structure have changed several times since its founding. At present the company's management believed it was settled into lines of business that would serve the company, its customers, and its investors many years into the future. The present businesses included medical technology (which consisted of improved x-ray and scanning devices), a computer software division that specialized in medical applications, and a division that manufactured hospital furnishings and equipment.

The company's capital budgeting cycle was completed annually and corresponded to the company's fiscal year. In essence, the divisions, after careful consideration and analysis of their expenditure proposals, submitted a list of those proposals to the corporate controller. The controller's staff, in conjunction with the head of strategic planning, subjected the individual capital expenditure proposals (projects) to additional analysis and scrutiny. The purpose was to ensure that each proposal met the return criteria set forth in the capital budgeting manual.

The firm's capital budgeting process was contained in the manual. Given the importance of the process, the manual was periodically reviewed and updated. This task was the responsibility of the corporate controller. It was usually initiated by the entry of a new person into the position of head of capital investment analysis, who reported directly to the corporate controller.

Now was just such a time. Lois Garrison had recently assumed the duties directly related to corporate-level capital budgeting. While there were several issues that she believed needed to be addressed, none, in her view, was as critical as a reasonable sensitivity analysis for all expenditure proposals. That is, the proper "what if" questions must be asked for each expenditure proposal that found its way onto the corporate-level approval agenda. While sensitivity analysis was a standard practice within the company, Garrison believed that its use must be broadened and thus made to correspond more closely with the company's current operating characteristics.

As an example of the basis for this concern, the company in recent years had dealt with a much more geographically diverse group of suppliers. In addition, an increasing amount of the company's raw materials came from overseas. Gone were the days of a relatively small number of domestic suppliers, many of whom were known personally to the purchasing personnel at Kirby Industries. As a result of this new environment, one in which most companies operated now, prices and supplies would occasionally change without much advance notice. Therefore, Garrison wanted to place the emphasis of sensitivity analysis as much upon the "cost" side as was now placed upon the cash inflow side of capital budgeting analysis.

The decision was made by Garrison to demonstrate the need for sensitivity analysis at the next staff meeting. As a means toward that end, she selected three previously approved expenditure proposals for her demonstration. In effect, those projects would be subject to an analysis based upon additional information concerning the following factors: cost increases for the various raw material and labor components; inflation projections that might affect both the cost component and the cash inflows; and any other quantifiable risk aspects that were not specifically referred to in the capital budgeting manual. The three projects selected for further analysis are illustrated in Table 1. The projects shown represent one project from each division. In addition, the projects are of the same risk as the average project within the firm, therefore, they are each evaluated at the firm's cost of capital, 10 percent. The cost (net outlay) data and the cash inflows were derived originally from probability estimates of the data, and the cash flow data represent the original estimates.

The three projects under consideration for sensitivity analysis were a part of the firm's overall capital budget. In reassessing the projects the following information was available. The expenditures for each of the projects were made in the year before the cash inflows were received. For example, Project B's cash flow projections at the time the expenditure was made appeared as follows:

Year	Cash Flow
0	($75,000)
1	30,000
2	42,000
3	32,000

Year 0 represents the present, the time of the original decision to approve Project B. The division financial staff performed a scenario analysis during the usual financial evaluation analysis concerning each project. As an example, during the scenario analysis the following was discovered for Project B:

	Worst Case	Best Case
Net outlay (including fixed and variable components)	$95,000	$70,000
Annual cash inflows:		
Year 1	$22,000	33,000
Year 2	30,000	47,000
Year 3	25,000	37,000

The worst case/best case data for each project were obtained from a careful study of pricing, revenue, and cost data. In addition, the macroeconomic data and information relevant for the industry, the region, and the company were considered. From those data and information a sensitivity analysis for the projects would be based upon some mid-range calculations for the worst and best cases for the projects. The analysts believed this to be a reasonable approach as long as the scenario analysis was reliable.

The idea of simulation analysis was also of interest to Garrison. With that methodology, each variable, cost and revenue in this instance, would be allowed to vary at the same time. With the aid of a computer, simulation analysis would permit a more detailed analysis and description of the "what if" question within a range determined by the scenario and sensitivity analyses.

Project A

1. By the time the project was put into place the <u>actual</u> net outlay was 15 percent more than the estimate that went into the net present value shown in Table 1.

2. The cash inflows per year could be 20 percent less in each year, relative to the Table 1 data.

Project B

1. The net outlay of $75,000 was based upon estimates that did not include the possibility of an interrupted labor supply—which did occur—thereby raising the cost by 10 percent at the time of completion.

2. The cash inflows for the project reached 90 percent of expectations in Year 1; 80 percent in Year 2; and 85 percent in Year 3. The shortfall potential was known at the time the project was submitted, however, its exclusion was due to disagreement concerning its likelihood.

Project C

1. A closer investigation of the net outlay for Project C indicated that 40 percent of the total outlay had a strong probability of costing 25 percent more than the original estimate. This was due to the impending nationalization of a certain mineral contained in the raw material by the exporting country.

2. The annuity of $45,000 received in Years 3 through 8 could have been 15 percent less, if one of the firm's major customers had continued in its inability to restart a manufacturing facility damaged by fire.

The use of sensitivity analysis will enable the analysts at the corporate level to obtain clearer information concerning the return on projects. That is, the additional analysis will allow a more realistic assessment of risk and return. The goal of the firm's financial managers is to correctly measure the firm's cost of capital, and to compare the project's returns, once correctly determined, with that cost. The use of sensitivity analysis as a necessary component of evaluating capital expenditures will be used for all of Kirby Industries' projects.

The idea that Garrison wanted to convey to division management was that of a closer comparison between risk and return. For example, she intended to use the relationship between the internal rate of return and the firm's marginal weighted average cost of capital to demonstrate the real importance of sensitivity analysis.

TABLE 1 Kirby Industries *Net Present Value Data*		
Project A	**Project B**	**Project C**
Net Outlay = $100,000	Net Outlay = $75,000	Net Outlay = $200,000
After-tax cash inflows per year: 1. $ 20,000 2. 15,000 3. 30,000 4. 60,000 5. 50,000	After tax cash inflows per year: 1. $30,000 2. 42,000 3. 32,000	After-tax cash inflows per year: 1. $15,000 2. 21,000 3. 45,000 4. 45,000 5. 45,000 6. 45,000 7. 45,000 8. 45,000 9. 42,000 10. 41,000
NPV @ 10% = $25,144.83	NPV @ 10% = $10,525.54	NPV @ 10% = $26,583.62

QUESTIONS

1. Why should sensitivity analysis be a part of the company's capital budgeting process?

2. Explain the role of weighted average cost of capital in the capital budgeting process.

3. Interpret the additional data and information given in the case for Projects A, B and C. Determine the sensitivity of Project B to changes in the annual cash inflows and to changes in net outlay. To which change is the project's economic value more sensitive? Why might this be the case?

4. Should any new conclusions be drawn concerning any of the three projects? If so, what are they?

5. In the two-dimensional sense (i.e., cost of capital and net present value/IRR), which of these has been altered by the calculations in Question 3? What does this result mean for the company's future capital budgeting efforts?

6. Is Garrison's decision to use previously approved projects as an example of sensitivity analysis sound? Why or why not?

7. How would the call for sensitivity analysis be incorporated into the firm's capital budgeting manual?

8. Why might there be resistance to this idea at various levels?

9. How should such resistance be handled and by whom?

10. Comment upon the need, or lack thereof, to update or revise the list of economic variables that go into the sensitivity analysis.

Case 16

Evaluating Capital Projects with Unequal Lives

The Winning Edge, Inc.

Mike Cramer was fit to be tied. He was screaming at his general sales manager, screaming at his executive assistant, and screaming into the telephone at his manager of executive travel. As founder, president, and CEO at The Winning Edge, Inc., a $60 million sporting goods retailer with sales outlets located in 42 states, you might think that Mike's flareup would intimidate his staff. In fact, they were used to his sudden outbursts. When he was out of the office, the firm's headquarters staff quietly joked that you could tell when Mike was getting ready to blow by watching his ears. Whenever his blood pressure started to rise, the tips of Mike's ears would turn bright red and start to twitch, and the angrier he became, the more they twitched. Yes, Mike was a hyperactive kind of guy, and The Winning Edge was a high-stress place to work.

As Mike slammed down the phone, none of the corporate officers in the room needed to check Mike's ears—it was quite clear that he was apoplectic. Here he was, he complained loudly to anyone within earshot, sitting at corporate headquarters in Amarillo, Texas, and he needed to be in Peoria, Illinois in just three hours for the regional sales meeting. The executive travel manager just informed him that this was physically impossible because the next scheduled flight to Peoria wouldn't leave Amarillo until 9:00 the next morning. He'd just have to miss the managers' meeting at the Peoria store—unless he chartered a private jet out of Amarillo. Unfortunately, chartered jets were tough to come by in Amarillo with little more than an hour's notice.

As Mike started to calm down, he began to realize that it might be a good time for The Winning Edge to consider a permanent change in the firm's corporate travel arrangements. At present, the firm's steadfast travel policy required all executives to fly coach on scheduled commercial airline flights—no chartered jets, no first-class upgrades, no ostentatious luxury. By 1996, however, the firm had grown to include retail locations spread across the better part of the continental United States, and most stores were located in modestly populated states like Iowa, Wyoming, Utah, and Arkansas. Trying to reach the far-flung corners of the corporate empire using commercial airlines was becoming a logistical nightmare, and The Winning Edge's executives were wasting far too much time sitting in airports waiting for connecting flights to their final destinations.

While Mike had an excitable personality, he was also a fairly astute business manager. He realized that corporate jets were quite expensive, and until recently, The Winning Edge had been unable to justify such an extravagant purchase. On days when the plane sat parked at the airport, the firm would have to pay its full-time flight crew anyway. When the chief pilot got sick or the plane went into the shop for maintenance, managers would still have to resort to commercial airline flights. Even worse, Mike knew that the no-nonsense institutional investors who owned a large block of The Winning Edge's common equity would take a dim view of pampered managers flying in corporate luxury at their expense. This thought made Mike's ears twitch.

Still, he realized that it was vital for the headquarters staff to communicate regularly with retail managers in the field, and more often than not, the best way to communicate was a face-to-face meeting. After all, the store managers needed to know when the boss was unhappy, and you couldn't see Mike's ears twitch over the telephone. To accomplish these site visits, Mike and his senior management staff were spending an increasing amount of time in the air. Table 1 provides a summary of current travel statistics at The Winning Edge, showing that executives made 48 round-trip flights from the Amarillo headquarters during the year. Even with careful efforts to reduce executive travel, airline usage at The Winning Edge was growing by 5 percent each year. Table 2 summarizes the firm's expected travel plans in each of the next 10 years.

Upon further investigation, Mike was able to assemble all of the travel cost and pricing data shown in Table 1. At this point, he was sincerely interested in establishing a new corporate travel policy for the coming decade at The Winning Edge. The change would be difficult, however, because the various options confronting him were somewhat technical and not directly comparable to one another. Moreover, Mike's ears began to twitch when he remembered that The Winning Edge just spent $250,000 in the previous fiscal year to revamp the way the firm managed executive travel, adding expensive computer hardware and a proprietary software scheduling system to help coordinate the busy executive travel schedule at the firm. Changing the corporate travel policy at this juncture would most likely make the firm's recent investment obsolete.

In spite of this potential loss, Mike felt it was time for a change. The software management system was simply not able to keep up with the frenetic schedule of The Winning Edge's executives, and the headquarters team needed to spend more time in the field. After reviewing his options, Mike identified three alternative courses of action he would consider:

1. Contract Flight Time on Commercial Carriers

This option would require the smallest change to The Winning Edge's current travel policy. Executives would continue to fly coach on scheduled commercial flights, but under a series of annually renewable contracts with a major domestic airline, The Winning Edge's average ticket price would be $1,000, and first-class upgrades would be available for an additional $300 per ticket. The frequent flier discounts shown in Table 1 could be used to reduce both of these fares; however, ticket prices were subject to annual price increases under the terms of the contract.

Even worse, The Winning Edge would be required by the airline holding the contract to book reservations as least three business days in advance of the intended departure date, and the firm's executives would be required to make all connecting flight arrangements through the same carrier. This final limitation meant that The Winning Edge's traveling executives could look forward to an average delay of four hours per round-trip flight as they awaited connecting flights in airport terminals. In addition, the firm would need to continue staffing the executive travel manager's position to coordinate executive travel arrangements. Given these drawbacks and the cost uncertainty associated with annual ticket price increases, Mike viewed this option as the most risky solution to the firm's travel woes.

2. Private Aircraft Purchase

As a second alternative, The Winning Edge could purchase a new Cessna Citation II corporate jet for $2.5 million. With a range of 1,600 nautical miles on a full tank of gas, the corporate jet could reach each of the retail stores without the need for intermediate refueling. The plane would have a 10-year useful life at The Winning Edge and would be depreciated on a straight-line basis over an 8-year period toward a 20 percent salvage value. At the end of its 10-year service life, Mike was assured that the plane would easily bring a price of $325,000 in the used aircraft market.

Unfortunately, jet ownership would require The Winning Edge to bear the costs of hiring a flight crew and maintaining the airplane. Table 1 details the fixed and variable operating cost estimates of jet ownership, as well as the forecasted annual price increases associated with these costs. There were a few advantages provided by this option, however. By purchasing the plane now, The Winning Edge would avoid any price increases associated with the rising price of jet aircraft over the next decade. In addition, a corporate jet would eliminate practically all of the "dead time" that the firm's executives were spending in airports. Even better, the plane would be available on a moment's notice, so Mike could get from Amarillo to Peoria with little advance planning. Finally, The Winning Edge would no longer need an executive travel manager to coordinate and manage executives' travel plans. The more Mike considered this possibility, the better it looked. He rated it the lowest risk alternative of the three options.

3. Corporate Aircraft Time-Sharing

A third and final option offered an intriguing possibility for The Winning Edge. For just $630,000, the firm could acquire a 25 percent ownership interest in a Citation II from Jet-Share, Inc., a Fort Worth firm providing corporate clients with time-shared use of jet aircraft. The Winning Edge would share ownership of the jet with other firms, and company executives could have exclusive use of the plane for flights anywhere in the continental United States with just two hours' advance notice. The Winning Edge would be charged $1,060 per hour of flight time for direct operating expenses, and the firm faced fixed costs of $134,580 in each year of the time-share contract. Each of these costs would remain constant for the duration of the time-share contract.

The good news was that The Winning Edge could depreciate its ownership share of the plane on a straight-line basis over the five-year term of the time-share contract toward a 20 percent salvage value. At the end of the contract, Jet-Share would repurchase the plane at its book value, and establish a new five-year time-share contract using a new plane. In addition, with only two hours' advance notice required for departures from Amarillo, the executive travel manager's position at The Winning Edge could be eliminated. The bad news was that the replacement time-share contract would carry prevailing market prices, and The Winning Edge would bear the risk of price increases for new aircraft, as well as aircraft operating expenditures, after just five short years. According to Jet-Share's promotional literature, customers could expect these price increases to average about 4 percent each year.

Given the novelty of the time-share contract, and the fact that Jet-Share didn't have much of a track record, Mike was a little hesitant to endorse this option. At the same time, this plan required virtually no connecting flights, and offered greater price protection than the contract arrangement with a commercial airline. All things considered, Mike rated the risk level of this option higher than the aircraft purchase option but lower than the contract option with a commercial carrier.

With all the facts on the table, it was time to get them organized and make a decision. The Winning Edge had enjoyed five years of steadily rising sales and profits, yet the firm's managers were not comfortable making multimillion dollar capital acquisitions at the drop of a hat. In addition, Mike was worried that a corporate jet might be viewed by outside directors and shareholders as an unnecessary extravagance. Most certainly, travel by private jet would provide first-class accommodations for the firm's management team, and the corporate travel policy had always required the austerity of coach flights, even for Mike. Finally, Mike realized that he could ill afford to disappoint the board with an inappropriate capital expenditure. Just last month, they gently but firmly admonished him to treat his employees with greater respect and control his temper. The board was clearly satisfied with the sales and profit growth The Winning Edge enjoyed under Mike's leadership, but privately many board members were beginning to express reservations that the financial end didn't necessarily justify the management means. As Mike retired to his office to consider his options, he realized he needed to make a decision—but more important, he needed to make the *right* decision.

TABLE 1

The Winning Edge, Inc.
Corporate Travel Statistics

I. Executive Travel Summary

Average round-trip flights per year (based on current fiscal year)	48
Average time lost awaiting flight departures (per round-trip flight)	4 hours
Annual growth in executive travel (percentage of flights per year)	5%
Average airtime per round-trip flight	4 hours
Average number of executive travelers per trip	4

II. Commercial Airline Cost Data

Average ticket price (round-trip; coach)	$1,000
Average frequent flier discount available to coach passengers	$200
Average ticket price (round-trip; first-class)	$1,300
Average frequent flier discount available to first-class passengers	$200

III. Internal Travel Costs

Executive travel manager (annual salary)	$40,000
Executive travelers (average annual salary per person)	$208,000

IV. Jet Aircraft Ownership Costs (Cessna Citation II)

Acquisition cost	$2,500,000
Range (nautical miles)	1,600
Passenger seating capacity (excluding crew)	7
Direct operating cost summary (per hour of flight):	
Fuel	$400
Crew	250
Maintenance	<u>167</u>
Total direct operating costs	$817
Annual fixed costs	$204,528

V. Projected Annual Price Increases for Travel-Related Expenditures (%)	
A. Salaries:	
Travel office personnel	4%
Flight crew	6
Executive travelers	8
B. Commercial Air Fares:	
Coach tickets	6
First-class tickets	6
C. Capital Expenditures:	
Jet aircraft prices	3
Fuel costs	8
Maintenance costs	5
Fixed expenses	4
Capital costs	3
VI. Risk-Adjusted Corporate Capital Costs (after-tax)	
Low-risk projects	7%
Average-risk projects	10
High-risk projects	14
Corporate tax rate	40

TABLE 2

The Winning Edge, Inc.
Executive Travel Forecast

	Year									
	1	2	3	4	5	6	7	8	9	10
Number of round-trip flights	50	53	56	59	62	65	68	71	75	79

QUESTIONS

1. Given that each of the three corporate transportation alternatives covers a different length of time, what time period should be used to compare these options?

2. In constructing the cash flows associated with each option, how should the analyst treat The Winning Edge's $250,000 expenditure for computer hardware and software to coordinate its executive travel schedule? Why?

3. In constructing the cash flows associated with the commercial airline contract option, should the analyst include: (*a*) the average cost of coach tickets; (*b*) the cost of upgrading a coach fare to a first-class ticket; and/or (*c*) both of these ticket prices? Be sure to explain your answer, and indicate how *each* of these costs would appear in the capital budgeting analysis.

4. In constructing the cash flows associated with the commercial airline contract option, should the analyst include the lost time that The Winning Edge's traveling executives spend waiting for connecting flights in airport terminals? If so, how should this time be represented in each year of the capital budgeting analysis?

5. What is the annual depreciation expense that The Winning Edge may claim against taxable income under each of the three travel options?

6. Does each of the three travel options contain a different risk level? If so, how should the analyst incorporate this risk differential within the capital budgeting analysis? Be sure to identify the appropriate discount rate necessary to evaluate each alternative in your answer, and explain your selection of each particular discount rate.

7. Should the capital budgeting analysis include the forecast inflation rates shown in Table 1? If so, demonstrate how each of these inflation factors will affect the various cash flows in the capital budgeting analysis.

8. What is the net salvage value that The Winning Edge can expect to receive from *(a)* the aircraft purchase option, and *(b)* the aircraft time-share option?

9. Based on your answers to Questions 1 through 8, prepare a schedule of corporate cash flows relevant to each of the three travel alternatives, and calculate the present value of total costs for each option. In developing the cash flows, assume that capital expenditures necessary to fund a change in The Winning Edge's corporate travel policy occur in the current period (Year 0) and all operating expenditures begin in the next fiscal year (Year 1).

10. In Question 9, should the analyst focus on before-tax or after-tax cash flows? Why?

11. The case mentions that The Winning Edge has enjoyed several years of growing profitability. How does this information influence your answer to Question 10? If the case included information that led you to believe that The Winning Edge would suffer several years of financial losses over the next decade, how would this new information change your estimates of project cash flows expected from each of the three travel alternatives?

12. In evaluating capital budgeting projects with different project lives, financial analysts often use a technique called the Equivalent Annual Annuity. Would this technique be useful in this case to evaluate the three travel alternatives? Why or why not?

13. Is Mike Cramer's assessment of the risk level of each travel alternative sufficient justification for the financial analyst to apply different discount rates to each of the three travel alternatives? Why or why not?

14. All things considered, which of the three options should Mike select? Be sure to justify your answer on the basis of *(a)* your capital budgeting analysis of the three travel alternatives, and *(b)* the contextual information provided by the case.

Case 17

Return-Based Measures of Project Evaluation

Gideon Research, Inc.

Carol Brainard, president of Gideon Research, Inc., could scarcely contain her excitement as she greeted her young research staff arriving at work early one spring morning in 1993. She had very good news to share with the researchers. Gideon's recent proposal to Mercantile Pharmaceuticals, a large East Coast drug manufacturer specializing in the biochemistry of genetic engineering, had been accepted. Mercantile would fund Gideon's synthetic drug screening project, and accept a percentage of future profits from any marketable new drugs that emerged from the project as compensation for the investment.

While Gideon was in the business of discovering life-saving new drugs, the only magic elixir that might save the young company was cold, hard cash. Gideon was founded in mid-1992 by a group of creative and restless biochemists at Mercantile who decided to leave the large, bureaucratic organization and go it alone. Unfortunately, Gideon's young researchers were unable to produce any new drug compounds in short order, and the consulting projects they relied on to meet payroll kept the scientists from doing any substantive research on their own. Without a new infusion of outside cash, Gideon was doomed to fail.

Full of promising new ideas and out of cash, Brainard had swallowed her pride and approached the Vice President of Research and Development at Mercantile with a proposal. Gideon's scientists would share the profits on any genetically engineered new drugs developed over the 1993–98 period, if Mercantile would agree to provide $75,000 in contract research funds to Gideon in 1993. There was only one small problem: Gideon needed the $75,000 up-front, before any research could begin.

Much to Carol's surprise, Mercantile accepted the offer—with a few strings attached. In order to avoid the lengthy review process associated with all new capital investments at Mercantile, the firm would provide $75,000 in contract research funds from its general operating fund. This required Gideon to book the cash infusion as taxable revenue, rather than show the $75,000 as an equity investment in the firm. While $75,000 in cash represented a great deal of money at Gideon, Mercantile could easily and quickly accommodate the expenditure from its operating budget. Mercantile's desire to assist Gideon was anything but altruistic. While Mercantile's senior managers privately felt Gideon's researchers were a bunch of young, loose cannons, the firm realized that these creative scientists had brains, enthusiasm, and most importantly, they were hungry. As such, Mercantile believed Gideon just might be able to move the science of synthetic drug screening forward.

Synthesizing new drug compounds in the mid-1990s was a tricky business. The screening process required Gideon to identify complementary chemical structures between potential new drug compounds and the surface of human cells, called receptor locations. When a drug matched a receptor, it would bind to the cell, in much the same way that a key fits in a lock. The ensuing chemical reaction between the cell and the drug would trigger the cell's genetic machinery to make a particular protein, change its structure, or simply self-destruct. Identifying and understanding the chemical linkages between new drug compounds and human cells was the key to predicting how new drugs might work, and how they might arrest the disease process.

Mercantile's cash infusion would go a long way toward getting Gideon's researchers back to work, but it wouldn't solve all of the firm's problems. What Carol didn't tell the research and development people at Mercantile was that the young researchers desperately needed $50,000 in new computer equipment to analyze and record the results of their experiments. She felt that this information would surely lead Mercantile to reject Gideon's request for contract research funding, because the top brass at Mercantile would quickly realize that Gideon didn't have the necessary tools to do any contract research. So, she did what many young entrepreneurs might do to save their businesses—she lied. Well, it wasn't exactly a lie—in the heat of the moment, she simply forgot to tell the stuffy old guys at Mercantile that her firm didn't have any computer equipment.

Now, however, the chickens were coming home to roost. Mercantile was planning to forward $75,000 to Gideon on Monday morning, and her research staff was ecstatic. She figured she could use most of Mercantile's $75,000 to quickly and quietly acquire the computer equipment, and still have enough left over to cover the 1993 operating expenses on the drug screening project. With luck, some good genetic engineering, and a little financial acrobatics, she could insure the short-term survival of Gideon.

Then the phone rang. Her R&D contact at Mercantile called to convey some last-minute instructions for Carol before Mercantile's CFO would release the $75,000 check. Mercantile wanted to make sure that Gideon had examined alternative cash flow scenarios associated with the project, and that the young researchers knew exactly what they were getting into. Carol needed to provide Mercantile with an estimation of the project's cash flows over the 1993–98 period under a worst-case scenario, demonstrating that the project's return would cover Gideon's risk-adjusted, after-tax capital cost of 11 percent even if the research produced no marketable new drugs through 1998.

Carol's heart sank. How could she possibly demonstrate the value of the project to Mercantile's managers if they had no new drugs to sell? Looking at the project's preliminary revenue and cost estimates, shown below in Table 1, the only revenues she could attribute to the project involved speaker's fees at meetings of the scientific community at which her staff would present the project's nonproprietary research results. Surely these minuscule revenues wouldn't provide a rate of return that covered Mercantile's capital cost. Even worse, Carol knew she had to disclose the planned computer purchase in the numbers she delivered to Mercantile.

A little financial analysis confirmed her worst suspicions. Developing the worst-case cash flow projection requested by Mercantile, Carol's spreadsheet was awash in red ink. She treated the $75,000 contract research funds from Mercantile as taxable revenue, and depreciated the $50,000 computer equipment using the MACRS depreciation schedule for 5-year property shown in Table 2. Since she planned to acquire this equipment immediately, she began recognizing depreciation expense in her 1993 cash flow projection. Gideon's marginal tax rate was 35 percent, and following Mercantile's instructions, she represented the project's capital cost as 11 percent.

The project looked like a definite money-loser. Even worse, when she tried to calculate the internal rate of return on the worst-case cash flows, her spreadsheet responded with an "ERROR" message. "Oh great," she thought, "the return's so low, this old computer can't even calculate it!" Full of despair, she wondered how she would break this devastating news to her exuberant young research staff.

TABLE 1						
Gideon Research, Inc.						
Projected Revenues and Expenses - Drug Screening Project						
Worst-Case Scenario						
	1993	**1994**	**1995**	**1996**	**1997**	**1998**
Speaker's fees (revenue)	$0	$965	$531	$0	$0	$0
Operating expenses	6,031	4,180	3,946	3,929	4,092	4,732

TABLE 2	
MACRS Recovery Allowance Percentages:	
Five-Year Property	
Ownership Year	**Recovery Percentage**
1	20%
2	32
3	19
4	12
5	11
6	6
	100%

QUESTIONS

1. Using the project cost and revenue estimates provided in Table 1, calculate the project's worst-case annual net cash flows over the 1993–98 period.

2. Calculate the net present value of the worst-case cash flows developed in Question 1. Based on this calculation, should Mercantile agree to fund the project? Why or why not?

3. Review your answers to Questions 1 and 2. Notice that the change in net income provided by the drug screening project indicates that Mercantile's investment is clearly a money-losing proposition, but the net present value obtained in Question 2 tells a very different story. How can this project show such poor profit potential, yet at the same time, produce a positive net present value?

4. Calculate the internal rate of return associated with the cash flows you developed in Question 1. Based on this calculation, should Mercantile agree to fund the drug screening project? Why or why not?

5. Develop the net present value profile associated with the worst-case cash flows obtained in Question 1. Does this profile provide any indication why Carol was unable to calculate the project's internal rate of return on her spreadsheet? Explain your answer.

6. Visually examine the project's net cash flows you obtained in Question 1. Do these cash flows provide any preliminary evidence to suggest that the IRR calculation may be unstable in this circumstance? What is this evidence?

7. Given the difficulties associated with the traditional IRR calculation in this circumstance, calculate the modified internal rate of return (MIRR) on the project's worst-case cash flows. Based on this rate of return, do you think that Mercantile should approve the project? Why or why not?

8. Return to the net present value profile you constructed in Question 5. Notice that the drug screening project's net present value reaches a maximum when the project's cash flows are discounted at approximately 30 percent. Does this finding suggest that Carol should telephone the CFO at Mercantile and urge him to raise Mercantile's cost of capital to 30 percent in order to maximize the value of this project? Why or why not?

9. Return to Question 1 and carefully examine the net cash flows associated with the drug screening project. Remember, Carol was asked by Mercantile's CFO to estimate the project's cash flows over the 1993-98 period under a worst-case scenario. Do the cash flows you constructed in Question 1 truly reflect the worst-case scenario at Gideon Research, given the project revenues and expenses reported in Table 1? Why or why not?

10. Based on your answer to Question 9, develop the net cash flows associated with your revised worst-case scenario for the drug screening project. Given these revised cash flows, how does (a) the project's net present value, and (b) the project's internal rate of return change?

11. Given your answer to Question 10, how would you advise Carol to report the worst-case cash flows to Mercantile's CFO? In particular, should she furnish Mercantile with (a) the capital budgeting analysis you prepared in Questions 1 and 2; or (b) the revised capital budgeting analysis you prepared in Questions 9 and 10? Be sure to justify your selection.

Case 18

Risk and Return in Capital Budgeting

Metal Fabricating and Recycling

The management of Metal Fabricating and Recycling (MFR) had enjoyed an extended period of revenue and earnings growth. This period of strong performance had lasted for the past four years and shown compound average annual growth of 12 percent. MFR's management was convinced that the recent strong growth was due to the company's entry into the recycling business and to its careful cultivation of its overseas customers.

MFR was a maker of heating and air-conditioning ductwork for commercial buildings and large residential buildings. The firm, in general a subcontractor on large building projects, had a strong reputation in the region in which it operated. That region was the area of the United States bounded by Buffalo, New York, and Cleveland, Ohio, in the north and Louisville, Kentucky, and Evansville, Indiana in the south. That area was the primary industrial region in the United States in the period from early in the twentieth century to the 1970s. The decline since that time had abated somewhat, and the region was believed to be at least "holding its own" in terms of economic viability. In any case, MFR operated in this environment from a position of dominance.

In terms of its operational strength and reputation, once the firm was contracted to participate in a construction project, its usual practice was to attend to the specific needs of the project through careful selection of materials. The desire was to pay special attention to the specific demands of the design, function, and purpose of the building and to the particular demands of the construction company. MFR designed, constructed (fabricated), and installed its product. Moreover, it guaranteed its work in a manner that assured a high level of serviceability for years to come.

In addition to its ductwork design and installation, the firm was also engaged in the reclamation of sheet metal, primarily ductwork, during the demolition of commercial buildings or large residential buildings. This recovered sheet metal was compressed into stacked sheets and sold directly to recycling companies. This portion of the business was highly profitable, and company management was considering ways in which to expand it geographically.

In addition to its dominance in its own geographic area, MFR had a very solid presence in an industrial region of France, the area roughly north of Paris and toward the Belgian border.

In fact, this region was similar in terms of economics to the area in the United States in which MFR operated. It was believed by some observers, however, that a recovery, or at least a strategy for an economic recovery, was not as well developed in the French region as in the U.S. region, known in the 1980s as the "rust belt."

In any event, the revenue from MFR's sales to its French customers was becoming an increasingly important part of its total revenue stream. An estimated 35 percent of the firm's cash flow would come from the overseas operation over the next three to five years. This was due to the gradual restoration of the French industrial region — unemployment was quite high in the region — and to MFR's well-established reputation as a reliable company. Table 1 outlines the firm's cash flow for the past year.

TABLE 1
Metal Fabricating and Recycling *Statement of Cash Flows* *1995* *($000s)*

Net income	$2,040
Depreciation	1,740
Increase acc. pay	520
Increase accruals	170
Increase acc. rec.	(1,040)
Increase inventory	(3,480)
Net cash flow from ops.	(50)
Fixed asset acquisition	(4,000)
Increase in notes payable	870
Increase in bonds	3,030
Payment of c/s dividends	(1,070)
Net cash flow from fin.	(1,220)
Net red'n. in cash & near cash	(1,220)
Cash & near cash; beginning of year	1,390
Cash & near cash; end of year	170

An assessment of the individual items for the firm's end-of-year cash flow determination caused Janet Dagna, the firm's controller to reflect once again on the issue of risk management. This issue had been the topic of heated debate recently between Dagna and her assistant John Taber. The topic of concern was that of managing (defining, measuring, assessing the effect on the firm's value) the risk of the firm's overall cash flows, and the overseas cash flows in particular. Again the items shown as captions in Table 1 set Dagna to thinking. What actually caused the variability in the overseas net income? For example, what effect did some of the other items on the cash flow statement have upon the end-of-year cash balance?

In addition to the concerns related to cash flow, Dagna and Taber wondered how the discount rate used to find the present value of cash flows might be better used to define and measure risk. Table 2 provides the latest balance sheet for the firm. The balance sheet data for the previous two years is not significantly different from Table 1, except in terms of depreciation's effect upon buildings and equipment, and the change in retained earnings.

TABLE 2

Metal Fabricating and Recycling
Balance Sheet
December 31,1995
($000s)

Total current assets	$ 1,066	Total current liabilities	$ 43
Land and buildings (net)	45,288	Long-term debt @ 8%	28,971
Equipment (net)	16,250	Common stock ($10 par)	26,640
Total fixed assets	61,538	Retained earnings	6,550
Total assets	$62,604		$62,604

The company's stock price is now $40 per share and the dividend expected in the next period is $2.50. The 15-year $1,000 bonds outstanding since 1992 are selling at par. The tax rate for MFR is 30 percent.

It was clear to Dagna that the standard method of defining and measuring risk in the finance literature was the variability in expected cash flows and the variance, standard deviation, and the coefficient of variation, respectively. Of a more pressing concern, however, was the relative variability of the items in Table 1. Was any one of the items more variable than another, and if so which ones?

QUESTIONS

1. Discuss Dagna's concern over the overseas cash flow variability. Is that concern justified? Why or why not?

2. If Dagna determines that the overseas cash flows are 20 percent more variable than the firm's average cash flow, how might that information be used to adjust for such risk?

3. From Table 1, which items if any may be more variable for an overseas operation. Why? Explain how trend data would be helpful in this instance.

4. What is the relationship between risk and return in financial decision making?

5. What is MFR's weighted average cost of capital? Is this a likely number for use as a discount rate in capital budgeting?

6.   Is it necessary to actually adjust for risk? Isn't awareness of risk in cash flows sufficient? Explain your answer.

7.   Generally, risk and return move together (are positively correlated) in finance. Explain this statement.

8.   Is it reasonable for MFR's management to assume that dividend growth and growth in cash flow are essentially identical? Why or why not?

9.   Based upon Table 1, what is the distinction between net income and cash flow?

Case 19

Capital Budgeting—Abandonment Value

Midwood Electronics

The internal investment decisions facing Midwood Electronics were not only influenced by the firm's business opportunities, but by the capital shortage, which usually accompanied strong revenue growth. Midwood Electronics was founded by Lee Moorer in the late 1960s. Mr. Moorer was presently serving as CEO, and his son Dan Moorer was the company's chief financial officer. The company, a leading manufacturer of advanced circuitry for the computers used to operate chemical processing plants and refineries, was located in the upper midwestern United States.

　　　　The decision that the firm now faced concerned the opportunity to invest in the manufacturing capabilities for a new type of computer-operated switching device. The device would be able to react more sensitively to variations in the temperatures of liquids that typically flowed through the many enclosures, strainers, traps, and the like in the chemical processing and petroleum refining businesses. The device was recently invented by Midwood's research and development (R&D) staff and had undergone the rigorous in-house testing that was standard for a new product. While the device, known as an M-7, was not for a new application, the firm's marketing staff was reasonably certain that there were ample opportunities in the overseas market. The staff also knew that such opportunities depended upon the on-site test results conducted by an independent consulting firm that had an impeccable international reputation for impartial evaluation of such products. In fact, the consulting firm's test of the M-7 would determine whether Midwood would proceed with production, regardless of the results of its own in-house test.

　　　　Midwood Electronics had an efficient and well-run capital budgeting process, which accommodated the firm's complex and extensive product base. In essence the firm operated with a relatively centralized management structure. The firm had an R&D division and a manufacturing division. The remaining functional areas were in direct support of those two areas. Those consisted primarily of the human resources department and the marketing function.

　　　　The capital budgeting staff was organized so as to "blur the line" between the analysis that in some firms would be made at the division level and that which would be made by the corporate controller's staff at the "corporate" level. This was possible due to the relatively simple organizational structure of the firm and to the similarity among the capital investments that came forward. Such proposals were generally prepared by the marketing research staff in consultation with R&D. It was Dan Moorer's job, as CFO, to see to it that the technical aspects of capital investment analysis were adhered to by the various analysts in this area. In addition, it was his task to ensure that the most reliable, relevant, and efficient theoretical developments were applied to his firm's operations. To that end, such issues as risk and return, measurement and other assessments of those items, the cost of capital, and their proper application to the decisions at hand were constantly on the mind of Moorer.

Of particular interest to the CFO was the question of risk and return. While these issues were standard concerns in capital budgeting analysis, the correct definition, measurement and application was another matter. Moorer was particularly concerned with the evaluation of the cash flows pertaining to the M-7. For example, the M-7 was to have a cash flow stream that had the following relevant characteristics: the firm's cost of capital is 14 percent and the M-7 cash flows were considered to be of average risk, relative to the firm's overall cash flow stream.

Moorer wondered whether the standard deviation or some other risk measure, perhaps the coefficient of variation, would better explain the project's risk. In addition to that concern, the consulting firm had provided Dan Moorer with net salvage value estimates, for each year, which are shown in Table 1. Those estimates are accompanied by the operating cash flow information for the M-7. Moorer understood that the net salvage value information was a reasonable proxy for abandonment value for the M-7 at the end of the respective year.

Dan Moorer was very concerned that a correct interpretation of the data provided by his analysts found its way into the evaluation of M-7. As with all discretionary capital expenditures this proposal would be subjected to a rigorous discounted cash flow analysis. A central part of such an analysis was a careful understanding of the risk of the project's cash flows. The question was how much variability would the cash flows exhibit? Therefore, the definition and measurement of risk were of equal importance in the analysis. Moorer wondered whether decision tree analysis or any related risk assessment would be useful in this context. He also wondered what would be the likely mood of upper management if the cash flows did indeed fall into the negative column after start-up. How did these concerns mesh with the report that the cash flow stream was of average risk? These and other questions caused Moorer to believe that the analysis of M-7 was somehow incomplete.

It was of particular concern to ensure that the question of abandonment was properly addressed in the event of disappointing cash flows. Thus, a discounted cash flow assessment of the full economic life of the project as well as the value of the project under abandonment was essential. He was determined, therefore, to make sure that the analytical work for the project proceeded on schedule and included all the necessary elements for a reliable decision. Tables 2 and 3 provide certain financial data for the firm.

TABLE 1

Midwood Electronics

Cash Flow and Salvage Value Estimates M-7

($000s)

Year	Operating Cash Flows	Net Salvage Value
0	($2,000)	$2,000
1	840	1,260
2	790	900
3	529	600
4	170	295
5	122	250

TABLE 2

Midwood Electronics
Income Statement Data
($000s)

	1992	1993	1994	1995
Sales	$140,000	154,000	167,000	185,000
Profit after tax*	$11,200	12,600	12,900	14,800

*(The firm's tax rate is 30 percent)

TABLE 3

Midwood Electronics
Balance Sheet
December 31,1995
($000s)

Current assets	$32,000	Current liabilities	$ 7000
Fixed assets, net	48,000	Long-term debt	28,000
		Common stock ($10 par)	11,250
		Capital surplus	4,500
		Retained earnings	29,250
Total assets	$80,000	Total liabilities	$80,000
		and capital	

QUESTIONS

1. Discuss the meaning and relevance of the standard deviation and the coefficient of variation as measures of cash flow risk. Does Moorer need these specific measures in this situation?

2.   In terms of risk, how would the M-7 be viewed by Midwood's management if it were a new product for a new market? Explain your reasoning.

3.   Does the M-7 seem to fit the normal operations of Midwood Electronics? Why or why not?

4.   What has been Midwood's sales and profit after-tax compound growth rates, based upon Table 2 data?

5.   Is it logical or in keeping with sound business practice for Moorer to include abandonment of the M-7 in his analysis? Explain your reasoning.

6.   Calculate the net present value of the M-7. The project can be abandoned at the end of any one of the five years.

7.   How should Moorer proceed concerning the M-7?

PART IV

INTERMEDIATE AND LONG-TERM FINANCING

Case 20

Evaluating the Cost of Bank Loans

Deal's Computerland

Amanda Deal, president of Deal's Computerland, had recently finished an arduous round of meetings with her financial staff. Those meetings dealt with the details necessary to produce an accurate and reliable forecast of the company's cash needs for the next twelve months. The firm's sales were generally not seasonal, and Deal and her finance staff had used annual pro forma financial statements to determine the amount of external financing needed.

Deal's Computerland had been in operation since 1981. Amanda Deal believed that the retail personal computer outlet had successfully weathered the business contractions and other manifestations of a changing economy that occurred throughout the 1980s. The firm's sales, $2.5 million in 1993, had grown at a compound rate of 10 percent since 1985; the profit margin had been less steady. Both the most recent sales growth and the profit margin represented improvements over the first several years of the firm's operations.

The need for external financing was a new phenomenon for the company. Previously, the firm's short-term funding needs were satisfied through reliance on trade-credit (a heavy buildup in accounts payable); or through the use of cash reserves over and above the cash needed for normal business transactions. At present, however, increased sales growth and the desire to avoid over-reliance upon the firm's suppliers made short-term financing from external sources necessary. It was this overall situation which placed Amanda Deal and her finance staff in the position of having to assess the various types of short-term loans offered by commercial banks.

In typical fashion, Ms. Deal wanted complete information on the various bank lending options. Many who observed her business practices believed that Amanda Deal's attention to detail and her skill at knowing when to delegate authority and duties largely accounted for the success of her business during less than hospitable economic times. In order to satisfy her need for information concerning the specific aspects of bank lending, Deal asked Lynn Kerr, the company's controller, to prepare a brief report illustrating the important aspects of bank lending. Kerr believed this to be a logical assignment given the work recently completed concerning the pro forma financial statements. Exhibit 1 below is Kerr's report.

EXHIBIT 1

Cost of Bank Lending Summary

TO: Amanda Deal

FROM: Lynn Kerr

DATE: February 9, 1994

RE: Bank Lending

Commercial banks are, in general, the primary suppliers of short-term loans to businesses. Short-term financing, as used in this context, refers to the various sources of external financing which are payable within one year. The need for such financing in the well-run firm arises when the spontaneous sources of financing prove insufficient. Firms may borrow from banks by using a line of credit, a revolving credit agreement, or a term loan.

The line of credit is for the purpose of providing short-term financing to those firms whose needs are reasonably predictable and recurring. In other words, rather than waiting until the funds are needed, the bank is asked by the firm to commit to the credit line. Thus, the bank makes a specific amount of funds available to the firm for a specified period. The time commitment on a line of credit rarely extends beyond one year. The rate on the credit line may be variable relative to the prime rate of interest. For the formal line of credit the bank will charge a commitment fee. Once the line is established, the firm can "draw down" any desired portion of the line of credit on very short notice to the bank. In most short-term revolving credit agreements the bank will stipulate that the borrower be "out of the bank" for a period of 30–60 days each year. That is, the loan must be paid up for that period. This allows the bank to clearly determine whether the loan is <u>actually</u> a revolving credit situation. If the borrower cannot pay the loan and avoid borrowing for a 30–60 day period then the loan may be converted to a term loan. A term loan is a commercial loan with a maturity greater than one year. Term loans from commercial banks rarely extend beyond seven years.

In terms of a more permanent line of credit, banks offer what is called a revolving credit arrangement. This is similar to a line of credit; however, the bank makes a commitment to the firm for a period of several years. There is a commitment fee attached to the revolving credit arrangement as in the case of the line of credit. In addition to the commitment fee, the borrower has to agree in writing to the credit arrangement. The written agreement contains loan covenants. Such covenants protect the lender and refer to such things as the level of working capital, dividend payments, and additional borrowing. These limitations on further financing activity protect the borrower as well. They may prevent activities not in keeping with sound financial practices.

EXHIBIT 1
(continued)

Page 2

A further aspect of bank borrowing has to do with the compensating balance. There are two types of compensating balances. One type is the balance that is a part of the check clearing activities of the bank. The compensating balance in this case provides the bank a means for earning a fee for the check clearing. The compensating balance funds are invested by the bank. The other type of compensating balance is part of the loan arrangement. As an example, in the case of a line of credit, the compensating balance may be expressed as some percentage of the drawn down amount of the line, or as a percent of the total line. Compensating balances also increase the effective cost of borrowing.

$$\text{Interest} = (P) \times (R) \times (N \div 360);$$

where: P = Principal (face) amount of the loan;
                R = Annual interest rate; and
                N = Number of days outstanding.

Based upon the foregoing example, if a firm borrows $50,000 for one year at an interest rate of 8 percent, the interest on the loan would be $4,000 (i.e., interest = $50,000 x 0.08 x (360 ÷ 360) = $4,000). If the term of the note were four months, 120 days, the interest would be $1,333.33 (i.e., interest = $50,000 x 0.08 x (120 ÷ 360) = $1,333.33). Interest is generally calculated using a 360-day year.

The annual interest rate charged on a loan is called the <u>nominal annual rate of interest</u>. The <u>effective annual cost</u> of the loan usually differs from the nominal rate. The effective annual cost depends upon the <u>net</u> amount of funds available to the borrower. The net funds to the borrower is affected by a compensating balance requirement, or by the loan being a discounted loan. The interest is paid at the inception of the loan in the case of a discounted loan. The borrower receives the principal amount minus the discounted interest. The effective annual cost of a loan which is discounted <u>and</u> has a compensating balance requirement as a specific provision of the loan would appear as follows:

Periodic annual cost = Annual interest rate ÷

[1 - discount percentage - compensating balance percentage].

It is the foregoing which influences the effective annual cost of borrowed funds. Banks discount loans or impose compensating balances based upon a number of factors. The state of the economy, the flexibility of the bank's lending policies, and the creditworthiness of the borrower are the primary reasons for a compensating balance or discounting to be part of the loans to businesses.

Deal read Kerr's memorandum with great interest. She then reflected upon the various factors which might influence her company's negotiations with the bank. Deal knew that the company's profit margin was less than outstanding in recent years due to a variety of factors. Most notable among those factors were the increases in rental costs for the company's administrative offices and retail location, relatively slow moving inventory, and increased training costs, all necessary in order to survive in a slow economy. She was relieved that very recent economic reports spoke of much better days ahead for the economy in general and for the retail personal computer business. Tables 1 and 2 illustrate certain aspects of the firm's operating characteristics. The company needed $150,000 on a short-term basis. The rates prevailing at the time were between 7 and 9 percent. Computerland would most likely be able to borrow at a rate of 8 percent. Deal had also read an article in a business publication which stated that banks had become "very cautious lenders." The article described the investment practices followed by many well-run banks which yielded returns sufficient to allow them the selectivity among borrowers to which the article referred.

TABLE 1

Deal's Computer Land
Income Statement Data
($000s)

	1989	1990	1991	1992	1993
Sales	$1,715	$1,780	$1,975	$2,200	$2,500
Less: Cost of goods sold	(858)	(925)	(1,086)	(1,144)	(1,287)
Gross profit	$857	$855	$889	$1,056	$1,213
Less: Total operating costs	(686)	(765)	(849)	(990)	(995)
Earnings before interest and tax	$171	$90	$40	$66	$218
Less: Interest expense	(10)	(12)	(8)	(5)	(4)
Profit before tax	$161	$78	$32	$61	$214
Less: Income taxes	(48)	(23)	(10)	(19)	(64)
Profit after tax	$113	$55	$22	$42	$150

TABLE 2

Deal's Computerland
Selected Financial Ratio Comparisons

	1991		1992		1993	
	Firm	Industry	Firm	Industry	Firm	Industry
Inventory-to-sales	25%	20%	21%	18%	20%	16%
Current ratio	2.0	3.2	2.1	3.3	2.1	3.5
Total debt-to-total assets	20%	30%	18%	28%	16%	25%

QUESTIONS

1. Comment upon the Kerr memo. What are its major points and how might these affect Deal's Computerland? Is the memo reflective of the manner in which banks lend money?

2. As a means of adding to Deal's information in this matter, calculate the APR for each of the following for the company's $150,000 loan:

    a. Simple interest at 8 percent.
        i.   No compensating balance.
        ii. 10 percent compensating balance.
    b. Discount interest at 8 percent.
        i.   No compensating balance.
        ii. 10 percent compensating balance.

    Which of the APR's might be most appropriate for Deal's? Explain your answer.

3. If banks are investing an increasing amount of funds in the money market versus lending to business borrowers, what will this mean to Deal now and in the future?

4. Why does the bank require a period of no drawdown? Is this reasonable? Should Deal change banks because of this provision?

5. Why is Deal concerned about "over-reliance upon the firm's supplies?" Discuss the advantages and disadvantages of bank borrowing, given her attitude about the suppliers.

6. Refer to your answer to Question 2. Is Deal in a position to seek the lowest rate shown? Why or why not?

7. Generally, what causes banks to be "cautious lenders?"

8. What type of information, and in what format, will the bank likely want before it seriously considers a loan to Deal's Computerland?

9. Of what importance will trend data be to the bank in this decision? Which trends will offer the most useful information to the bank?

10. Describe, without the use of numbers, the difference between the nominal annual rate of interest and the effective annual cost of the loan.

Case 21

Small Business Financing

Clearline Filters, Inc.

Clearline Filters, Inc. (Clearline) began operations in 1985 in a midsized city in the southwestern United States. The firm manufactured a wide variety of filters, constructed of paper and metal, for an even wider variety of industrial and automotive uses. The firm was primarily a one-product company. This approach was the management policy of the firm's president, Bill Drummond. In the management philosophy that gave rise to Clearline, Drummond wanted to make the most of the expertise that he had acquired as an operations vice president for a major manufacturing firm located in the industrial section of the mid-western United States. In his rise to that position, Drummond had accumulated experience in marketing research and cost accounting. As an independent, well-educated, and experienced person he was eager to start his own company. From that experience and motivation Clearline Filters, Inc., came into being.

The company's operations were located in a modern, well-equipped building, which was purchased from a manufacturing firm whose management had decided to move its operations to the east coast. The entire operation of Clearline was under one roof. From all accounts this added to the efficiency with which the company was managed. The company employed 75 persons and was highly automated. At the end of 1995, revenues were $5 million. Table 1 illustrates the sales and earnings pattern of the firm for most of its history.

Management of Clearline consisted of a management team made up of the president, Drummond, a manager of accounting, a manager of operations, and a manager of marketing. This group met twice each month to discuss the general operations and to assess the overall conformity to the company's strategic plan. The accounting manager met once every two months with the company's external auditor. The results of those meetings were reported to Drummond on a regular basis. The firm's strategic plan was for a three-year period with semi-annual updates or revisions as the business climate dictated. The strategic plan was constructed by the management team with the participation of the external auditor.

The company's product was a paper and metal filter used in lines that transported fluid. This very ordinary product had a great number of uses. One of its most well-known applications is that of the primary component in the gasoline and diesel engine oil filter. Indeed, this application accounted for approximately 25 percent of Clearline's revenue and production volume. The machinery on which the product was made, like the plant itself, was quite modern and up-to-date. In fact, it was a primary focus of the firm's strategy to maintain a first-rate manufacturing environment in order to offer a product of the same quality. The attention to the manufacturing environment included all aspects of the operation. This very much included safety concerns for the employees and concern for the natural environment as well.

The firm's strategy, set for the next several years, was based to a great extent upon the forecast for an increased level of sales growth. The consulting department of the accounting firm that performed the auditing function for Clearline had prepared an economic forecast for the management team. The focus of that report was the health of the national economy and certain overseas economies over the next 3 to 5 years. The outlook was quite positive; revenue growth for Clearline would likely be in the range of 18-22 percent compounded annually. Moreover, the industrial output of most economies was to remain strong, and in some countries to become even stronger. In addition to that encouraging news one of Clearline's competitors, a privately owned firm, had exited the business due to an entanglement concerning the estate of the original owner. This seemed to leave Clearline in an even stronger position in the coming years.

Based upon the optimism evident in the consultant's report and the focus of the plan that Drummond and his managers had set forth, it was clear that an expansion of the present manufacturing facility was necessary. The building from which the company now operated was at capacity. The management team had been aware of the need for additional space for at least a year. It was their decision, however, to wait until they received the consultant's report before coming to a firm conclusion on how best to proceed. It was clear to the managers now that expansion should not be delayed any longer than necessary.

The primary decision that had to be made concerned how to finance the expansion. In terms of the logistics of what they needed to do, the choices were between building an addition onto the present structure or finding a buyer for the present structure and moving the operation to a larger facility. The preliminary assessment of this part of the decision had been carried out by the management team while they were waiting for the consultant's report. The team had decided to expand the present facility. The cost would be $700,000. The specific nature of the financing decision would likely revolve around a limited number of options.

The firm's stock was closely held. The majority of the common stock was held by Drummond and Bob Randel, the accounting manager. Table 2 outlines the firm's financial structure. Of the 500,000 common shares outstanding, at a par value of $1, Drummond and Randel owned 61 percent. The remaining shares were held by a few close friends and family members of the two majority owners. In most things having to do with the strategic direction of Clearline, Drummond and Randel were very much of one accord. The specific financing alternatives, however, would revolve around an equity issuance, the use of borrowed funds, or some as-yet-unspecified source.

Concerning an equity issue, the closely held nature of the company meant that there was no ready market for the firm's stock. In addition, the question of how to expand and continue to maintain a controlling interest in the firm was of major concern to Drummond and Randel. The concern over what price to charge for the shares was an issue that needed resolution. Would a sale of shares at book value be sufficient to attract investors? Given that Drummond and Randel would likely not significantly increase their stake in the company, the number of new shares that would have to be sold was also of interest, at least for the two majority stockholders. The possibility of the use of borrowed funds was also under consideration. The company's banking officer, with which it had a line of credit, had mentioned to Randel the size of the firm's existing debt level. While the banker did not consider the firm's debt level excessive, she did suggest that Randel keep "a close watch on the matter." The management team also knew that the Small Business Administration was a possible source of funds. This was especially true since the SBA had a special lending category for firms who exported a portion of their product. The projected increase in Clearline's sales was due in large part to its having taken full advantage of the growth in the overseas segment of the business. Table 3 provides data concerning overseas sales for Clearline.

TABLE 1
Clearline Filters
Revenue and Earnings

Year	Revenue	Earnings
1988	$1,879,700	$225,564
1989	2,161,655	259,399
1990	2,422,670	298,308
1991	2,735,791	343,055
1992	3,200,875	394,513
1993	3,681,006	453,690
1994	4,196,347	521,743
1995	5,000,000	600,000

TABLE 2

Clearline Filters Inc.
Balance Sheet
December 31, 1995
($000s)

Current assets	$ 150	Current liabilities	$ 100
Land	1,600	Debt	2,100
Building (net)	1,600	Common stock	500
Equipment (net)	1,545	Surplus	150
		Retained earnings	2,045
Total assets	$4,895	Total liabilities and equity	$4,895

TABLE 3		
Clearline Filters Inc.		
Selected Revenue Data		
Years	1990	1995
Total revenue	$2,422,670	$5,000,000
O'seas revenue	$ 341,974	$1,150,000

QUESTIONS

1.   Why is Clearline Filters, Inc., referred to as a closely held company?

2.   Based upon certain general but widely used categorizations, is Clearline Filters, Inc., a small business? Why or why not?

3.   What has been the compound average annual growth rate in revenue and earnings after-tax for the firm?

4.   Calculate the book value per share of the outstanding equity. If the firm finances the expansion with equity and book value per share is used as the issuing price, how many new shares must be issued in order to secure the necessary funds?

5.   Based upon your answer to Question 4, what will be the ownership percentage held by Drummond and Randel after the new issue? Assume no new shares purchased by Drummond and Randel.

6.   Calculate some financial ratios that may be useful to the management team in an assessment of the current performance of the company and in the decision on how to finance the expansion. Explain the reason for your choice of ratios and the meaning of the ratios that you have chosen. In 1995 if earnings before interest and taxes were $1 million and the firm's interest expense was $143,000, what is the times-interest-earned ratio? Assume further that the ratio will be 5.5 if borrowed funds are used. Please discuss.

7.   In general, do the projected overseas sales pose any additional risk to the firm? Consider exchange rate risk in your answer. How should the management team address such risk if it exists?

8.   What financing choice should the management make: debt; equity; or an SBA loan?

Case 22

Equity Valuation in a Public Stock Offering

Suburban Electronics Company

Suburban Electronics Company was founded in 1979 by John Marris, a graduate of the College of Engineering at a nearby university. It had been Marris' dream to own a business, and after just two years of employment with an electrical engineering design firm, he went out on his own. Suburban Electronics designed and built a variety of electronic warning devices, burglar alarms, and the like. All of the items manufactured by the company were designed by Marris and one assistant, and were then built on the premises.

John Marris had earned a degree in electrical engineering, and his assistant, H. J. "Hank" Mack, was a mechanical engineer. The small company's products were sold in several ways. Some of the smaller, more commonplace products were sold to major wholesalers and retailers and were "private branded" by those companies. That is, the products were sold under the brand name of the major company. In that aspect of its business, Suburban Electronics Company had a reputation as a reliable, high-quality producer of electronic products. In fact, one of the company's best selling private branded items was an electric garage door opener sold by two very large general merchandise retail chains under their own brand names.

The other aspect of the company's business revolved around doing contract work for large manufacturers. For example, the company had just secured a contract to manufacture the alarms that sound when a car door is opened while the keys are in the ignition. This contract was with a Japanese automobile manufacturer, and John Marris considered the contract his best ever and firmly believed that it would launch his company into its next phase of development.

Suburban Electronics had increased its sales and earnings at a steady pace since its inception. As a result of that growth and the desire to expand the size and scope of the business to the highest proportions it could reach, Marris desired to take the company public. Marris and Mack realized a need to raise additional capital in the future, but also wanted to make their ownership in the company more liquid. A public market for the stock would accomplish both objectives. Table 1 is the balance sheet for Suburban Electronics. Table 2 is a summary of sales and earnings data for the company. Table 3 illustrates certain operating characteristics for a composite of firms related in customer type and other operating characteristics to Suburban Electronics.

Planning to go public, John Marris and Hank Mack had several conversations with Sandra Tracy, a principal in a "boutique" type investment banking firm headquartered in the southeastern city in which Suburban Electronics operated. Tracy's company was known as a boutique because of its highly specialized line of business. That business consisted of taking small firms public, and valuing private companies for various purposes.

With Marris' wish to go public, attention turned to the valuation of Suburban's stock. While Tracy was well-versed in the valuation of companies, Marris and Mack were not. As a result, Tracy wanted to be sure that her approach to the task was not only clear and correct, but that it was understandable and reasonable to the two owner/managers. She had learned, for example, that price-earnings multiples for several public firms in Suburban Electronics' area of the country were in the 12–14 range. The market value per share to book value per share for those firms ranged from three to five. When it was explained clearly, Tracy believed the owners would readily understand this information. In addition, it was Tracy's opinion that the company could pay at least 20 percent of its earnings as dividends. This would compare with a payout of 15–25 percent for several similar companies with which Tracy was familiar. Those firms offered their equity holders a total return of approximately 20–22 percent.

All of the existing shares were owned by Marris and Mack. Marris' interest in the company amounted to 270,000 shares. The funds for the initial capitalization had originated with a mortgaged home in the case of Mack, and the sale of inherited farmland in the case of Marris. There was a great emotional inclination to maintain control of the firm on the part of Marris and Mack. It was clear to them, however, that the real need was to have the firm continue to grow and prosper. Therefore, they both believed, and Tracy had provided additional urging, that a public offering of the stock was the most logical course of action.

TABLE 1

Suburban Electronics Company
Balance Sheet
December 31, 1992
($000s)

Current assets	$400	Current liabilities	$300
Fixed assets	2,500	Mortgages	250
		Common stock	
		($1 par value)	300
		Retained earnings	2,050
		Total liabilities and	
Total assets	$2,900	equity	$2,900

TABLE 2
Suburban Electronics Company
Sales and Earnings History

Year	Sales	Net Income After Tax	EPS
1982	$1,292,000	$155,040	$0.52
1983	1,550,000	217,000	0.72
1984	1,861,000	241,930	0.80
1985	1,900,000	247,000	0.82
1986	2,010,000	241,000	0.82
1987	2,350,000	258,500	0.85
1988	2,820,000	338,400	1.13
1989	3,584,000	430,080	1.43
1990	4,600,000	552,000	1.83
1991	6,250,000	717,200	2.38
1992	8,000,000	811,448	2.70

TABLE 3
Suburban Electronics Company
1992 Composite Data
Electrical Component Manufacturers
(based upon 10-year averages)

Market value common shares	$15 to $25
Total debt as a percentage of total assets	25%
Compound growth in sales	15%
Compound growth in earnings per share	16%
Return on equity	25%

QUESTIONS

1. Evaluate Suburban Electronics' growth rate for sales, net income after-tax, and EPS.

2. Develop a range of values for Suburban Electronics' common stock per share.

3. Which of the values in question two seem most reasonable? Why?

4.   Discuss the appropriateness of using data for firms similar to Suburban Electronics to develop a common stock price for Suburban.

5.   What additional data and information would you prefer for the valuation requested in Question 2? Explain your reasoning.

6.   Do the historical data in Table 2 seem sufficient for such an important decision as assigning value to a firm's stock?

7.   Marris and Mack would like to maintain control of the company. Discuss this motivation relative to their desire to have the firm grow.

8.   What role should Marris and Mack reasonably expect for themselves now that sales and earnings are expanding at a significant rate?

9.   Should the owners consider an outright sale of the company?

10. Discuss the influences imposed upon the company by the larger economy.

11. How do the company's chances for survival and prosperity into the future (i.e., 5 to 10 years) seem based upon the information provided?

Case 23

Underwriting and Issuing New Common Stock

Neptune's Locker, Inc.

Floating serenely in the shimmering blue seas off the coast of Jamaica one bright April morning in 1717, the 100-foot, three-masted galley *Wyandot* was an impressive sight. She had just unloaded cargo carried from the Mediterranean to the New World, and was now loaded with ivory, indigo, and thousands of pounds of gold and silver bound for an Atlantic crossing to England. While the *Wyandot's* profile was indeed breathtaking in the calm Jamaican waters, it was the ship's cargo—not her profile—that attracted young Samuel Bellamy's attention.

Bellamy was a former sailor in the British navy who left His Majesty's service in 1715 seeking fame and fortune in colonial Massachusetts. He persuaded a wealthy British landowner to finance a ship, and he left Cape Cod early in the summer of 1715 with a crew of free men looking for sunken treasure off the coast of Florida. Seeking sunken treasure in 1715 was one thing, finding it and recovering it was an altogether different task. As you might expect, Bellamy's crew wasn't particularly successful in this line of work, and they soon started looking for the kind of treasure that was floating on top of—rather than beneath—the ocean.

That's a nice way to suggest that Bellamy—now known as Black Bellamy—became a pirate. Not just any pirate, mind you, but a most successful pirate. In just over a year as captain, Bellamy had captured over 50 ships and "acquired"—oh, all right, *stolen*—over 28,500 pieces-of-eight. This sum paled in comparison with the cargo of the *Wyandot*, which was rumored to include over 30,000 pounds sterling, as well as Spanish gold and various other metallic treasures. In Bellamy's eyes, the *Wyandot* was ripe for the picking.

And pick, he did, in the Spring of 1717. After a three-day chase up the North American coastline, Bellamy's crew captured the *Wyandot* and made her the flagship of their burgeoning pirate fleet. Heading to New England for a little R&R, however, the buccaneers ran smack into a full-scale nor'easter, with blinding rain, 70 mile-per-hour winds, and waves cresting to 40 feet. The top-heavy and cargo-laden *Wyandot* was quickly swept into the shoals off Cape Cod, where Bellamy, now known as *Wet* Bellamy, and his treasure earned a swift trip to the ocean floor.

Only one sailor lived to tell the tale of the *Wyandot*, but as it turned out, that was enough. The legend of the sinking, and talk of pirate treasure sitting on the ocean floor less than five miles off the coast of Cape Cod, was passed down through generation after generation of New Englanders. While everyone knew the story, no one knew quite where to find the sunken wreckage of the *Wyandot*. No one, that is, until Robin Beechley.

Robin owned and operated a small marine salvage company, Neptune's Locker, Inc., located in Wellfleet, Massachusetts. The firm specialized in marine exploration and recovery of industrial cargos, as well as the disposal of hazardous marine waste, off the shores of Cape Cod. Robin was a reluctant mariner, having inherited Neptune's Locker from her father who founded the firm in the days following World War II.

As a life-long resident of Massachusetts, Robin knew the legend of the *Wyandot*, and her passion for colonial American history combined with her access to contemporary marine search and recovery tools led to the ship's discovery in 1989. While Robin's small firm had definitively accomplished a seemingly impossible feat by producing the ship's bell from the *Wyandot* and retrieving a few of the gold coins scattered around the site of the wreckage, Neptune's Locker was totally unprepared for the chain of events that followed the discovery.

First, Robin had to file a report with the U.S. District Court in Boston, laying claim to all sunken treasure she might recover for Neptune's Locker. Following this court filing, the Commonwealth of Massachusetts initiated proceedings in state court to claim ownership rights to 25 percent of the value of the *Wyandot* salvage project. Neptune's Locker faced a Superior court battle to prove that sovereignty over the wreckage was vested in the federal government, and that under federal law at the time of the *Wyandot's* discovery, the ship belonged to Robin as finder of the wreckage.

Even worse, definitive identification of the ship's remains prompted the Massachusetts Board of Underwater Archeological Resources to block Robin's exploration and excavation of the wreckage site until Neptune's Locker had thoroughly documented the underwater resting place of the ship. Documentation required remapping the site according to standard archeological methods, including a string-grid location map recording the exact coordinates of each nautical artifact resting on the ocean floor. Finally, recovery of the sunken treasure would require more technologically sophisticated equipment than Neptune's Locker currently owned. Robin's shopping list included electronic navigation tools, a side-scan sonar, and a sub-bottom profiler, and oh yes, one more thing: a bigger ship to carry all these new gadgets to the site of the wreckage.

Robin estimated that the total cost of the *Wyandot* salvage project would be $4 million. Raising this kind of cash for a risky recovery operation was a real stretch. As Table 1 shows, Neptune's Locker didn't generate nearly enough income to raise $4 million from operating cash flows. Borrowing the necessary capital was also out of the question. Given the project's risk, debt financing could easily land Neptune's Locker—and Robin's entire family—in bankruptcy court. There was a third financing option, however, that appeared somewhat promising: a public offering of common stock in Neptune's Locker, Inc.

Shortly after the local press reported news of Robin's discovery of the *Wyandot*, a prominent Boston investment banking firm—Lee, Purvis, and Day—paid Neptune's Locker a call. Given the publicity surrounding the discovery and the well-known legend of the *Wyandot*, the investment bankers offered to lead a firm commitment syndicate that would provide Neptune's Locker with $4 million in new funds. The strength of the equity offering was based on the probability distribution of the salvage project's cash returns, shown below in Table 2. According to the investment bankers' estimates, there was a 70 percent chance that the project would be profitable, and this strong likelihood of profits would attract enough investors to guarantee Robin $4 million in new capital.

The investment bankers also explained that Lee, Purvis, and Day would accept 50 percent of the offering for direct sale to the public. The remaining new shares would be divided among two other firms interested in the underwriting syndicate, both well-known regional investment banking houses located in Boston. The syndicate would include Reynolds and Thrasher, which would purchase 30 percent of the issue, and Collins and Bainbridge, which would acquire the remaining 20 percent on a firm commitment basis. The syndicate's shares would all be distributed among a selling group composed of four large retail brokerage firms located throughout the New England area.

At first, Robin was somewhat confused by the notion of taking Neptune's Locker public. In truth, before the discovery of the *Wyandot*, the firm was little more than a family business. While the corporate charter permitted Robin to issue up to 600,000 shares of stock, only 60,000 shares were currently outstanding. These shares were all held by members of Robin's immediate family, and the thought of transforming her father's family business into a public corporation was a bit intimidating. Still, she knew that the salvage operation would require far more cash than she could raise in any other way.

Thinking seriously about the public stock sale, Robin asked Lee, Purvis, and Day for the specific terms of the offering. The investment bankers indicated that new public shares in a high-risk venture like Neptune's Locker would sell in the market for around 6 times earnings, and the gross underwriting spread charged by the lead investment bank would run 10 percent. When Robin inquired about this charge, the investment bankers gave her the summary of underwriting costs shown below in Table 3.

Now Robin was even more confused. When it came to the subject of public stock issuance, she was, well, like a fish out of water. She needed time to sort out her options; but the longer she took to secure financing for the salvage project, the longer the delays in completing the court battles, the longer the wait in acquiring new salvage equipment, and the more time it would take to excavate the site of the wreckage. While she waited, Robin knew that the underwater landscape was quickly changing. Shifting sand carried by swift tidal currents would soon obliterate her discovery and redistribute valuable marine artifacts over a distance of several miles. In spite of her reservations, she knew she had to act quickly and decisively if she hoped to recover the wealth and historical treasures she found in the wreckage of Black Bellamy's purloined *Wyandot*.

TABLE 1

Neptune's Locker, Inc.
Statement of Revenue and Expense
January 1, 1992 to December 31, 1992

Net sales revenue		$1,416,750
Less: Operating expenses:		
Depreciation	($925,625)	
Wages and salaries	(226,129)	
General and administrative costs	(109,625)	
Total operating expenses		(1,261,379)
Earnings before interest and taxes		$155,371
Less: Interest expense		(12,188)
Earnings before tax		$143,183
Less: Taxes		(53,183)
Net income		$90,000

TABLE 2	
Lee, Purvis, and Day Investment Bankers *Underwriting Fees for New Common Stock Sale by Neptune's Locker, Inc.*	
Underwriting Charge	**Cost as a Percentage of the Initial Offer Price**
Out-of-pocket expenses	0.50%
Management fees	1.17
Underwriting fees	3.89
Selling commission	4.44
TOTAL	10.00%

TABLE 3	
Neptune's Locker, Inc. *Potential Income Generated by Wyandot Salvage Operation (net of project costs)*	
Net Income (loss)	**Probability**
($4,000,000)	0.10
0	0.20
1,000,000	0.40
5,000,000	0.20
10,000,000	0.10

QUESTIONS

1.   Where should Neptune's Locker offer its new common equity—in a regional, national, or over-the-counter stock market? Why?

2.   What is the current earnings per share for shareholders owning Neptune's Locker stock?

3.   What is the initial offer price at which Lee, Purvis, and Day recommends selling new common stock in Neptune's Locker?

4.   How much will Lee, Purvis, and Day pay to acquire Neptune's Locker new equity; and how many new shares must the firm issue to raise $4 million in new financing?

5. Using the information provided in Table 2, determine:

    a. The price that members of the underwriting syndicate (Reynolds and Thrasher, and Collins and Bainbridge) will pay for each new share of stock in Neptune's Locker they acquire from the lead underwriter (Lee, Purvis, and Day).

    b. The price at which members of the underwriting syndicate will resell shares in Neptune's Locker to members of the retail selling group.

    c. The price at which members of the selling group will offer each share of Neptune's Locker stock to the public.

6. Given the public sale of new common stock, will current shareholders of Neptune's Locker retain a controlling interest in the firm? What proportion of the firm's equity will they control after the public stock sale?

7. If maintaining corporate control of Neptune's Locker is important to the Beechley family, how might they proceed with the public stock sale and still achieve this objective? What are the disadvantages of the approach?

8. What is the gross underwriting spread on the public sale of common equity by Neptune's Locker, and how is this spread divided among the out-of-pocket costs, management fees, underwriting fees, and selling concession associated with the public offering of common stock?

9. Based on the *Wyandot* salvage project's expected profitability and return on invested capital, should Neptune's Locker proceed with the new stock issue? Why or why not?

10. What rate of return must Neptune's Locker earn on the net proceeds it receives from the public stock sale to avoid any post-issue earnings dilution?

Case 24

Preferred Stock Issuance

Burkeville Power and Light

Leon V. Moran, Chief Financial Officer (CFO) of Burkeville Power and Light (BPL) believed himself a manager with few options. At a recent meeting of the small utility's executive committee, presided over by the company's CEO, Adele Lee, the question of additional long-term financing was hotly debated. The company needed funds for an overdue replacement of several of its substations and several other expansion or replacement projects.

BPL began its operations in the period immediately following the second World War and has operated profitably since that time. It serves a largely rural community made up of the border areas of two adjoining states in the Midwest. Table 1 illustrates the revenue and after-tax earnings of BPL over the past decade.

The debate over long-term funds revolved around the type of security to use in the acquisition of the funds. In addition, there were several external considerations related to market timing raised by several members of the financial staff. The items under discussion were very much interrelated, Moran believed, and it was necessary to resolve them as soon as possible.

The company's financial staff was managed by Moran and Bill Frederick, the corporate controller. Frederick also served as the treasurer. Joyce Millis was the manager of corporate accounting, and handled fixed asset expansion (capital budgeting) with a staff of four. It was this group which found itself on occasion, as now, involved in the acquisition of long-term funds through the capital markets.

The major concerns of the company's financial staff had to do with conditions in the capital markets, as opposed to any major internal or company-specific considerations. The company, based upon the opinion given by several financial rating agencies, was sound. In addition, modest but steady growth was forecast for the long-term future. The company relied upon the regional (including a county-by-county assessment) forecast of the Federal Reserve Bank in the district. At present the company's price/earnings ratio was 12.

To return to the external items which the financial staff found important, the stock market index was at a low for the year, and interest rates on corporate bonds were historically high. On the face of it, these considerations did not preclude the issuance of common stock or long-term debt. BPL, however, was a "local" company as were many of its investors. As a result company management believed more was involved than a financial decision; there was a strong sense of loyalty toward the company's investors, and deference to their opinion often influenced financial decisions.

In discussions with financial consultants, company management obtained clarification on the possibility of an issue of callable debt. In other words, if debt were issued it could be "designed" to be exchanged for common stock at some future time. The usual intent in such a situation was to gain insight into the time it would take for common stock prices to improve in the overall market. The debt would be called at that time. In addition, the consultants commented upon the improvements made in the transmission of power from one utility to another in recent years. An increasing number of smaller utility companies were purchasing kilowatts from other utility companies.

As noted previously, the market for common stock was in a depressed state. As measured by the usual indices, the market was at a two-year low. In addition, the company's debt to total assets ratio was at a level beyond which the financial staff believed a downgrading of the company's bond rating would be possible. Therefore, a preferred stock issuance was seen as a reasonable alternative. There were, however, several aspects of issuing preferred stock that each member of the financial staff wanted discussed and clearly understood before there was any action taken toward raising funds. Among these were the following: (1) Would there be a sinking fund and if so, how would it affect the decision? (2) Would the preferred stock dividends be cumulative? (3) Should the preferred stock be convertible? (4) Finally, how does preferred stock compare, exactly, to common stock and debt? It was certain that some members of the utility's board of directors would ask these questions. It was important to answer them as honestly as possible. In addition to sound financial stewardship, the board of directors and the relatively small group of investors expected the most highly ethical behavior from management. At present, BPL had no preferred stock on its balance sheet. While that situation was somewhat unusual for a utility, the company had managed to maintain a modern plant with funds provided by debt and common stock up to this point. In terms of pricing the preferred stock issue, Moran knew of a similar utility which had a recent issue of preferred stock outstanding. The preferred stock of that firm had a price of $50 and a semiannual dividend of $3. Moran believed that BPL's preferred issue, if decided upon, should be priced at $100. Tables 2 and 3 below provide the latest balance sheet and income statement, respectively, for BPL.

The period 1987–1992 had been one of lackluster financial performance for public utilities (including electric, cogeneration, and water companies). Specifically, earnings per share (EPS) and return on equity (ROE) had declined on average for utilities during the period. The decline was due, in large measure, to the economic slowdown which began in the latter half of the 1987–1992 period. There was a curtailment of industrial demand, a slackening in home construction, and certain less significant decreases in the demand for electricity throughout the economy. When taken in sum, those decreases in demand quickly eroded the profitability of the capital-intensive utilities industry. Table 4 provides certain financial data for utilities.

BPL was situated in an area of the midwestern states wherein variations in electrical usage were related primarily to the seasons of the year, not to economic activity. In fact, the only major change in demand experienced by the company was the reactivation of a once closed military base in the area served by the company. As a result, demand forecasts were relatively straightforward. This meant that capital expenditure needs could be forecast with equal confidence.

It was against this background that Moran, Lee, and the other decisionmakers had to decide whether a preferred stock issuance was in the best interest of BPL and its customers. The decision seemed to include only the preferred stock issue, or no action at all. Moran believed there was sufficient evidence to indicate that taking no action would endanger the company's ability to provide the best service to its customers and the best financial return to the investors.

TABLE 1

Burkeville Power and Light
Preferred Stock Issuance
($000s)

Year	Revenue	Earnings After Tax
1983	$21,576	$1,632
1984	23,733	1,661
1985	26,107	2,089
1986	28,718	2,441
1987	32,164	2,573
1988	36,657	2,749
1989	39,233	2,654
1990	42,372	3,390
1991	45,338	3,174
1992	48,512	3,881

TABLE 2

Burkeville Power and Light
Balance Sheet
December 31, 1992
($000s)

Utility plant, net	$97,636	Current liabilities	$8,713
Investments	10,430	Long-term debt	75,623
Current assets	9,286	Deferred credits	1,985
Deferred charges	2,828	Equity	33,859
		Total liabilities	
Total assets	$120,180	and equity	$120,180

TABLE 3

Burkeville Power and Light
Income Statement
December 31, 1992
($000s)

Operating revenue	$48,512
Operating expenses	42,612
Interest on long-term debt	4,219
Capital credits	1,719
Net operating margin	3,400
Net nonoperating margin	481
Net margin (earnings after-tax)	$3,881

TABLE 4

Burkeville Power and Light
Utility Companies
Selected Data 1987 and 1992

	1987	1992
ROE	14%	11%
P/E	13x	15x
EPS	2.91	2.00
Debt-to-assets	49%	24%

QUESTIONS

1. Calculate the ROE and total debt/total assets ratios for BPL for 1992.

2. What is the feasibility of a debt or common stock issuance for BPL?

3. If long-term funds must be acquired at this time, is preferred stock a feasible alternative? If the $50 preferred stock of the similar utility is a perpetuity, and BPL's issue will also be a perpetuity, what is the yield on each issue of stock?

4. Is preferred stock a fund-raising mechanism used only by utilities?

5.   List some important characteristics of preferred stock. Why are these characteristics important? If the BPL issue is cumulative, what are the implications for voting rights of the preferred stock holders?

6.   What is the long-term effect upon financial structure of a preferred issue convertible to common stock? What is the purpose of the convertible feature?

7.   Comment upon the relative debt burden of BPL compared to the industry data given in Table 4. Comment further upon the ability of utilities to carry fixed-income obligations.

8.   Discuss alternatives to a preferred stock issue for the company.

9.   Discuss the feasibility of a long-term debt issuance convertible to common stock.

10.   What is the likelihood of a preferred stock issue being well-received by investors?

11.   What is the role of the financial intermediary in BPL's capital needs situation?

12.   Discuss the fact that BPL is a regulated industry? What effect does this have upon their financing plans?

Case 25

Common Stock Rights Offering—Corporate Control

Commercial Builders, Inc.

Of the ten or so major construction firms in the southeastern United States, Commercial Builders, Inc. (CB, Inc.) has approximately 30 percent of the market. The growth rate in the construction of commercial office space and other commercial buildings was 12 percent annually since 1988. This southeast building boom showed no signs of abating. This was especially apparent in such areas as Charlotte, NC, Atlanta, GA, Jacksonville, FL, and other cities within the eastern "sunbelt."

CB, Inc., began operations in 1975. The firm was started by brothers Barry and Michael Krew. Their interest in carpentry and the intricacies of wood construction led to their desire to turn that interest into a vocation. Neither of the Krews ever imagined that their small start-up company would evolve into one of the major players on the United States construction scene. As the years passed and opportunities became available, the firm acquired the assets of smaller, less well-run firms in the mid-Atlantic region. CB, Inc., sold its common stock to the public for the first time in 1980. Tables 1 and 2 illustrate the firm's most recent balance sheet and income statement, respectively.

TABLE 1

Commercial Builders, Inc.
Balance Sheet
December 31, 1995
($000s)

Cash	$10,264
Accounts receivable	35,584
Inventory	41,848
Total current assets	$87,696
Net fixed assets	$75,168
Total assets	$162,864
Accounts payable	$22,752
Notes payable	10,972
Accruals	7,963
Total current liabilities	$41,687
Long-term debt	15,800
Common stock	13,808
Retained earnings	91,569
Total liabilities and equity	$162,864

TABLE 2

Commercial Builders, Inc.
Income Statement
December 31,1995
($000s)

Revenue	$113,760
Cost of operating	97,274
Earnings before interest and taxes	$16,486
Interest	2,112
Earnings before taxes	14,374
Taxes @30%	4,312
Earnings after tax	$10,062

The firm had shared in the growth of the geographic region. Both sales and earnings have shown a 12 percent annual compound growth over the past six years. In fact, a practice of using all assets to the fullest and the steady sales and earnings growth were the primary reasons for the strong financial statements shown in the tables. The strength of the firm's financial statements, however, gave rise to a concern that the owners had not previously faced or even considered. Barry and Michael Krew served as the firm's chief operating officer and chief financial officer, respectively. It had recently come to their attention that one of the firm's stockholders had begun purchasing the firm's shares at a rapid rate.

For some time there had been a particular point of contention between the managers and some stockholders concerning the firm's strategic plan. The Krew brothers did not want to expand their business outside of the geographic region in that it now operated. Their belief, based on various studies that they had commissioned, was that commercial construction had a particularly strong regional element. Specifically, financing, access to and quality of the labor force, and the general ethos of the commercial customers were defined by the region in which they operated. The Krews "understood" their region and were convinced that this insight was, in large measure, responsible for the success of CB, Inc. They considered expanding market share within the region as good business. In fact, they wished to completely dominate the business in the region if possible. They had made a conscious decision to not seek acquisition candidates outside of the southeastern United States. A small group of their stockholders strongly disagreed with this strategy.

In order to thwart what they believed to surely be an attempt to gain effective control of the firm's Board of Directors through ownership of a relatively large block of shares, the managers sought to revise the firm's bylaws. They believed it imperative to put an "antitakeover" amendment in the corporate charter. The idea of the amendment met with virtually no resistance from the board. The amendment's design was essentially that of a "poison pill." Its primary purpose was to discourage an unwanted or hostile takeover of CB, Inc.

The specific aspects of the antitakeover amendment included the following: The stockholders of record would receive one right for each share of common stock owned. That right would permit the purchase of 1/15th of a share of a planned new issue of non-cumulative preferred stock. The cost of the portion of a share would be $200. Further, in the event that a shareholder purchased as much as 15 percent of CB, Inc., outstanding common shares, the rights holder may buy CB, Inc., common shares for one-half of their market price. The authorization to issue the shares to be purchased at one-half price would be the central part of the antitakeover amendment. In addition to the foregoing, in the event of an unwanted takeover, the CB, Inc., common shareholders were being encouraged to seek the option of a share purchase in the acquiring firm for one-half of the shares' market price.

The managers hoped that the antitakeover amendment would achieve the desired results. Moreover, they had concerns about the stockholders' view of what they were doing and the manner in which they were going about it. Was it ethical? Was it in the best interest of the business? Concerning the best interest of the business, Barry Krew had recently read an article that discussed ways in which business performance, and consequently the performance of the management team, could best be measured. The performance measure mentioned in the article was referred to as "Economic Value Added," or EVA. In essence, the EVA measure compared operating profit, less taxes, with the dollar cost of the capital used to generate that profit. If the net number was positive — that is, more profit than costs remained, then economic value had been added to the firm, and conversely. Had the present management team added value to the firm? This was an issue that was certain to come up, especially if there was contention between stockholder groups intent on control and the management of the company. Table 3 presents selected data from a nationwide sample of similar firms.

TABLE 3			
Commercial Builders,Inc.			
Selected Industry Data			
	1993	1994	1995
ROE	11.5%	10.5%	11.0%
ROA	8.2%	7.5%	7.5%
EVA*	$1.5	$2.0	$2.2

* In $ millions: EVA is defined as follows:

Operating Profit   -   Weighted cost of capital
      - Taxes   x Total Capital

=A   =B

A-B=EVA

QUESTIONS

1.   Discuss management's desire to change the corporate bylaws.

2.   What role should stockholders play in the development of the firm's strategic plan?

3.   Why is the amendment being considered referred to as a "poison pill"? Who is expected to be discouraged by the amendment, and will it likely achieve the desired effect?

4.   Managers are considered "agents" of the shareholders. If this is so, what is expected of managers at all times as they occupy the agency role? (Assume the stock price reflects the rights-on price.)

5.   If the firm issues new shares at half-price to counteract a purchase by one shareholder of 15 percent of total shares outstanding, what effect will this have on the wealth of the existing shareholders?

6.   Is the general strategy adopted by management, regional expansion only, in the best interest of the stockholders? Why or why not? Consider the data and information in Table 3. (Assume CB, Inc., has a cost of capital of 9 percent, and total capital in use of 1995 total assets plus 5 percent. The 5 percent accounts for such "capital" items as employee training and the like).

7.   The data and information in Table 3 are national data. Is this a relevant concern in the evaluation of CB, Inc.?

8.   Should the Krews remain as managers of CB, Inc.? Why or why not?

Case 26

Evaluating Corporate Takeovers

Buffalo River Steel Company

The prosperity in the Buffalo River section of the lower midwestern United States had always been due to the "smokestacks." That is how regional residents referred to the steel mill, which for so long had provided the primary employment in the region. In 1962, the Buffalo River Steel Company employed 2,800 people. By 1988, the number of persons employed at the mill was approximately 1,600. The reduction in the employment rolls was not due to attrition or plant modernization, but to a much less positive set of factors then pervasive in the U.S. steel industry.

From the mid-1970s to the late 1980s, the number of persons employed in the U.S. steel industry was reduced by approximately one-half. The primary reasons were competition from overseas steel makers and a reluctant policy of domestic capital investment. These phenomena were in direct contrast to the dedicated, skilled, but perhaps overpaid, workforce in the steel industry in the United States.

While steel is a commodity item, the sales of which typically rise and fall with the cyclical and secular movements in the economy, its overall demand is directly linked to a strong world economy. There seems to be, both now and in the past, sufficient room for every efficient producer of this truly global product. Unfortunately, the Buffalo River Steel Company had simply failed to maintain its plant in a reasonable manner, and costs of production rose steadily over the years while worker morale fell. By 1990, it was clear to observers of the industry that the company would be likely to face a major transition.

In the spring of 1991, Greg Matwick had occasion to visit the Buffalo River mill. He was a regional inspector for the state's environmental oversight department. In addition, he had grown up in the region and was familiar with the mill's value to the community. Being an employee of his home state, Matwick was an astute observer of the economic scene in the state and region. His academic background, at the undergraduate and graduate levels, was in the areas of finance and economics. It was due to his interest in economics and his "levelheadedness" (as one of his friends had described him as having) that had allowed him to turn a modest inheritance into a substantial personal net worth.

Matwick's many visits to the mill led him to believe that the entire situation there was not suited for survival in the world economy. His apprehension was caused mainly by the mill's physical condition and overall financial condition. The publicly owned company was relatively easy to assess financially, and the mill's physical appearance completed the picture. After a long and thoughtful period, including consultation with some of his friends in the investment banking and venture capital businesses, Matwick decided to make an offer to buy Buffalo River Steel Company.

An offer to buy the company would have to take into account many important factors. Among these would be how and where to acquire financing (an offer of $60 million seemed reasonable at the early stages of the process) and the extent of the necessary refurbishing of the aging mill. Such upgrading would of course include the full range of pollution control equipment, relative to local and federal regulations, as well as adherence to an ethical means of operation concerning the natural environment.

Matwick did not have a long-standing ambition to be the owner of a steel company. On the other hand, he believed this particular enterprise to have satisfying potential on several fronts. First, it was Matwick's belief that the plant could become highly profitable again. In the second place, the opportunity to return the region to its former prosperity, or at least its former employment level, was an enticing prospect. Of course, the two motivations, profitability and a fully employed workforce, were inextricably interrelated; Matwick understood that and knew that his plan had to proceed carefully.

The first step in arranging financing would be to have a clear idea of how the debt, if any, would be serviced. Profitability would, of course, heavily influence that issue. Tables 1 and 2 illustrate the firm's most recent income statement and balance sheet, respectively.

In considering where to turn for the necessary financing, Matwick decided to develop a clearer view of where the company was headed in terms of profits and overall operating characteristics. To that end, the offer of $60 million was put before the company's board of directors. The board agreed to give it every consideration and further agreed to provide Matwick with any financial information deemed necessary by him or anyone designated as his partner or representative. That amount was equivalent to book value, and it was the market price per share as of the end of the year 1992.

Book value and the presumed price of the firm were numbers that did not necessarily have a close connection. Matwick understood that and, as a result, had the plant managers, in conjunction with his investment advisors, develop additional data to assist in the cash flow/valuation/debt-service analysis.

Toward that end, Table 3 illustrates the data for worldwide steel production. The data provided are for modernized plants. Such plants are defined as those that have adopted the cold-roll process and state-of-the-art smelting techniques. The major movement in the steel industry in the past two decades had been toward clean production processes. The natural environment was to be protected. Table 4 provides an estimate of revenue for Buffalo River over the period shown. Matwick believed cash flow after tax would equal approximately 3 percent of revenue for each year.

Based upon the revenue projection of $190 million for 1994, Matwick believed that the markets would come to a less-than-favorable conclusion concerning the firm's prospects for the coming year. As a result, he was convinced that obtaining financing for the purchase would rest entirely on his ability to clearly demonstrate the long-term prospects for the company.

The specifics of the financing package were as follows: (1) The $50 million of long-term debt currently on the company's books would have to be renegotiated. This was especially important since it seemed reasonable to expect an interest rate of 8 percent on the new debt. (2) Of the remaining $70 million of new funds needed (2.5 million shares purchased at $24 per share and $10 million for plant modernization), Matwick was prepared to invest $5 million; a consortium of savings and loans had expressed some interest in lending $30 million, a private investor had indicated a willingness to provide $10 million, and three large insurance companies would likely provide $25 million.

After many rounds of discussion and negotiation, certain facts became clear to Matwick. First, all of the potential investors considered the purchase of a steel mill a high-risk undertaking. As a result, they were not willing to even discuss interest rates of less than 10 percent. (During this period yields on medium quality corporate bonds of 10 years' duration or more were 8.3 percent). Therefore, Matwick became convinced that 10 percent would be the interest rate on the debt from the new investors, and refinancing the existing debt was moot. It would be a matter of trying to convince the original debt holders to transfer responsibility of the debt over to the new owners. The financial advisors who had joined the buyout project were convinced that such transference was highly likely and that it would occur without any change in the 10 percent rate of interest. As a result of those developments, Matwick understood that the annual debt service, post buyout, would be $11.5 million.

The servicing of $115 million of debt, including $50 million of existing debt and $65 million of new funds (net of Matwick's $5m) would, of course, depend upon the sales level and operating efficiencies obtainable by the new owners. Matwick estimated the most likely sales for 1995 at $205 million. By that time, the $10 million invested in plant modernization would most likely raise the plant's annual fixed costs to $109 million, and variable costs would be reduced to 40 percent of revenue. Industry projections for shipments of steel convinced Matwick that the actual revenue for Buffalo River could be $20 million less than projected. He was convinced, however, that the post buyout figures provided by two mechanical engineers, each with 15 years experience at the plant, were reliable.

TABLE 1

Buffalo River Steel Company
Income Statement, December 31, 1993
($000s)

Sales	$200,000
Fixed costs	(90,000)
Variable costs	(100,000)
Earnings before interest and taxes (EBIT)	$10,000
Interest	(5,000)
Earnings before taxes	$5,000
Taxes (35%)	(1,750)
Earnings after tax	$3,250
Earnings per share*	$1.30

Note: * 2.5 million common shares outstanding.

TABLE 2

Buffalo River Steel Company
Balance Sheet, December 31, 1993
($000s)

Current assets	$30,000	Current liabilities	$20,000
Net fixed assets	100,000	Long-term debt	50,000
		Common stock	25,000
		Retained earnings	35,000
		Total liabilities	
Total Assets	$130,000	and capital	$130,000

TABLE 3
Buffalo River Steel Company
Worldwide Steel Production
Modernized Plants (millions of tons)

1988	1992	1994 (Projected)
200	424	590

TABLE 4
Buffalo River Steel Company
Projection of Revenue
(in millions)

Year	Revenue
1996	$230
1997	257
1998	288
1999	322
2000	361

QUESTIONS

1. Given the financial information presented in the case, outline Buffalo River Steel's debt composition after the purchase. Based upon the projections, what will be the likely level of EPS, year-end 1995?

2. Given the risk perceived by the potential investors, why would they most likely be interested in this investment?

3. What is the compound average growth rate in worldwide steel production from 1988–1992 as shown in Table 3? What does this growth rate imply for the investors in Buffalo River?

4.   Using the projections from the case, consider the following:

    a.   Do the cash flow data and other information seem to warrant an asking price of $60 million?

    b.   Given the limited horizon for the projection, should a selling price for the plant be a part of the valuation information? Why? Why not? If so, what selling price or liquidation value should be used?

5.   If steel production contributes significantly to environmental pollution, is such production better left then to other countries? How important should the issue of clean steel production be to the new managers?

6.   How significantly should environmental pollution figure into the new owner's written company policies?

7.   Discuss the capital intensity of this industry. What are the implications for the proposed plant modernization?

8.   What is the role of steel production in a country's economy? Is steel production important for an industrialized economy?

9.   Discuss the nature of the interrelationship between environmental issues and profitability for Buffalo River.

10.   Specifically, what additional information would be useful and relevant for Matwick's decision, and why?

Case 27

Mortgage Financing and the Investment Decision

Village Plaza Shopping Center[*]

Christine Barnes reviewed her notes. Her boss, the treasurer of Hampton Heating and Air Conditioning, had just made Village Plaza Shopping Center Christine's responsibility.

The assignment was not unexpected. Since being hired by Hampton, Christine had compiled the property's operating statements, contracted for various maintenance items, and made certain that property taxes, insurance, and debt service were paid on a timely basis. Until now, this had been just another part of her job. The idea that this was now her responsibility did not really trouble her.

The disturbing aspect of her new, official assignment was that the mortgage loan on Village Plaza would be coming due within the next two months. The original mortgage, held by a large, national life insurance company, specified a 20-year amortization with a balloon payment of principal due at (or near) the end of the fifth year. The original lender was willing to refinance the balloon amount at a new interest rate, but would need to see evidence that the property was still a viable and attractive investment. Christine would have to assemble and justify this evidence.

Christine had also been in contact with a group of real estate brokers concerning the potential sale of the property. They had produced a long list of prospective buyers and several promising offers. In fact, she had on her desk the most recent cash offer from an investment group in a neighboring state. This offer promised a price of $1,540,000, net of all related sales costs; and she was certain that the sale would go through if accepted by Hampton's shareholders. She had received no fewer than five such offers in the past few weeks, and all had been very similar in terms and dollar amounts. It was up to Christine to determine whether the company should refinance the mortgage and keep Village Plaza, or sell the property, repay the mortgage, and invest the equity in something else.

Hampton Heating and Air Conditioning was a regional contractor located in Smedley, South Carolina, a small, rural town approximately forty miles from the state capital, Columbia. The family-owned business had been in operation for almost 50 years, and eventually came to specialize in heating and air conditioning systems for commercial and multi-unit residential buildings. Most of the land in and around the actual town of Smedley (population 12,500) was owned or controlled by the members of the Hampton family.

With the completion of a four-lane highway near the town in 1986, Smedley had begun to grow toward Columbia. Workers from the capital city's major corporations, tired of life in the suburbs, moved to the surrounding rural towns en masse. Over the course of several years,

---

   * This case was prepared by Timothy B. Michael, The University of North Carolina at Charlotte, whose cooperation is acknowledged with appreciation.

it had become evident that Smedley would become a prosperous bedroom community. After this growth was obvious, the Hampton family decided to develop some of its land holdings.

Most investment by the family had taken the form of developments of single-family housing units (Hampton Acres, Hampton Estates) and these were managed and funded by separate corporations or partnerships. Village Plaza Shopping Center, owned and controlled by Hampton Heating and Air Conditioning, was the family's sole commercial property experiment and the only real estate investment managed through the main family business.

Village Plaza, built in late 1988, was a retail shopping center with 33,000 square feet of leased space occupied by a chain grocery store and a popular discount drug store. The building had been constructed several miles outside the city limits of Smedley on the rear portion of a 6-acre parcel which faced the town's major four-lane thoroughfare. Access to the shopping center was through two entrances from the main road into the parking lot and by a service road behind the building from an adjoining street. Only the building and its parking lot were on the site, leaving several large and attractive landscaped areas around the front and sides of the property. By 1993, other businesses had built nearby, but Village Plaza was the only shopping center within five miles of the town.

The center had cost a total of $1,230,000 in 1988. The land was purchased for $40,000 per acre (from family members), and the building had cost roughly $30 per square foot to build. At the time, it had been the insurance company's policy to lend a maximum of 75 percent of the value of any property. Accordingly, the original mortgage totalled $922,500 at an annual rate of 10.35 percent, to be repaid in annual amounts corresponding to a 20-year amortization. The first annual payment of $110,956.42 was made at the end of 1989. An additional provision of the loan was that the principal remaining after five payments would be due and payable by the end of the fifth year.

A mortgage banking firm in Atlanta was negotiating with the insurance company on behalf of Hampton. As in many commercial real estate transactions, the lender was concerned with the value of the mortgaged property rather than the repayment ability of the borrower. According to the mortgage bankers, the insurance company would refinance the balloon amount, $827,346.65, if Hampton could show that:

1.   The $827,346.65 to be borrowed would not be more than 75 percent of the total value of the property at the time of the new loan.

2.   The expected annual cash flow generated by the property would be *at least* 1.5 times the amount of the new annual mortgage payments (debt service).

The new mortgage loan, if made, would probably carry an annual rate of 9.15 percent. Again, payments would be based on a 20-year repayment schedule, with a balloon payment due in five years.

Christine had several tasks to accomplish before the current loan came due. First, she had to calculate the amount of annual debt service for the new mortgage. Next, she had to determine whether the property could be refinanced given the projected annual debt service amount and the current value of the property. Finally, she would have to decide whether or not Hampton Heating and Air Conditioning should continue to invest in the shopping center. Calculating the specifics of the loan would be simple, but determining the investment value of the property would require many assumptions and a great deal of analysis.

The income from the property could be divided into three parts: fixed rents, percentage rents, and expense reimbursements. Fixed rents were designed to guarantee the owner of the property a certain minimum amount of return each year, while percentage rents allowed the landlord to share in the (potential) success of the store and the location. The amount paid by each tenant was stipulated in the individual lease agreements.

Good Foods, a grocery store, occupied 25,000 square feet. The food store was part of a large regional chain, and was extremely creditworthy. According to the store's 20-year lease, the total rent paid in any year would amount to the greater of 2 percent of the store's annual revenues or a fixed rent amount of $3.50 per square foot per year. As shown in Table 1, the amount of fixed rent and the additional percentage rent were usually given separate lines in the operating statement. The sum of fixed and percentage rents would total 2 percent of Good Foods' sales revenue in 1993. Rent payments were usually made at the end of each year.

Corner Drugs, a discount drug store, occupied the other 8,000 square feet in the shopping center. This tenant was also part of a regional chain, and was considered to have an excellent credit reputation. This store's 20-year lease required a fixed rent of $4.50 per square foot per year or a percentage rent of 3 percent of annual store sales, whichever was greater. Table 1 shows Corner Drugs' expected rent payments for 1993.

Village Plaza had few direct operating expenses, due to the nature of the lease agreements with each tenant. Known as net leases, the leases required each tenant to pay for all property taxes, insurance, utilities, routine maintenance, and repairs. Hampton was fully reimbursed by the tenants for all property taxes and insurance. Each tenant paid a share of taxes and insurance based on its leased square footage as a percentage of the building total. Most of the other expenses were paid directly by the tenants without passing through Hampton; the mortgage lender required regular proof of payment of insurance and property taxes, and this was best obtained by having Hampton pay and be reimbursed for its payments.

Several operating expenses were not paid by the tenants. The owner regularly paid for landscaping and lawn maintenance, maintenance and electricity for the shopping center's illuminated sign, and for the regular cleaning and sweeping of the parking lot.

Hampton was also responsible for any future capital repairs such as roof replacement or parking lot resurfacing. Given the age and condition of the shopping center, it was not likely that any major repairs would be needed in the next five or six years, but problems could be expected after twelve or fourteen years of operation.

The projected year-end operating statement for Village Plaza Shopping Center is given in Table 1. This statement shows the current level of percentage rents and the expected annual expenses. There is no property management expense listed, because that function is filled by the treasurer's office of Hampton Heating and Air Conditioning. If the building were to be managed by a third party, this expense would likely amount to 5 percent of annual rents (before expense reimbursements) each year.

Net Operating Income (NOI) was the measure used by the mortgage holder to determine the debt repayment ability of the property. The expected NOI for 1993 is shown in Table 1. Note that NOI does not include depreciation, debt service, or tax considerations, because the insurance company is interested in the actual cash return potential of the property. In the event of a borrower default, the mortgage holder would become the owner of the property, and all of the income tax, depreciation, and debt service amounts and conditions would immediately change.

Debt service coverage, as measured by the mortgage lender, was the ratio of net operating income to the annual mortgage payment. Given an original annual debt service of $110,956.42, Village Plaza could have paid its debt service 1.77 times in 1993. Christine hoped that next year's cash flow would produce a ratio at least this high, if not higher.

She had yet to develop a method of determining the investment value of the property. In the analysis section of the original loan proposal, Christine noted that a form of discounted cash flow analysis had been used to defend the investment. This analysis had considered the original cost of the shopping center compared to its projected annual cash flows, and had assumed that the property would be sold for replacement cost (less depreciation) after five years. The analysis had used Hampton's original desired equity return of 12 percent to discount the cash flows.

Evaluating the property using this method would be fairly simple. A five-year cash flow projection, based on 1993 numbers, could be developed using a spreadsheet and a set of basic assumptions. Given an estimate of construction and land costs after another five years, she could calculate a future sale price (terminal value). Also, given the structure of the loan agreement, the cost of the loan, and Hampton's desired return on equity (which hadn't changed) she could develop a reasonable cost of capital to use in her evaluation.

Regardless of what the mortgage holder wanted to see, to properly account for the annual cash flows provided by the investment Christine would have to calculate the income taxes generated by the property and take account of the depreciation tax shield in any given year. The building was currently being depreciated on a straight-line basis over 31.5 years on an original construction cost of approximately $990,000. The tax consequences of any interest payments would not be included in the annual cash flows. Hampton had a marginal tax rate of approximately 30 percent.

The determination of the future price was more difficult. After extensive research, Christine discovered that average land prices near Smedley had been increasing 4.5 percent per year and this trend was expected to continue. Also, construction costs had been increasing 2.5 percent per year over the past five years and were expected grow at this rate over the next five years. To account for the effects of use, she decided that the amount of annual depreciation already calculated for the property was adequate.

TABLE 1	
Village Plaza Shopping Center *Projected Operating Statement* *Year Ending December 31, 1993*	
Income:	
Fixed rents (total)	$123,500
Percentage rent:	
Good Foods (from sales of $7,500,000)	$62,500
Corner Drugs (from sales of $2,000,000)	24,000
Expense reimbursements (taxes & insurance)	23,860
Total rental income	$233,860
Operating expenses:	
Property taxes	$(15,165)
Insurance	(8,695)
Parking lot maintenance	(2,400)
Landscaping	(9,600)
Sign maintenance and electric service	(1,650)
Total operating expenses	($37,510)
Net operating income (NOI)	$196,350
Depreciation	(31,429)
Income before taxes and debt service	$164,921

QUESTIONS

1. One of Christine's tasks involves determining the value of the shopping center today. What should she consider when evaluating the present value of the property? What is the property worth?

2. Why would a commercial lender prefer a balloon-payment mortgage over a standard (full amortization) mortgage? Why would borrowers agree to a balloon-payment mortgage? Create an amortization schedule for the first five years of the proposed new loan, and be sure to show the balloon payment which would be due at the end of 1998.

3. Christine has argued to her boss that management expense should be listed among the various costs of operating Village Plaza. He firmly believes that this expense is immaterial; in fact, it is at his insistence that current operating projections do not include the cost of management. How should she account for the cost of property management in her cash flow projections?

4. Construct a five-year cash flow projection for Village Plaza Shopping Center. Assume that the total sales of each store will increase by 4 percent per year over the period, and expenses (except management expense) will increase by an average of 3 percent per year. Based on your answers to Questions 1 and 2 and your cash flow projection for 1994, will the insurance company be willing to refinance the mortgage when it comes due?

5. Hampton's mortgage bankers have suggested that Village Plaza should be evaluated using a cost of capital which reflects the risk of the shopping center's cash flows. Although the fixed rents and expense reimbursements are contractual and would be paid regardless of whether the tenants leave the center before the leases expire, any estimates of future expenses or percentage rent must be based on simple assumptions. Accordingly, the mortgage bankers have pushed for a cost of capital of approximately 13 percent, due to the small town location of the property. Christine has argued that the investment should be evaluated at a weighted-average cost of capital. Her boss feels that the owners of Hampton Heating and Air Conditioning would appreciate a 12 percent return on their investment. What factors influence the cost of capital decision? For this analysis, what cost of capital is appropriate?

6. Using your answer to Question 1 and the cash flows from Question 4, and assuming that the property is sold after another five years for replacement cost less accumulated depreciation, should Hampton sell or refinance Village Plaza? For simplicity, further assume that there will be no tax consequences from the sale of the property, and that commissions paid on the sale will amount to 6 percent of the sale price.

7. A few Hampton family members have said that they would like to keep as much land as possible "in the family." In other words, the land itself may have some additional value to them as part of their total holdings. How should Christine measure this intrinsic value, and how should it influence the investment decision?

PART V

FINANCIAL STRUCTURE, THE COST OF CAPITAL, AND DIVIDEND POLICY

Case 28

The Bond Refunding Decision

The Orient Express

Marketing new consumer products in a strange land to an unfamiliar culture can be an expensive and risky business. Consider the recent experience of Procter & Gamble Company's ill-fated entry into Poland's personal hygiene market with its Wash & Go shampoo product. P&G blanketed Polish television with expensive TV commercials and distributed samples by mail to local households. The ad campaign showed a young woman emerging from a swimming pool and ducking into the shower.

Unfortunately, most Polish households don't have showers; they have bathtubs. Even fewer Poles have swimming pools. Needless to say, Wash & Go received a chilly reception from confused Polish consumers. Many raided neighbors' mailboxes to steal the Wash & Go samples to sell. Still other consumers thought P&G was trying to sell products in Poland that the firm was unable to market in the West. Even worse, the Wash & Go nameplate became the target of a local joke: "Wash your hair, and it goes away." The product was derided to such an extent that local Warsaw bars began serving a vodka drink called, you guessed it, the Wash & Go. Procter & Gamble didn't think any of this was very funny.

If Tim Novak, divisional vice president at The Orient Express company, thought P&G's misfortunes in Poland were funny, he didn't express it to his staff. He, too, was engaged in the business of selling consumer products in an unfamiliar land, and also faced the product rejections and failed marketing campaigns that P&G's management team faced. The Orient Express represented a wholly owned subsidiary of the Crawford Soup company that was formed to develop and market new soup flavors for the Asian market. With over two billion consumers in China and other Pacific Rim countries, the market's potential was huge, and The Orient Express had enjoyed steadily increasing sales and profits over the last ten years. Novak, as well as his superiors at Crawofrd Soup, fully expected this impressive financial performance to continue in the future.

Unfortunately, the risks in this market equalled its potential returns. Asian consumers were not like their American counterparts, and had different tastes, customs, and preferences for food products. The wealth of consumer research maintained by The Orient Express' parent company was practically useless in Asian markets. Western consumers preferred good old chicken noodle, while Eastern tastes included such delicacies as duck-gizzard soup, scallop broth, radish-and-carrot soup, and the market favorite: pork, fig, and date soup. In some Asian markets, Novak's market research team had learned there was even a thriving potential market for cream-of-snake soup.

As you might imagine, Tim faced an uphill battle trying to convince key executives at Crawford that the subsidiary should boil a few snakes in its test kitchens and whip up a batch of cream-of-snake for distribution within a few test markets. He faced an even more difficult task in trying to obtain capital funds from the corporation to finance his new products.

Inevitably, some wiseguy at corporate headquarters would crack a joke about buying futures contracts on snakes, lizards, and duck-gizzards, and Tim's funding requests would be politely rejected. From his perspective, it seemed like all Crawford was interested in doing was selling chicken noodle soup in Hong Kong, and this particular product-market combination didn't leave him much room to gain new business.

There was one option that Tim felt the finance staff in New York had missed. When Crawford capitalized The Orient Express subsidiary ten years ago, the subsidiary immediately issued $10 million in long-term bonds. These $1,000 par value bonds represented the only debt in The Orient Express' capital structure, and given the optimal debt and equity mix at Crawford, they were to remain a permanent financing fixture within the subsidiary. They were also expensive, carrying an annual coupon rate of 10 percent.

Tim realized that Crawford's CFO viewed these bonds as a mechanism through which The Orient Express subsidiary could obtain a capital structure that mirrored that of the parent company. The bonds represented nonrecourse debt of the subsidiary, which explained the relatively high coupon interest rate and the fact that they originally sold in the market at a $20 discount from face. Flotation costs of the issue totaled $100,000, and the bonds contained an unusual call feature. They were callable beginning 5 years after the date of original issue, and continuing for a 10-year period until the bonds were 15 years old. During the first year of the call period, the call premium represented one year's coupon interest payment. This premium declined by 10 percent in each of the 10 years in which the call window was open. Each bond carried an original maturity of 30 years, and to date, none of the bonds had been called by the firm.

In order to fire-up his Asian test kitchens and start boiling some tasty snakes, Tim needed to raise $250,000 in two years time. He figured that additional market research was necessary before he could commit corporate resources to risky new product development, and this research would require a few years to complete. While Crawford allowed its subsidiaries ample funds for market research, Tim knew that any product development expenditures would require him to raise new external funds.

How could he raise the $250,000 in just two years time? Headquarters would never approve a request for external funding to develop cream-of-snake soup mix. What would they call the securities in the new-issue prospectus, reptile bonds? Maybe debt issuance was out of the question, but Tim thought Crawford's CFO just might permit the subsidiary to refinance its existing debt and invest any resulting cost savings back into the subsidiary's operations. If Tim could issue new bonds as recourse debt, where the bondholders could claim a legal interest in Crawford Soup company's cash flows if The Orient Express defaulted on its bond payments, he figured he could sell $10 million in 20-year bonds at par carrying a 7.5 percent coupon rate.

Preliminary talks with Crawford's underwriting specialists led Tim to believe that the total flotation cost to the subsidiary would run $150,000 for the new issue. He also learned that debt retirement of the old bonds, which would occur subsequent to the new bond issue, would require a five-month overlap period. Thus, The Orient Express would face double interest payments for a five-month period, during which time the firm could invest the net proceeds received from the new bond issue in marketable securities paying 4.5 percent (before-tax). The subsidiary's corporate tax rate was 35 percent, and its staff accountants amortized all bond issuance costs on a straight-line basis.

Leaning back in his chair, Tim contemplated the risk he would be taking by investing any financing cost reduction in the development of snake-flavored soup. Procter & Gamble's experience selling shampoo in Poland had taught him how easy it was to have an extremely embarrassing experience with the most innocent product. From a Western perspective, cream-of-snake soup sounded much more radical than shampoo—and much riskier. He could just imagine the jokes they'd be telling about him, his lizard stew, and his brief career if he tried and failed. Still, his market research staff told him that snake was a culinary delicacy in many parts of the Asian world—a world populated by 2 billion hungry consumers who probably thought that eating boiled chicken surrounded by egg noodles was a little weird, too.

QUESTIONS

1.   What is the value of the tax shield that The Orient Express would realize by immediately expensing the unamortized issuance cost of its existing bonds?

2.   What is the value of the annual tax shield that The Orient Express would realize from the issuance costs on the new bonds?

3.   What is the total interest expense that The Orient Express must pay on the old bond issue during the overlap period? What is the firm's net interest expense for this period, given the short-term investment plans for the proceeds received from the new bond issue?

4.   What is the value of the call premium payment that The Orient Express must offer to retire its existing bonds?

5.   What is the value of the tax shield that The Orient Express would realize by immediately expensing the unamortized portion of the discount on its existing bonds?

6.   Based on your answers to Questions 1 through 5, what is the total incremental outlay required by The Orient Express to refinance its current debt?

7.   What is the total reduction in interest and amortization expenses that The Orient Express would realize in each of the next 20 years if the firm refinances its existing debt?

8.   Given your answers to Questions 1 through 7, what is the total value of the refinancing option for The Orient Express? Should the firm refinance its existing bonds?

9.   If The Orient Express pursues the refinancing option, will the firm realize sufficient cash savings to fund $250,000 in product development costs in two years' time?

10. Given your answer to Question 9, should Tim Novak abandon his plans for refinancing The Orient Express' bonds? Why or why not?

11. The case reports that The Orient Express has enjoyed steadily increasing sales and profits over the last ten years, and that the firm expects this financial performance to continue in the future. Suppose that this were not the case, and that The Orient Express' current and continuing future profitability is highly uncertain. How would this uncertainty change your evaluation of the bond refunding opportunity facing the firm? Would you still reach the same decision concerning the refunding effort that you reached in Question 8? Why or why not?

Case 29

Costs, Volume, Profits —Breakeven Analysis

Specialty Chemicals, Inc.

The management at Specialty Chemicals, Inc. was faced with an exciting opportunity. Management's experience, however, made it aware of the accompanying challenges. The company planned to relocate part of its operations to the lower mid-western United States. The move would certainly expand sales opportunities and very likely provide operating efficiencies as well.

Specialty Chemicals began as a small firm in the 1930s. During its early years, the firm's primary line of business was selling blasting chemicals to state highway departments for road building. In the middle region of the eastern United States the period 1950 to 1965 saw major interstate highway expansion. In order for the road building to proceed, great quantities of rock and the many mountainous areas had to be removed by way of blasting.

During the period since the early 1960s the company acquired several smaller firms in similar businesses. It also acquired patents on various chemicals and chemical processes from companies and inventors. Throughout this period the firm maintained a reputation as a dependable, high-quality producer of chemicals for the construction industry, the wood processing industry, and other industries where high-quality, dependable delivery and innovation focused upon industry needs were paramount.

At the present facility, the firm had managed to build and maintain a stellar reputation thanks largely to its skilled and loyal workforce. While many firms in this relatively small industry had chosen to compete by employing a technology-driven strategy, Specialty Chemicals had opted for a different approach. The company management's policy had placed more emphasis on a labor-intensive strategy, choosing to rely on its people more than on the latest technology. The company's sales and earnings for the past five years are shown in Table 1. The industry revenue and earnings compound growth rates for the same period were 12 percent and 10 percent, respectively. Industry earnings as a percent of sales had been approximately 7.5 percent for the past four years.

TABLE 1

Specialty Chemicals, Inc.
Sales and Earnings
($000s)

	1990	1991	1992	1993	1994
Sales	$30,000	$33,800	$36,500	$42,148	$47,100
Earnings, After tax	$1,800	$1,960	$2,064	$2,215	$2,362

The firm's plans for the new facility included an approach to office management and production different from the present operation. The new facility would be more technologically advanced. As a result, a relatively smaller work force would be needed.

The firm's operations manager, Linda Merwin, and the human resources manager, George Banwick, wondered about the effect the planned move would have on the firm's reputation as a "people-oriented" company. Both managers knew that a number of the present employees wished to be transferred to the new site. The managers also knew that there was an abundance of highly skilled labor in the area of the new plant. In addition, the more technologically updated plant would need fewer workers. Even so, Banwick and Merwin were very interested in the equitable and ethical treatment of their employees. Further complicating the matter was the fact that skill levels and years of seniority varied widely among current employees.

The operating characteristics between the old and new facilities would be different in terms of fixed costs. This was clearly a trend in the industry. Consolidation within the industry, which made the planned move attractive and necessary, was due in part to an unwillingness — or inability — on the part of many firms to adapt to emerging managerial, technological, and financing trends. Specialty Chemicals wished to avoid any such problems if at all possible. One management practice that Merwin wanted to improve upon in the new location was the manner in which the "risk" aspects of the firm's operations were assessed. For example, the firm relied heavily upon break-even analysis when assessing the relationship among cost, volume, and the resulting profit or loss. This was especially useful in the introduction of new products for which there was a ready market of a known size.

Merwin's concerns involved two important additional issues. First, the new facility would have more fixed costs in its operation than the present facility. Second, the reliance upon break-even analysis as the primary assessment of the cost-volume-profit relationship may prove less beneficial than in the past. Merwin wanted the concept of leverage, the use of fixed costs in financing or operations, to become a part of the risk measures typically used by the firm as it sought to remain competitive in the changing business climate.

In addition to the anticipated use of a greater level of fixed costs in the production process, the firm's weak earnings growth and profit margin had lead to a greater focus on improved internal risk assessment. In fact, the planned method of operating at the new facility was a direct result of the concern over earnings growth and profit margin.

As an example of the difference in fixed cost usage at the two facilities, Merwin devised the following information, which she hoped would illustrate the two different operating characteristics. Table 2 represents the cost-volume relationship at the present plant, and Table

3 shows similar information for the new plant. The numbers in the tables are not sales, cost, and profit numbers for the company, but the *relationship* among the numbers was identical to those of Specialty Chemicals, Inc. The examples in the table were constructed by Merwin while attending a recent management seminar. Those attending the upcoming meeting would complete the two tables at that time as a means of fostering understanding of the interrelated data and information.

TABLE 2

Specialty Chemicals, Inc.
Old Operating Mode
Cost-Volume-Profit

Selling Price per Unit = $432
Variable Cost per Unit = $324
Total Fixed Cost = $500,000

Units Sold	Operating Cost	Total Revenue	Operating Profit
0	$500,000	$0	$(500,000)
5,000	$2,120,000	$2,160,000	$40,000
7,000	-----	-----	-----
8,000	-----	-----	-----
14,000	-----	-----	-----

TABLE 3

Specialty Chemicals, Inc.
New Operating Mode
Cost-Volume-Profit

Selling Price per Unit = $432
Variable Cost per Unit = $175
Total Fixed Cost = $1,728,000

Units Sold	Operating Cost	Total Revenue	Operating Profit
0	$1,728,000	$0)	$(1,728,000)
5,000	$2,603,000	$2,160,000	$(443,000)
7,000	-----	-----	-----
8,000	-----	-----	-----
14,000	-----	-----	-----

QUESTIONS

1. Discuss the possible reasons for Merwin's desire to move beyond the break-even concept and to evaluate the importance of financial and operating leverage.

2. In what way is the break-even number of units produced a measure of risk?

3. Construct a break-even volume chart for the old facility and the new facility. Discuss your findings.

4. What is the relationship between increased fixed costs and break-even volume.

5. Calculate the compound average annual growth in sales and earnings after tax for the firm. What is the possible relationship between sales and earnings growth and break-even volume?

company's growth rates relative to the industry? (Ignore possible disruptions in sales and earnings increases due to start-up.)

7. Calculate and interpret the degree of operating leverage (DOL) for the present operating mode and the proposed operating mode. Assume units sold of 8,000 and use Merwin's tutorial data from Tables 2 and 3.

8. The DOL for the industry in which Specialty Chemicals, Inc., operates is 6.10; comment upon this in relation to your answer to question 6. Does the change in operating policy, to the mode of operation planned for the new facility, seem reasonable in view of the industry DOL? What will be the likely effect upon the company's 1995 earnings after tax.

9. What is the relationship between DOL and the break-even volume? Does Merwin seem to recognize the relationship and its importance?

10. Does Specialty Chemicals, Inc. face an ethical dilemma in its desire to have fewer workers at the new facility? (Discuss this issue in terms of existing employees who may wish to move to the new facility.)

11. Use the information from the new mode of operation to calculate the degree of financial leverage and the total leverage. Again, use the data from Table 3. Also assume an interest level of $200,000. Interpret your results. Assume 8,000 units sold. Discuss how the firm might exert some control over its operating leverage.

12. Discuss the firm's planned new operating characteristics in terms of continued revenue growth. What should Merwin do if she discovers that some costs are not completely "fixed" or "variable"?

Case 30

Capital Structure, Agency, and Free Cash Flow

McDermott Manufacturing, Inc.

The concern uppermost in Sonia Burdett's mind at present was how to effectively communicate to the firm's Board of Directors the soundness of her financial policies. Ms. Burdett is CFO of McDermott Manufacturing, Inc., (MM, Inc.), a position she has held for the past five years. In three days the Board of Directors would meet to consider several issues, all of which had implications for the strategic direction of the firm. Sonia Burdett's role in that meeting would be to provide assistance to the firm's president as he sought to explain the relationship among the firm's free cash flow, capital investment opportunities, and capital structure.

MM, Inc., had operated profitably since 1985. Its primary business was the manufacture and sale of turbines for the electric utilities industry. The firm enjoyed a reputation for high-quality products and very reliable service once a unit was sold. The capital intensity of the industry eradicated ease of entry for potential new competitors. As a result, the industry enjoyed relatively stable revenue and earnings growth, and such growth was relatively easy to forecast.

In terms of forecasting sales and earnings growth for the industry, trade groups and others indicated in published material that the industry would grow at the approximate rate of the nominal GDP for the foreseeable future. The generation of electric power in the United States would be based upon improved operating efficiencies within the plants that currently existed. New construction, nuclear or otherwise, was at a virtual standstill for a number of reasons. It seemed that the utilities industry was poised for some type of major transition, as yet unknown. The replacement of turbines and related machinery, including software and other ancillary items related to the operation of the turbines, was now the major source of revenue for MM, Inc., and the firms against which it competed.

The upcoming meeting, for which Burdett intended to be "doubly prepared," as she had remarked to a colleague, concerned issues that were being considered and discussed across a wide range of industries. Such issues bore directly upon corporate financial policy and reflected a fundamental change that was still evolving in terms of the relationship between stockholders and managers. If managers were "agents" of the stockholders, what were the implications of that relationship for such matters as compensation, monitoring of management's performance, and the overall financial viability of the firm? For example, what effect, if any, should the agency relationship have upon the firm's capital structure? Moreover, was such a consideration an appropriate area of inquiry for the Board of Directors? It was these questions to which Burdett had, for the past weeks, given her full attention. Table 1, provides the firm's most recent balance sheet.

TABLE 1			
McDermott Manufacturing, Inc.			
Balance Sheet			
December 30, 1995			
($000s)			
Cash	$ 1,860	Accounts payable	$ 2,976
Accounts receivable	417	Accruals	744
Inventory	2,187	Notes payable	3,255
Total current assets	$ 4,464	Total current liabilities	$ 6,975
Land	12,927	Long-term debt	7,734
Buildings	15,438	Total liabilities	14,709
Equipment	22,971		
		Common stock	13,284
Total fixed assets	$51,336	Retained earnings	27,807
		Total equity	$41,091
Total assets	$55,800	Total liabilities and equity	$55,800

Burdett believed that the board was particularly interested in the firm's financial policies relative to its future use of the firm's free cash flow. [Free cash flow is described as Earnings Before Interest and Taxes (1 – tax rate) + Depreciation – Capital Expenditures – Additions to Net Working Capital]. Such cash flow had accumulated due to the comparatively small number of capital expenditure projects available to MM, Inc. The slowdown in industry growth was the main contributor to that situation. The board's use of the term "free cash flow" referred to cash flow available after all acceptable capital projects were funded.

The day of the Board of Directors meeting was finally over, and Sonia Burdett wondered about the long-term effect some of the discussion would have upon MM, Inc. Most prominent among the directors' concerns was the use to which the firm's financial staff would put the firm's free cash flow. The members of the board seemed to believe that such a substantial amount of money should not just become "play money" for the financial staff, as one board member had put it. Free cash flow had increased by 15 percent compounded over the past five years. Specifically, the consensus among the board members seemed to be that the firm should increase its level of long-term debt. An increase in long-term debt would accomplish two very important goals, according to the board's thinking. First, a portion of the outstanding common stock could be retired, thereby increasing the return on equity (ROE) for the remaining shareholders; and second, the payment of interest on the additional debt would assure that the increasing free cash flow would be put to good use.

Ms. Burdett considered the foregoing suggestions in view of the changing nature of the relationship between shareholders and managers. In essence, shareholders were intent upon holding managers more closely responsible for their actions, and making sure such actions were in keeping with the goals of the shareholders. Shareholders could easily monitor the relationship between free cash flow and debt service payments. Such monitoring was not so easily accomplished when the cash flow was available for expenditures the risk and return for which was essentially unknown to shareholders.

Burdett wondered what effect the additional long-term debt would have upon the firm's debt rating, its interest coverage ratios, and its capital structure in relation to other firms in the industry. These were questions that were of great concern to company management, because even with the forecasted modest growth, the firm wished to maintain its reputation in the industry. The need to raise funds quickly and at competitive rates was important in that regard. Selected industry data are shown in Table 2 below.

TABLE 2

McDermott Manufacturing, Inc.
Selected Industry Data *

Total debt-to-total assets	35%
Times interest earned	9
Return on equity	25%

---

*Data for companies that make up 80 percent of industry capacity, year-end 1994.

In addition to the foregoing data and information, the average interest on M.M., Inc.'s debt in 1995 was 7 percent. The yield curve was relatively flat during this period. Burdett believed that long-term funds borrowed within the next 12 to 18 months would carry an interest rate of approximately 8 percent. Profit after tax in 1995 was $11,152, and the firms tax rate is 30 percent for the combination of federal and all local taxes.

QUESTIONS

1. Why are managers considered "agents" of corporate stockholders? Is the description justified? Explain your reasoning.

2. The firm's Board of Directors wishes to have more control over the managers' use of the firm's free cash flow by the increased use of debt. Is there a "cost" to this aspect of the agency relationship? If so, how would the cost be described? Discuss any alternatives to incurring such a cost.

3. Of what relevance is the information provided in Table 2, given that it is 1994 data?

4. What is the meaning of a "flat" yield curve? How is such a curve relevant to Burdette's concerns?

5. Assume that Burdett will double the firm's long term debt and use the funds to retire equity. (Assume that the common stock data shown in Table 1 is market value data.) What is MM, Inc.'s total debt-to-total-assets ratio, times interest earned, assuming no change in EBIT, and ROE before and after the acquisition of the additional debt?

6. Assess the change in the ratios calculated in Question 6.

7. Would the board members' concerns be better addressed if they requested detailed and ongoing information concerning the firm's capital expenditures? What are the likely costs and benefits to such a request?

8. Are there any specific recommendations that Burdett should make to the board? Why?

Case 31

The Debt versus Equity Financing Alternative

High Rock Industries

Kathleen Crawford, president and CEO of High Rock Industries, reflected upon the company's growth since its inception in 1975. That growth, indicative of the activity in land development in the mid-Atlantic region of the United States, carried with it a persistent need for expansion capital.

High Rock Industries (HRI), named for the founder's tiny hometown in Southeastern Virginia, was engaged in the purchase of undeveloped acreage which was then developed for industrial use. Over the past fifteen years, the company had become the dominant mid-Atlantic developer of office parks.

The company began with Crawford's grandfather's purchase of farmland in the 1960s for the purpose of residential development. As the rural areas of Maryland, Virginia, and North Carolina declined in population, and hence the ability to attract industry, Crawford's strategy had to be revised. Much of the originally purchased land was liquidated, and the cash was used to purchase land within a reasonable proximity of urban areas. The company wanted to take advantage of business relocations of many companies from the industrial region which had Cleveland, Ohio as its approximate center.

By 1975, the complexity of the business demanded incorporation and an appropriate managerial staff. It was at that time that Crawford finished her MBA and was in search of meaningful employment. Her grandfather was eager to turn the business over to her so that he could spend more time enjoying travel and his rare book collection.

While some land development firms had excess acreage, HRI did not. The economic period which followed the oil embargo of 1973 brought about many changes in the way business was done in the United States. The changes, however, could be broadly categorized as locational changes, and revisions to the scale of businesses. Many businesses were changing locations for any number of reasons, and the operations of many companies were becoming smaller. It so happened, however, that the land owned by HRI was located in the region to which many businesses were moving.

The company's plan, from inception, had been to deal in only the most potentially profitable land acquisitions. While such a strategy appeared obvious to some observers, its execution was another matter altogether. Crawford was intent upon having the infrastructure necessary to make the company's strategy work. To that end, having the best people on staff was the key element.

The staff had not only well-qualified accountants and marketing people, but appraisers and specialized analysts who addressed leasing, zoning requirements, and population patterns. As a result of the level of expertise which was found in the company, strategy had always been defined in terms of specific competencies, which led to clearly defined products and markets.

As a result of that phenomenon, the revenue and profits of HRI increased at a steady pace. As is typical in the land acquisition and development business, strong profits provide access to higher-priced, and hopefully, better-situated property, which often means even faster profit growth. HRI was in a most enviable position relative to the competition. Tables 1 and 2 present a balance sheet and income statement, respectively, for HRI. The debentures currently outstanding have a coupon rate of 9½ percent and carry a triple A rating, according to a nationally known bond rating agency. Most firms with which HRI competed had similar bond ratings and capital structures which included no more than 55 percent debt. The firm's equity is widely held due to active over-the-counter trading. The current trading range of the stock is between $32 and $34 per share.

In recent weeks Kathleen Crawford learned of a tract of land which had become available in the general vicinity of Washington, D.C. In fact, the land was to the west of the D.C. metro area along the border shared by Maryland and Virginia. The development in that area was primarily commercial and had become the site of some very well-situated office parks and federal office buildings. In addition, the area was occupied by several U.S. offices of foreign governments and businesses.

The small tract of land in which Crawford had become interested was occupied by a well-constructed building occupied by good tenants. There was also a parking garage owned by another company; in addition, the area was well served by the area's rapid transit system. HRI considered the asking price of $6 million to be most reasonable. In addition, based upon the present revenue which the building generated, Crawford's financial staff assured her of an increase in HRI's earnings before interest and taxes (EBIT) of 20 percent. This post-purchase EBIT forecast was based upon the occupancy rate of commercial property in the immediate area, a forecast of commercial construction, and HRI's skill in managing such property.

On the basis of the foregoing, HRI had been in very close contact with the property's owners and it appeared that a deal could be made before the property was placed with a commercial real estate broker. While the normal process of property acquisition would include a brokerage service, the current situation was one of those obviously fortuitous circumstances that demanded a quick decision.

The attention of HRI turned to the means by which the funds would be raised. The company's financial staff believed that the present debt level of the firm was within acceptable limits. In addition, they saw a continuing need for long-term funds in the future. The investment bank with which HRI usually worked outlined possibilities and conditions for the acquisition of the $6 million, which are provided below.

Within the commercial land development industry, firms' capital structures differed widely. This was due in part to the managerial structure of the firms which made up this particular industry. That is, some of the most profitable and well-run firms were thinly managed. Their success seemed to stem from the personality and connections of the principal shareholder/manager. This, however, implies no lack of ethics and standards in the business. In terms of HRI, the company's operating characteristics placed it among a select group of stable companies for which there were reliable data provided by industry analysts. Such operating characteristics included earnings stability, method of financing, and revenue and earnings growth.

The idea of having connections in the business referred most often to the ability to simultaneously, or so it seemed, identify a desirable property and arrange for financing. The idea of stand-by financing was often cited as a reason for the success of many firms. In these cases there was not necessarily a line of credit, but lenders or equity investors stood ready to commit funds on short notice based upon the reputation of the firm. Thus, industry average capitalization had less meaning than did say, coverage ratios for a particular firm. The coverage ratios were reliable due to the fact that most firms held fairly constant financing patterns even though such patterns differed among firms.

The Alternatives

Debt: Six million dollars of straight debentures, with a 7 percent coupon and a 15 year maturity, could be placed with an insurance company. The flotation cost on such an issue would be $200,000. There was also the possibility of a sinking fund of $400,000 per year. All parties concerned thought this unlikely, given the existing level of interest rates and the reputation of HRI within the financial community. (There are no explicit interest charges for current liabilities.)

Equity: An equity issue could be sold to the public. HRI would net $30.

**Preferred
Stock:**   While HRI had no preferred stock in its capital structure at present, this did not rule out the possibility of such an issue. One-hundred-dollars per share preferred stock could be sold to net the company $93.50 per share after brokerage fees. The yield on preferred stock of equivalent quality is 8 percent.

		TABLE 1		
		High Rock Industries		
		Balance Sheet		
		December 31, 1991		
		($000s)		
Current assets	$1,500	Current liabilities		$500
Net fixed assets*	52,000	Long-term debt		25,000
		Common stock ($20 par)		20,000
		Retained earnings		8,000
Total assets	$53,500	Total liabilities and equity		$53,500

Note: * Primarily holdings of undeveloped acreage and leased property.

TABLE 2
High Rock Industries *Income Statement* *December 31, 1992*

Revenue	$10,000,000
Less: Cost of sales	(5,589,300)
EBIT	$4,410,700
Less: Interest	(2,375,000)
Taxable income	$2,035,700
Less: Taxes (30%)	(610,710)
Profit after-tax	$1,424,990

QUESTIONS

1. Does the proposed acquisition seem to fit HRI's business pattern? Why or why not?

2. Should the proposed acquisition be financed with debt, preferred stock, or common equity? What are the relevant decision criteria?

3. What information and data are most useful in answering Question 2?

4. Calculate HRI's debt to total assets ratio and the times interest earned ratio before and after the new capital is acquired. Assume a 20 percent increase in current liabilities and a 20 percent increase in current assets. Discuss your findings.

5. What is the effect of a sinking fund requirement upon your calculations in Question 2? Why might interest rate levels or company risk factors influence the imposition of a sinking fund?

6. What additional information would have been useful in your analysis of HRI? Explain.

7. Consider your answers to Questions 2 and 3 above, then comment upon the meaning and usefulness of a probability estimate of the level of EBIT after the purchase.

8. Is there information, in addition to the specifics of the financing alternatives, that should be provided by the investment bankers?

9. If the stable developers such as HRI have a total debt-to-total assets ratio in the range of 48-55 percent, how much flexibility for future financing will HRI have if debt is issued at present?

10. If such flexibility, risk, and income are major factors in selecting a financing alternative, how should these considerations be defined and measured?

Case 32

Target Capital Structure
(Book Value versus Market Value)

South East Merchandisers

Ginny Carson, chief financial officer of South East Merchandisers, knew instinctively that the firm for which she had worked for the past 10 years was undergoing an evolution in the manner in which it conducted business. The strategic directive that the firm had developed to carry it through the next five years or so placed increased attention upon the setting of financial policy. Carson believed that the interrelationship between the overall corporate plan and the financial plan took on increasing importance during periods when revenue and earnings growth slowed to levels approaching those of the industry.

South East Merchandisers began operations in the mid-1970s as a retailer of general merchandise, ranging from jewelry to exercise equipment. Since the company's founding, the number of stores, all located in the south eastern United States, had grown to eight. The firm's revenue at the end of fiscal year 1995 was $300 million, and its earnings after tax were $24 million.

The company competed in the "discount store and fashion retailing" industry. The industry consisted, as of early 1995, of 55 companies, ranging in size from $200 million to $60 billion in sales. The selection of merchandise carried by the companies in the industry category varied by the merchandising specialty that each company had staked out.

The dominant firms in the industry, relative to sales level, were firms that had been in business for a long period of time and whose business had evolved along with the customs, tastes, and buying habits of the American public. In recent years, however, the discount general merchandise retailer, which did not sell clothing, had entered the general retail scene and had experienced tremendous success. The primary reason for this success had to do with price; modern, well-lighted stores; and a wide selection of high-quality merchandise.

Sales level was not the only characteristic that distinguished the various companies. Debt level, return on equity, price/earnings ratio, and other important measures of financial performance differed widely among the many firms in the industry. As an example, the return on common equity (ROE) at the beginning of 1995 ranged from 60 percent to a -80 percent. In addition, an inspection of the audited financial statements of many of the firms showed vastly different asset and liability structures.

Industry analysts and others qualified to comment upon significant trends and developments, predicted that the entire industry would experience a slowdown in sales and earnings growth. It was clear that the firms that did well in the coming years would be those whose management concept encompassed the whole organization. Sales and earnings, products and customer service, and promotion would continue to be major areas of emphasis in the future. The firm's finances would have to be managed with the same care and long-term outlook.

The issue facing Ginny Carson at present was the question of how best to operationalize part of the management of the financial plan. That addressed the issue of capital structure. Carson knew that a part of the management of financing with borrowed funds was maintenance of a specified level of debt relative to total financing; setting a benchmark for the optimal level of debt to equity was not easy. The optimal debt to equity ratio depended on market conditions, the management's operating philosophy, and the actual business conditions faced by the firm's management.

Of particular interest to Carson was the nature of the debate within the treasurer's office around the issue of "which capital structure" was to be viewed as the bench-mark. The financial staff knew the meaning of both the "book" and "market" capital structures, but were less sure about which of those should serve as THE capital structure and why. Table 1 illustrates the firm's book value capital structure at the end of 1995.

TABLE 1

South East Merchandisers
Book Value Capital Structure ($000,000s)
December 31, 1995

Long Term Debt	$ 60
Common Stock	10
Capital Surplus	5
Retained Earnings	65
Total	$140

*The Long-term debt, $1,000 face value, consists of 10-year debentures issued in January 1992 at par with a 7 percent coupon. The common stock is $2 par.

Carson wished to make it clear to all levels of South East's financial management that the two central issues surrounding the current discussion of the target capital structure were *(1)* the optimal capital structure is that structure that maximizes the firm's value to its shareholders, and *(2)* variations in capital structures differed among firms in the same industry. South East's management needed to understand why such variations existed. Carson knew that inflation, sales and profit levels and growth rates, as well as the firm's tax rate were influences upon the optimal capital structure.

The chief financial officer who preceded Carson had worked to maintain a target capital structure for South East of 40 percent long-term debt and 60 percent common equity. It was clear to Carson, however, that her predecessor had not thoroughly addressed the book versus market value issue of the optimal capital structure question. In fact, it seemed reasonably clear that management considered the data in Table 1 as an indication that the firm was operating very close to its target capital structure.

Resolving the issue was of considerable concern to Ginny Carson because of her commitment to the value maximization principle to which conscientious and competent financial management should adhere. The absence of volatility in the target capital structure is, for many managers, its most desired characteristic. Regardless, however, the firm's internal investment decisions are dependent upon a cost of capital that is itself dependent upon a value-maximizing capital structure.

South East's management, for all the lack of clarity concerning how to gauge the target capital structure, understood that the "basic" financial tools were quite useful in measuring the efficacy of the firm's decisions. Certain financial ratios were useful in assessing the debt capacity aspects of capital structure decisions. Carson made a note to herself to emphasize that point at the next staff meeting. She also decided to have a frank discussion at that time concerning business and financial risk, and their definition and meaning in capital structure decisions.

QUESTIONS

1. Discuss several factors that managers may consider when setting the firm's target capital structure. Be sure to explain why each is important to the decision.

2. Is the target or optimal capital structure for a given firm likely to be a "point estimate" or a range of values? Please explain.

3. Without the use of numbers, what is the difference between book and market values in terms of the capital structure?

4. Given the following, calculate the market value capital structure for South East Merchandisers for December 31, 1995: Debentures equivalent to those now outstanding yield 9.0 percent after tax. South East's common equity has a current market value of $25 per share.

5. How does the capital structure you have developed in question 4 compare with the firm's desired target capital structure?

6. Why do capital structures differ among firms in the same industry? Please be specific.

7. Describe how financial ratios would be useful to Carson in assessing the firm's capital structure decisions. Calculate the return on equity and the debt-to-equity for South East on a book value and market value capital structure basis. Discuss the difference in your results and the likely effect upon financial decision making. (The book value and market value return on equity are 30 percent and 19.2 percent, respectively.)

8. The setting of a target capital structure requires judgment. It also requires consideration of the debt coverage, future flexibility in financing, and profitability. How would each of those items be influenced by South East's capital structure?

9. Would Carson be correct in arguing for use of the market value capital structure as the firms target? Explain your answer.

Case 33

Cost of Capital Considerations

Touring Enterprises

Ed Mettway was concerned about his firm's ability to acquire the necessary property, plant, and equipment to take advantage of steadily increasing sales. Touring Enterprises, established in 1970, began as a mail-order house for motorcycle parts and accessories. In the early years, growth was slow and the business, though profitable, plodded along. Ed Mettway was the chief financial officer and treasurer. In the last 10 years, compound average annual sales and earnings growth had been 18 percent and 15 percent, respectively, a dramatic change from the earlier years.

Motorcycle parts and accessories sales in the early 1970s consisted primarily of parts sales to do-it-yourself repairpersons. In addition, sales of outerwear—jackets, pants, rain suits, and boots—were also offered by most mail-order houses in this business.

As the decade of the 1980s progressed, the nature of motorcycle sales, and consequently the accessories purchased, began to change. The elements of that change were as follows: (*1*) motorcycle ridership began to rapidly lose its "radical" image; and (*2*) the market for motorcycles began to noticeably segment among touring riders, around-town riders, and others. In addition, more motorcycle dealerships began to emerge. As a result, motorcycles became more widely advertised and more accessible to consumers. Also, the European practice of riding "sportbikes," the faster more powerful type of motorcycle preferred by younger riders, started to catch on in the United States. This group of riders preferred more stylish and protective riding apparel.

These developments were a boon to the manufacturers and merchandisers of riding apparel, parts, and other accessories. Touring Enterprises was ideally situated to serve this growing market. Mail-order parts and accessories companies were successful if the goods were carried in wide variety and were of high quality, and if shipments and returns were handled quickly and with minimum inconvenience to the customer. The emergence of small package delivery companies was a definite complement to the industry. Touring Enterprises' revenue and earnings grew along with these positive developments in the industry.

As the company's sales and earnings increased, so did the demand for capital. The firm's needs included inventory as well as additional space to house the inventory, computer facilities, and order processing areas. In the late 1980s the firm decided to include in its business some light fabrication of certain parts. The purpose of this was to handle certain customers' needs for specialty items. Such items were generally those made of fiberglass or aluminum. On-premises fabrication of such items gave the firm the ability to purchase parts from a wider array of suppliers without the constraints imposed by concerns for fit, style, color, and the like.

The recent growth, however, had placed severe demands on the firm's ability to manage all aspects of its finances. Mettway had formed solid relationships with banks and other lenders, and the firm's stock had been traded on a regional stock exchange since the initial public offering in 1978. As the firm's strategic plan indicated the desirability of a new facility on the East Coast, Mettway's attention turned increasingly to a careful articulation of an internal financial policy. The policy would serve as a guideline for acquiring capital in the short-term as well as during and after the establishment of a new business location.

Of specific concern to the company's treasurer was the matter of how to communicate to the firm's financial analysts and accountants the proper manner in which to calculate the weighted average cost of capital. The desire was to not only have the concept widely understood by all financial staff members, but to understand how the current liabilities and depreciation fit into the calculations, if at all. The firm's balance sheet is shown in Table 1.

TABLE 1

Touring Enterprises
Balance Sheet
December 31, 1995
($000s)

Cash	$ 810	Bank loans	$1,830
Marketable securities	2,647	Accounts payable	1,070
Accounts receivable	2,500	Accrued expenses	1,763
Inventory	8,519	Current maturities of	
Re-Paid expenses	500	long-term debt	460
Total current assets	$14,976	Total current liabilities	$5,123
		Long-term debt	4,600
		Total liabilities	$9,723
Gross fixed assets	$13,343		
Less: Accumulated			
depreciation*	(5,499)	Common stock	$ 2,024
Net fixed assets	7,844	Paid-in capital	3,952
Other assets	677	Retained earnings	7,798
Total assets	$23,497	Common equity	$13,774
		Total liabilities	
		and equity	$23,497

---

*Annual accumulated depreciation, approximately $400,000 for the past 3 years.

What concerned Mettway was the unspecific nature of certain aspects of the cost of capital calculation in practice — that is, how best to present the general rules of cost of capital in a manner that the finance staff would see as logical and widely applicable. The firm's cost of funds obtained through a stock issuance or offering of long-term debt was relatively easy to assess. At present the firm's stock price was $22 and the annual dividend was $1.10. Further, the yield on debt of the type that Touring Enterprises had recently issued was 7.5 percent. The firm was in the 35 percent tax bracket. (This included federal, state, and local taxes.)

The bank loans shown on Table 1 were revolving lines of credit, which the firm maintained at a relatively constant level of draw-down year to year. The same was true for accrued wages and taxes, and accounts payable. Mettway recognized that textbook expositions of the weighted average cost of capital exhibited a (necessarily) simplistic approach, which showed the interrelationship among equity, long-term debt, and the total of those two as the basis for the weighted average capital cost calculation. However, the operating practices of firms differed across industries and among firms within the same industry. Such differences often influenced capital cost calculation. The primary causes of such differences were capital structure, composition and level of current liabilities and depreciation, and the firm's effective tax rate. Mettway believed that developing a clear policy on the firm's cost of capital calculation would require careful consideration of the specific operating characteristics of Touring Enterprises.

The company's treasurer understood that the inclusion of current liabilities in the firm's financial planning affected the capital budget. Mettway knew that in any given period the amount of external funds at a given cost would be influenced by the inclusion or exclusion of current liabilities. For example, if Touring Enterprises used accelerated depreciation for its tax reporting, and straight line depreciation for reporting income to stockholders, a deferred tax (a current liability) charge would appear on the report to stockholders. Deferred taxes are a noncash charge; therefore, net income, but not net cash flow, would be altered due to the difference in depreciation.

QUESTIONS:

1.   What is the major value of the weighted cost of capital calculation for the firm?

2.   Describe "capital structure."

3.   How is the firm's weighted cost of capital influenced by the firm's capital structure?

4.   Describe the role of the firm's tax rate in cost of capital calculations?

5.   Calculate the cost of long-term debt and common equity for Touring Enterprises. Calculate the weighted average cost of capital.

6.   Provide an argument for including or not including current liabilities in the cost of capital calculation.

7.   Touring Enterprises' capital structure is believed to be optimal. What is the meaning and importance of an optimal capital structure to the cost of capital calculation?

8.   What economic circumstances will likely cause a change in the firm's optimal capital structure?

9.   Explain the effect of accelerated depreciation versus straight-line upon net income. How does this create "deferred taxes" on the firm's balance sheet?

10.   Should Touring Enterprises consider current liabilities as a part of its permanent financing? Why or why not?

Case 34

Determining the Corporate Cost of Capital

COBA Corporation (Part A)

W. F. Kenner, president and general manager of COBA Corporation paced back and forth as he considered the business awaiting him in the afternoon meeting. The meeting was to include Julie Tiffin, COBA's treasurer, Jan Bergerson, COBA's controller, and Kenner. The discussion was to center around the calculation of the appropriate cost of capital for the corporation.

The company, whose name was formed from the names of the smaller enterprises that were combined to form the present company, manufactured a variety of items for the health care industry. The firm's operations were divided into two segments: Division A, which manufactured hospital clothing such as surgical gowns, masks, and other outer covering for surgical staff; and Division B, which manufactured sterilized items such as scalpels and hypodermic needles.

The present company was formed in 1978. Its stock was first offered to the public the following year. The company joined several more well-established firms in an industry that had experienced steady growth since the 1950s. The industry was characterized by efficient production practices, prompt delivery of its products, and limited flexibility in terms of pricing the various products.

COBA's manufacturing operations were modern and efficient by industry standards. The two operating divisions were located in the same city and the corporate office was in the suburban northern end of the city. The company's sales and earnings had increased at a significant rate over the past few years; Table 1 illustrates that trend.

Given the sales and earnings growth experienced by COBA, finding viable internal investments (capital budgeting projects) was not a problem for the company. It was the issue of capital budgeting, however, which had given rise to the upcoming meeting. During the company's brief history its proposed capital budget was developed in the following manner: (1) Tiffin and Bergerson developed a funding plan for the company. That is, they determined the amount of funds available for investment in property, plant, and equipment and the source of those funds for the coming fiscal year. (2) The divisions developed a capital needs plan based upon the marketing research and replacement expenditure information put together by the division controller. (3) The division budgets were modified to conform to the funding plan developed by Tiffin and Bergerson. (4) The final capital budget represented those expenditures for each division selected based upon their net present value (NPV) or their internal rate of return (IRR).

It was the task of the company's treasurer and controller to assess the primary influences upon the company's stock price, risk and, return (COBA operated without a vice president of finance; those duties, planning and policy-setting, were shared by Tiffin and Bergerson.)

Tiffin and Bergerson both held degrees in finance; therefore, they understood the relationship among risk, return, marginal cost, and marginal revenue. More important, they understood how those factors affected the continued success of the firm. It was now necessary to explain these considerations to certain division personnel who were in need of a clearer orientation concerning the finance function within the firm. This effort was part of a plan by the treasurer and controller to have marketing research, cost accounting, and finance all "on the same wave length," as Bergerson had put it. The overall purpose of the orientation was to improve coordination and planning of capital expenditures within each division. It was seen also as an opportunity to bring Kenner up-to-date on the details of financial decisionmaking within the firm. The focus of the discussion was to be upon the firm's historical or book cost of capital as represented by the capital structure shown in Table 2.

Tiffin and Bergerson wanted to make sure that each functional department understood why the cost of capital calculation was important and how the cost was calculated. For example, one member of the Division A accounting staff had frequently questioned the assumed relationship between the cost of capital and the required return on the firm's capital budgeting projects.

In terms of a further clarification of the cost of capital issue, the difference between the two divisions held some relevance. Division A was the "mature" portion of the firm's business. That is, its growth prospects were not outstanding and most incremental cash flows from the division were based upon the replacement type of expenditure. This referred to the pursuit of better ways to manufacture standard items for an existing market. Cash flows from Division A were stable. By contrast, Division B was experiencing rapid growth and there were many high-return projects available to the division. The question of the opportunity cost of capital versus the firm's overall cost of capital warranted discussion among the division's financial analysts.

To add to the list of things that needed to be clarified, the component costs of capital—the cost of individual capital items, debt, equity, and preferred stock—needed to be understood. As an example, in cost of equity calculations, the dividend model, also called the Gordon Model, was the company's preferred method for determining the equity cost. The questions concerning the use of the dividend model often centered around the calculations of the growth component of common stock returns.

There were, of course, other questions related to the cost of capital calculations. In a seminar that he had attended at a local university, Kenner heard a heated argument between two of the participants over the role of the firm's capital structure, divisional risk, and the difference between the book value capital costs and the market value capital costs as an influence on capital costs. On occasion, Kenner would run these ideas and concerns past Tiffin and Bergerson to gauge their thinking on them. As a result, the two managers believed these same issues would be raised in the meeting. In the case of COBA, and specifically for the upcoming meeting, the following facts were believed to be useful by Tiffin and Bergerson. A study of each division's cash flows over a period of five to seven years verified the difference in variability of the two divisions' cash flows. The two managers concluded that this had some effect upon the cost of capital for the divisions. The managers defined cash flow as the sum of profit after tax, plus depreciation; the variability in cash flow was measured by the standard deviation.

The firm has had no additional issuance of stock since its inception. Investment in new assets had been accomplished through the retention of approximately 60 percent of earnings after tax, and borrowing on a long-term basis. The current stock price, at year-end 1995, was $20 per share. The firm was in the 35 percent tax bracket (including federal, state, and local taxes).

While the foregoing information provided a useful background against which Tiffin and Bergerson might explain the cost of capital concept, there were more specific areas that would have to be addressed. A question that was often debated during the budgeting season was the relationship of the discount rate used in the capital budgeting analysis to the firm's cost of capital. Why was Tiffin's motto "Marginal cost equals marginal revenue?" What did that have to do with anything?

An issue that the two financial managers wanted to settle before the meeting was whether an ongoing relationship with an investment banker was necessary. While there were no specific plans being made to raise additional capital, the firm's strategic plans made such an event likely within the next two years. As a result, information about such things as debt rating, debt costs, and risk characteristics in the industry as seen by external analysts was needed. Therefore, it was against this background that the top-level management of COBA sought to establish a consensus among the members of the divisional financial staff on the cost of capital.

TABLE 1

COBA Corporation
Sales and Earnings History

Year	Sales	Earnings per Share	Dividends per Share
1987	$15,000,000	$0.90	$0.37
1988	16,800,000	1.01	0.40
1989	18,750,000	1.13	0.45
1990	21,600,000	1.30	0.53
1991	24,600,000	1.48	0.60
1992	26,850,000	1.61	0.65
1993	32,500,000	1.95	0.79
1994	33,100,000	2.00	0.81
1995	37,140,000	2.23	0.91

TABLE 2

COBA Corporation
Balance Sheet
December 31, 1995
($000s)

Total current assets	$800	Total current liabilities	$250
Land	$8,000	Long-term debt (at 9%)	$21,750
Buildings (net)	26,000	Common stock	
Equipment (net)	12,200	(2m shares outstanding)	20,000
Total fixed assets	$46,200	Retained earnings	5,000
Total assets	$47,000	Total liabilities and net worth	$47,000

QUESTIONS

1. Comment on the desirability of building a consensus among the financial staff concerning the cost of capital.

2. How does the cost of capital relate to capital budgeting? (Please explain in detail.)

3. What is the probable meaning of Tiffin's motto?

4. What is the projected dividend growth rate?

5. Calculate the weighted average book cost of capital for COBA. Discuss each of the component costs.

6. What is the relationship, if any, of the current liabilities to the company's cost of capital?

7. Comment on the optimal capital structure as it relates to the cost of capital.

8. What are some advantages of establishing a relationship with an investment banker?

9. What is the meaning of the opportunity cost of capital for the divisions relative to the firm's overall cost of capital?

10. What is the role of the opportunity cost in capital budgeting?

11. Discuss the cost of retained earnings versus the cost of new equity. If these costs differ, why do they differ?

12. What, if anything, would cause a fundamental (permanent) change in the firm's cost of capital?

Case 35

Risk Management and Corporate Capital Costs

COBA Corporation (Part B)

After the meeting, Tiffin and Bergerson were feeling some relief and some apprehension over the way things went. They were relieved because they believed that Kenner now fully understood why they made financial decisions in such a manner. In addition, the more experienced financial staff from each of the divisions were also "tuned in." Their apprehension arose, however, from a series of questions raised by Kara Sims, a finance major and summer intern from a nearby university. Sims' questions seemed to imply that COBA's approach to cost of capital calculations was less than up-to-date.

The young summer intern was especially interested in Tiffin and Bergerson's views concerning the book versus market cost of capital. For example, how did these differ, and did the difference, if any, influence the manner in which capital budgeting was conducted, or the results that were obtained? In other words, Ms. Sims wanted to make clear the following points: (1) the dividend model had some inherent shortcomings; and (2) capital investment decisions, the primary use for the cost of capital, should be made with regard to marginal cost as well as marginal revenue.

These issues and concerns were not new to Tiffin and Bergerson. They were sure that each of Sims' points was relevant, and they decided that all matters concerning the cost of capital had to be cleared up immediately. Only then could it be decided whether another meeting with Kenner and the divisional finance and accounting staff was warranted. In order to resolve things in the most efficient manner possible, a special project was designed for Sims.

In essence, Tiffin and Bergerson wanted Sims to design a cost of capital manual for use by COBA management. The issues to be dealt with in the manual were those alluded to by Sims earlier. These could be enumerated as follows:

1. Explain the difference between book value cost of capital and market value cost of capital.

2. Discuss an alternative to the dividend model of use in calculating the cost of equity. Specifically outline, in clear detail, the Capital Asset Pricing Model (CAPM) approach to the cost of equity.

3. Concerning item 2, describe the sources for the parameters of the CAPM or its relevant component, the Security Market Line (SML).

4. What effect, if any, will any changes to the cost of capital calculation have upon the firm's capital budgeting activities and the number and type of projects it ultimately accepts?

The issues that Sims wanted to clarify for the company would influence the policy set by the firm concerning financial matters. As a result, the firm's strategy would also be influenced. The proper considerations of risk in capital budgeting was important; it was also multifaceted. Sims wanted a clear, cohesive set of guidelines for the firm to follow.

The cost of capital for the firm was influenced by the cost of capital for the two divisions. Each division's cost of capital would, in a CAPM setting, be based upon the particular characteristics of the individual division. The idea and practice of comparing an operating division to a firm that operates solely in that line of business was known as the "pure-play" technique. Therefore, the debt level of a division's pure-play, and the cost of debt that resulted from that debt level, helped to determine the division's cost of capital. In general, the greater the debt level of a division, the greater the division's beta coefficient. (Beta measures the nondiversifiable risk of a security, such as a company's stock, or an operating division of a company.)

Sims began work on the assignment immediately. She believed that a thorough job would be good for the progressive and well-run company and would also assure her a more permanent position there. As a result of these motivations, Sims wanted to be as systematic as possible in her task. As a first step she wanted to recast the company's balance sheet, shown in Table 1, in the most current manner possible.

It was clear to Sims that the long-term capital items in the capital structure would appear differently if the value of each was calculated using market weights. She knew, for instance, that debt identical to the 9 percent debt now outstanding for COBA could be issued with a 7 percent yield. The market value of the common stock was $20 at present. As a result of that information, a market value capital structure would have to be calculated as a part of her task. (Recall that the firm's income tax rate is 35 percent.)

In addition to the capital structure explanation, Sims wanted to make sure that the delineation of the cost of equity calculations was clear. She wanted to illustrate a smooth transition from the dividend model to a more market-oriented model. The capital asset pricing model, which Sims' finance professor insisted was superior to internally influenced models such as the dividend model, was the analytical approach she wanted to emulate. Specifically, the individual company aspect of the CAPM known as the security market line would be used to calculate the firm's equity cost, the required yield on equity.

Sims knew, for example, that the parameters for the SML included a risk-free (or, very low risk) interest rate, the return on a market average of common stock, and the firm's beta. Further, it was clear that a low risk proxy used in the SML was the return on U.S. Treasury bills. The bonds outstanding have an assumed maturity value of $1,000 and a remaining maturity of 15 years. In addition, the imbalance on the balance sheet resulting from the market value of capital would be corrected by assigning replacement value to the land, buildings, and equipment.

The firm's beta could be calculated or simply found in one of several publications that carried financial ratios and similar information. The return on the market index could be calculated or assumed to be represented by the ROE of a broad market index (such a number was approximately 12.5 percent at the end of 1992). Sims, equipped with the foregoing data and information, believed she was ready to prepare an up-to-date cost of capital for the company.

The return on the market calculation may be handled in at least two ways: (1) by subtracting from the historical average return on common stock the historical average return on high-grade corporate bonds and adding the difference to the currently prevailing rate on high-grade corporate bonds; or (2) a specific pool of stocks (all industrial stocks or all utility stocks) might be assessed for their level of return over some time period. In any case, the objective is to obtain as representative a figure as possible relative to the factors that influence stock returns.

TABLE 1			
COBA Corporation *Balance Sheet* *December 31, 1995* *($000s)*			
Total current assets	$800	Total current liabilities	$250
Land	$ 8,000	Long-term debt (at 9%)	$21,750
Buildings (net)	26,000	Common stock	
Equipment (net)	12,200	(2m shares outstanding)	20,000
Total fixed assets	$46,200	Retained earnings	5,000
Total assets	$47,000	Total liabilities and net worth	$47,000

QUESTIONS

1. What is the purpose of using market values in cost of capital calculations?

2. What is COBA's cost of equity using the dividend model (see COBA A)? Using the SML? Explain the difference between these numbers. (Assume that the risk-free rate of interest is 5 percent, and the firm's beta is 1.41.)

3. What is COBA's weighted average market value cost of capital using the information in Question 2?

4. What is the beta for each of COBA's divisions if, in a pure-play sense, division A has a market value debt of $11.5 million, and division B has a market value debt of $14.7 million and the firm's total market value equity is invested equally in each division? (The unlevered beta is 1.0.)

5. Answer item 4 from the case.

6. If the company had only three capital expenditure projects up for consideration prior to Sims' work and the respective IRRs on the three were 16.3 percent, 11.7 percent, and 11.4 percent; how would Sims' calculations affect the disposition of these projects?

7. What capital structure assumption is implicit in the task assigned to Sims?

8. What is the rationale for preference of the externally influenced SML in the cost of capital calculation?

9. In general, how have interest rates on long-term debt behaved over the past five years? That is, what are the high and low levels of such rates over the period?

10. Consider your answer to Question 8. What is the implication for the cost of capital calculation?

11. Is the weighted average cost of capital the only correct discount rate to use in capital investment decisions?

12. Comment upon the rationale for historical data and trends being reflected in the return on the market calculation used in the SML equation.

Case 36

Determining Multi-Divisional Capital Costs

Cole-Williams, Incorporated

Cole-Williams, Incorporated, began operations in the 1920s. The firm began as a maker of industrial paints and coatings designed to resist corrosive chemicals and withstand other harsh conditions. In those early years, the company was a single-product firm. At that time operations were conducted from a single location in the midwestern United States. That location served as headquarters and manufacturing site for the company.

In the ensuing years, the company underwent many changes. Such revisions related to strategy, product offerings, management philosophy, and general scope of operations. The company now reflects many of the major and substantive trends that have affected U.S. businesses over the years. Those include product/market diversification, geographic diversification, and multilayers of management.

The company's sales and earnings pattern reflects its long and varied history. The data in Table 1 reflect more recent results, however, and the pattern is indicative of the much longer trend. In its present configuration, Cole-Williams is a multimarket, two division firm. Figure 1 illustrates the present makeup of the firm's finance areas. The managerial makeup of the divisions was similar. That is, each division had a controller, a marketing research department, and a staff that managed the division's manufacturing operations. The corporate staff, however, figured prominently into the arrangement.

The corporate finance staff, shown in Figure 1, was the administrative section for the corporation as a whole. In the past year or so, there was particular concern in the corporate finance area regarding the firm's internal investment approval process. In other words, what was the relationship between the nature of each division's business or products and the manner in which funds for capital budgeting were allocated to the divisions? The nature of the concern with the capital budgeting process is best examined in terms of the three relevant parts of that concern. Those parts are: (1) the businesses in which each division operates; (2) the "risk and return" profile of the earnings stream generated by each division; and (3) the company's desire to have an orderly process for internal investment analysis and to express that process within a capital budgeting manual.

The two divisions operated in relatively distinct product/market areas. The Plastics Division marketed to a wide variety of industrial users. The poly-compound plastic was manufactured at the division's two plants and resulted in interior wall coating material or as the plastic body of a telephone or handheld calculator. The wide range of applications for the division's product caused two major occurrences relative to capital budgeting — a constant demand for internal investment funds and a relatively stable sales and earnings pattern. The industrial rubber division manufactured a wide range of rubber products for many industrial applications including the mining industry. The products were primarily hoses, belts, and similar items used in many different industries. The sales and earnings of the Rubber Division, as it was known within the company, exhibited cyclical trends reflective of the industries that were the division's primary customers. The historical earnings pattern for the Rubber Division had shown more variation than that of the Plastics Division.

A major concern for Cole-Williams was how to best allocate capital to each division relative to its capital budgeting process. That is, how should the risk/return characteristics of each division influence the capital allocation process? Compensation for division managers was related to division performance. As always, the primary elements in the capital budgeting "mechanics" were the estimation of the expected cash inflows and the discount rate used to place those inflows on a present-value basis. Generally, the net outlay of cash for an internal investment project was known with greater certainty than inflows of cash. This was due to the fact that most outlays were contractual amounts and they occurred in the near term.

In its capital budgeting activities a major concern of the corporate staff was the determination of the cost of capital. Since it is the responsibility of corporate level financial management to write the capital budgeting manual— it was essential to be as clear and specific as possible. The divisional financial staff conducted their activities based upon that manual. For some time a debate existed over the cost of capital for the divisions. Finance theory had developed to the point where practitioners understood that the variation in expected future cash flows influenced the discount rate necessary to place those cash flows on a present value basis. At present the corporate cost of capital (the overall cost of capital for the firm) was based upon the most recent "market value" data as shown in Table 2.

In order to manage the capital allocation process in a manner equitable to both divisions it was necessary to outline the relevant issues, including the latest developments in finance theory. The task was left to the corporate finance staff and would become an appendix within the firm's capital budgeting manual. The issues and concerns are outlined in Table 3.

Based upon the foregoing, the corporate finance group began to collect data and information that would permit the divisional analysts to understand and make use of a cost of capital related to the specific line of business in which the division operated. To that end, information was gathered concerning other firms that operated in the same lines of business as Cole-Williams, including the overall cost of capital for those firms. Data for the Vandell Company and the JBG company are as follows:

$$\text{Vandell} \quad = \quad \text{MWACC} \quad = \quad 0.4P + 0.6I$$

$$\text{JBG} \quad = \quad \text{MWACC} \quad = \quad 0.2P + 0.8I$$

The "translation" of the above is as follows: The Vandell Company's overall marginal weighted cost of capital is based upon the proportion of its assets that are invested in plastics (P) plus the amount invested in industrial rubber (I). The same holds true for JBG. The overall cost of capital is 12 percent and 14 percent for Vandell and JBG, respectively. The Cole-Williams investment in plastics was 70 percent of its total market value assets and 30 percent for the industrial rubber products division.

Certain recent academic articles addressing corporate finance indicated that a solution for the divisional cost of capital based upon product lines was possible if the component costs of capital and the proportions of the firms' value across product lines could be correctly measured. Further, these academic articles added to a history of research in this area. The importance of the risk-adjusted hurdle rate to the practitioner is well known to academics. The correct, or efficient, allocation of capital to various operating units is essential if firms are to provide the required return to investors. The exposition of the value-additivity principle, based upon the idea of a firm being a collection of operating units, independent of the overall corporation, was the basis for the Cole-Williams financial staff's desire to find capital costs for each of the two divisions.

TABLE 1		
Cole-Williams, Incorporated *Sales and Earnings History* *($000s)*		
Year	**Sales**	**Earnings after Tax**
1989	$400,000	$32,000
1990	450,000	35,200
1991	504,250	39,425
1992	549,635	44,945
1993	605,960	79,500
1994	675,055	55,000
1995	780,500	66,385

TABLE 2			
Cole-Williams, Incorporated *Corporate Cost of Capital*			
After-tax cost of debt:	$k_d \times (1 - t) \times w_d$	$= [0.07 \times (1 - 0.34)] \times 0.40$	$= 1.85\%$
Cost of common equity:	$[R_f + \beta (R_m - R_f)] \times w_e$	$= [0.05 + 1.1 \times (0.113 - 0.05)] \times 0.60$	$= 7.15\%$
Marginal weighted cost of capital:	$k_d \times (1 - t) \times w_d +$ $[R_f + \beta (R_m - R_f)] \times w_e$	$= 1.85\% + 7.15\%$	$= 9.00\%$

where:

k_d	$=$	Interest rate on debt
t	$=$	Corporate tax rate
w_d	$=$	The proportion of debt-to-total assets
k_e	$=$	Required return on the firm's equity
$R_f + \beta (R_m - R_f)$	$=$	The Security Market Line
w_e	$=$	The proportion of equity-to-total assets

TABLE 3

Cole-Williams, Incorporated
Assumptions— Multidivisional Cost of Capital

---

1. The Cole-Williams Company operates in two distinct lines of business. The operating and risk characteristics of the lines of business are the most important distinguishing features.

2. The proportion of the firm's assets dedicated to each line of business is measurable and fixed.

3. The firm is a collection of divisions for which the acquired rates of return are independent of the overall corporate required rate of return.

4. The business and financial risk of similar lines of business are the same across all firms.

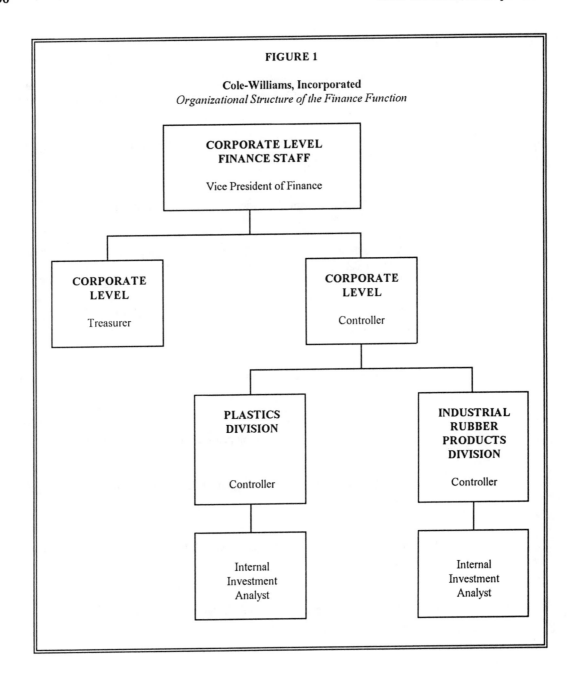

FIGURE 1

Cole-Williams, Incorporated
Organizational Structure of the Finance Function

QUESTIONS

1. Discuss the company's organization as shown in Figure 1. Is the organization conducive to a reasonable flow of information concerning the evaluation of capital expenditures?

2. What are some ways in which the firm may have measured the variability in sales and earnings for the two divisions?

3. What is the cost of capital for each of the company's divisions?

4. Compare the answer in Question 3 with the relationship between sales and earnings after tax from Table 1.

5. What are some benefits of the firm's use of the correct cost of capital for the two divisions?

6. How does use of the appropriate capital cost for each division affect managerial compensation?

7. Comment on the "product lines" approach to capital cost determination.

8. Is it likely that the company's divisions differ in terms of the cash generating ability of each? Why or why not?

9. In terms of Question 8, is there also a likely difference in the cash needs of each division? Why or why not?

10. What would cause a fundamental change in the way in which the firm is considering calculating its capital costs?

Case 37

Corporate Financial Restructuring

Orchard Mill Development

In December 1992, Orchard Mill Development Corporation (OMD), a regional development company, was evaluating several new investment projects for possible adoption in 1993. The corporate treasurer, Susan Shue, was very interested in resolving certain aspects of the firm's financial and capital structures, which she believed affected its ability to compete.

OMD was a land developer. In essence, the company bought parcels of undeveloped real estate in favorable locations, prepared the site for residential or commercial construction, then sold the individual parcels to builders. Involved in this process were such issues as zoning laws, road and street availability and adequacy, and various other municipal and state regulations. These issues were left to the company's competent legal staff. The resulting financial matters were the responsibility of Shue.

Of major concern to Susan Shue were the questions of investment projects, the rate of return to the firm, and the cost of capital to the firm. She understood, also, that these items were influenced by the firm's capital structure—the mix of debt, equity, and preferred stock.

In the early years of the firm's operations, and until very recently, the company faced a surfeit of high-return, low-risk investment opportunities. That was an ideal situation, to say the least. Now, however, it was clear that such lavish opportunities had become fewer in number. This did not mean that business has "fallen off" for OMD, it meant that it was now much more necessary to pay attention to marginal revenue _and_ marginal cost.

During the prior period, the firm operated without paying a great deal of attention to its capital structure. The equity holders had been happy with the return that the company provided. Within that method of operation had been a cost of capital that reflected a capital structure that stood in contrast to firms similar to OMD. Those firms operated, on average, with approximately equal amounts of debt and equity.

Shue understood that the firm's capital structure influences the cost of capital; this was the case due to at least two manifestations that occur simultaneously. In the first instance, a capital structure that was not optimal meant that the cost of capital would be higher. In the second place, if the cost of capital is based upon a suboptimal capital structure, some investment projects might have to be foregone—which would ultimately raise the cost of capital even more due to a weakened competitive position. As a result, the question of how to restructure the firm's capital structure was of immediate importance to Shue. Figure 1 illustrates the cost of capital for the company based upon a projected level of new financing.

It was clear from Figure 1 that the firm's cost of capital would reach a relatively high level when new financing approached approximately $8 million. In addition to the concern over the cost of capital for the firm, Shue wondered how the present capital structure would affect the ability to invest in capital projects. That is, if strategic considerations were an integral part of the capital budgeting process, and they should be, then would the investment in such projects be hampered by an inordinately high cost of capital? In order to better understand the implications of such a situation, Shue considered the information in Table 1, which provides data concerning independent capital expenditures being considered by the firm.

Based upon the foregoing information and concerns, Shue began to think seriously about a restructuring of the firm's long-term financing. She considered this because she believed that each of the investment opportunities shown in Table 1 were of equal strategic importance. That is, those expenditures bore directly upon the firm's survival in the product/market areas in which it had chosen to compete.

Now that the firm had reached the point of maturity in its life cycle, Shue reasoned that a capital structure more reflective of the industry average was probably appropriate for OMD. It was clear, for example, that many of the investment opportunities now "on the drawing board" offered a more modest return than previous expenditures in the firm's early operating history. It was now time to manage both risk and return. Based upon projections of a slower but steady growth in the firm's EBIT, earnings before interest and taxes, it seemed prudent to provide the equity investors the advantage of financial leverage.

In her decision to restructure the firm's capital structure she settled on equal amounts of debt and equity. It had come to Shue's attention that the academic finance literature had illustrated a quantifiable relationship among risk, stock price, and capital structure. There were other elements involved in this matter also; such items as the P/E ratio, EPS, and the like were relevant. In other words, there were identifiable elements that influenced stock price and the value of the firm and the method of financing was an important consideration. Shue believed that the capital structure now under consideration would produce the marginal weighted average cost of capital relative to the proposed new financing needs as shown in Figure 2.

Based upon all of the foregoing, Shue hoped to settle on the capital structure change after the next meeting of the firm's finance committee. It still remained to be seen, however, how the restructuring would affect the capital expenditure proposals shown in Table 1. She knew that the firm had reached a level of sophistication in all aspects of its operations, wherein the financing decisions would have a long-range and far-reaching influence upon the company's future.

There were other concerns related to the financial restructuring that seemed to be beyond the control of the firm's financial staff. For example, Shue recognized that the capital markets often reacted to news of corporate restructuring in ways not necessarily reflective of the firm's real intention. Moreover, how would the company's stockholders react to the move? Shue had learned, from her past academic work and through observation of similar activities by other firms, that the level of the stock price could be adversely affected by news of corporate financial restructuring. In other words, what was the nature of the information content of OMD's plans? Further, would such information content be reflected in the short-term or the long-term plans?

It seemed, from the literature on the topic, that the financial markets adjusted quickly to new information. Shue was still not sure what this would mean for the price of OMD's stock. It was clear, however, that the firm's earnings were strong. That is, earnings would show little variability in the near future and would not decrease. In fact, a modest upward trend was forecast.

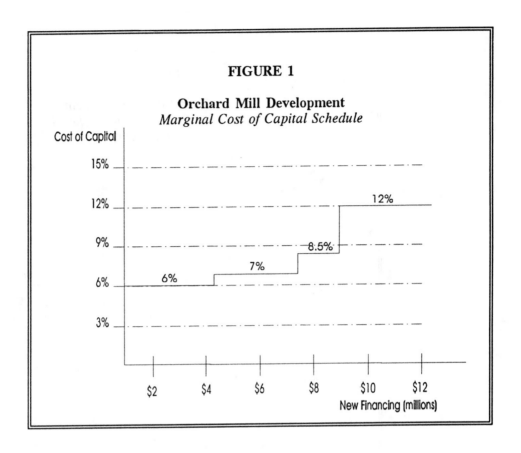

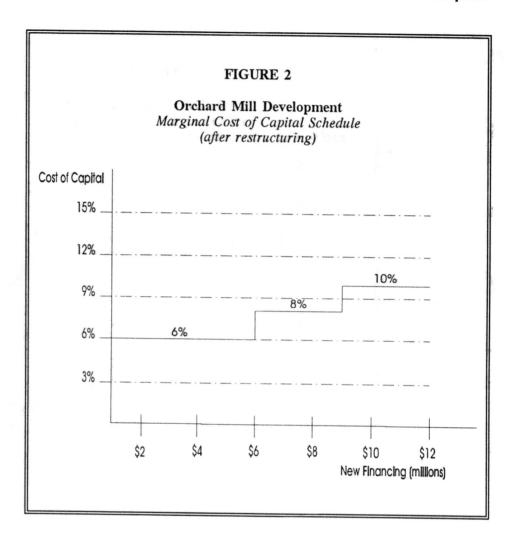

FIGURE 2

Orchard Mill Development
Marginal Cost of Capital Schedule
(after restructuring)

TABLE 1

Orchard Mill Development
Corporate Financial Restructuring
Planned Capital Expenditures

Project	Cost	Duration	Annual Cash Inflow
A	$1 million	5 years	$298,311
B	$2 million	3 years	$861,475
C	$3 million	6 years	$729,678
D	$3 million	4 years	$987,719
E	$0.5 million	3 years	$194,016

QUESTIONS

1. Discuss the relationship among method of financing, earnings level, risk, and stock price. How do those considerations relate to maximization of the value of the firm?

2. What is the primary disadvantage of not restructuring the firm's capital structure?

3. Calculate the internal rate of return (IRR) for projects A through E. Plot an investment opportunity schedule (IOS) on Figures 1 and 2. Comment upon your findings.

4. What action should Susan Shue take?

5. Why is the firm's capital cost lower under restructuring?

6. Should strategic considerations, as well as return, be a part of the capital budgeting process? Why?

7. Will the restructuring likely cause a change in the company's stockholder clientele? Why or why not?

8. What will be the likely duration and effect of any "disruption" in the company's stock price?

9. How should Shue prepare for such disruptions? Consider the following:
    a. The role of the media.
    b. The company's annual report.
    c. The stockholders' annual meeting.

10. Discuss the aspects of the larger economy that may influence the restructuring.

11. Discuss the difference between what Shue knows about the company (continued strong earnings) and what the investing public may know (a change in the financial structure).

Case 38

Dividend Policy and Corporate Capital Structure

FuzzyTronic, Inc.

David Myers, the CFO at FuzzyTronic, Inc., faced a real problem. Returning to his office one afternoon in late 1996, Myers knew he would spend another long night at his computer revising the firm's four-year financial forecast. While he realized this was a challenging task, he was nevertheless energized by the events that had transpired at the day's long staff meeting. He sensed that FuzzyTronic's computer programmers had just cracked a major developmental problem in designing software for the automobile industry, and the firm finally stood on the verge of becoming a major supplier of automotive transmission software to virtually all the major automobile manufacturers.

FuzzyTronic was founded in 1990 by Wong Xau, a young Chinese graduate student in mathematics who emigrated to the United States in pursuit of a dream. Xau started a small company, FuzzyTronic, Ltd., in his basement apartment in San Francisco to test the commercial possibilities of fuzzy logic, a new branch of mathematics that promised to make elevators run faster, furnaces modulate air temperature more accurately, and, yes, automobile transmissions shift more smoothly.

The trouble was, Xau knew little about American business practices, and even less about international marketing. He met David Myers, a recent college graduate with a background in finance, through a mutual acquaintance. Xau soon realized that Myers offered the business expertise and professional skills that he himself lacked. The two young graduates got along quite well, and by 1992 Myers had supervised the initial public offering of FuzzyTronic's common stock. From 1992 through 1996 the firm achieved one success after another, selling fuzzy logic software primarily to Japanese and Hong Kong manufacturing firms.

Unfortunately, it was tougher to sell fuzzy logic to American firms. Despite the odd name, fuzzy logic used crisp and detailed mathematical statements to deal with approximations—concepts such as many, most, few, and slightly—by assigning a series of numbers to clusters of overlapping gradations. Fuzzy logic software allowed computers to deal with shades of gray, such as when to turn on the air conditioner in a warm office building on a sunny afternoon and how fast to operate the fan delivering cold air to the building.

Both Xau and Myers often cursed the phrase "fuzzy logic" and regretted their naive decision to name the firm FuzzyTronic, Inc., because American managers seemed to connect fuzzy logic with fuzzy thinking. It was difficult enough for the young corporation to sell new technology to American industry without the negative connotation inspired by the word "fuzzy." Xau often argued that a better label for his software would be continuous logic; however, the term fuzzy logic was accepted and respected in the Asian markets where FuzzyTronic generated most of its sales.

By 1996, FuzzyTronic's future was a topic of concern for both Xau and Myers. In spite of its early product successes, Japanese competitors began developing their own fuzzy logic systems in early 1994, and FuzzyTronic knew that it needed a new star product to remain a key player in its industry. The innovation that FuzzyTronic's programmers stumbled upon quite by accident in late 1996 involved a software control mechanism that would shift automobile transmissions more smoothly than the mechanical linkages used in current vehicle transmissions. The programmers argued persuasively that the new software would be an instant hit in the market, if only Myers could find the money that the programmers needed for development.

To Myers, that was a big *if*. He had just completed two months' work preparing FuzzyTronic's projected financial statements, as shown in Tables 1 and 2 below with the firm's actual operating results from 1996. Now he faced the job of revising all the numbers. In addition, he had to report back to the programmers in three days about whether or not FuzzyTronic could afford the $175,000 investment necessary to fund the transmission software project in 1997.

Myers knew that FuzzyTronic's current financial forecast called for a healthy jump in dividend payments, and he also knew that the firm's stockholders expected this dividend increase. Between 1992 and 1995, FuzzyTronic paid its shareholders no dividends, reinvesting all of the firm's earnings back into the business to fund research needs and sales expansion. Myers worked hard in 1995 to realign the firm's capital structure in anticipation of FuzzyTronic's first dividend payment in 1996. He used the firm's healthy 1995 profit margins to trim long-term debt and boost FuzzyTronic's capital base, so that when the firm initiated dividend payments in 1996, FuzzyTronic was operating with an optimal capital structure.

FuzzyTronic's optimal capital structure involved very little debt because of the substantial operating risks facing the firm. At the same time, Myers knew that the cost of equity capital (i.e., retained earnings) at FuzzyTronic was 14 percent, and this relatively high cost—as well as the future dividend burden imposed by the firm's shareholders—was a big concern. FuzzyTronic's original public shareholders were patient folks who realized it would take several years before the firm could offer any significant dividend payments. But Myers knew that stockholder patience had its limits; by 1996, shareholders clearly expected the $0.90 dividend payment. In order to remain satisfied with their investment, Myers also knew the firm's shareholders expected healthy dividend boosts in 1998 and 1999.

That's why he was especially pleased with the pro forma statements shown in Tables 1 and 2. It took several weeks' work to compile projections that reflected FuzzyTronic's conservative growth in sales revenue over the 1997–2000 period, maintained the firm's optimal capital structure, and offered shareholders the significant dividend boost they expected. Now Myers was afraid the transmission software project would upset this delicate balance. He knew the software engineers really wanted the project to fly, and he suspected that they may have understated the project's true cost and overestimated its sales potential to win his support.

At the same time, Myers was aware that FuzzyTronic really needed the new project. In preparing his original pro forma financial statements, Myers felt that the firm's sustainable growth in sales and earnings was only 5 percent. According to the programmers' sales pitch, the transmission software project would boost this figure to 16 percent each year through 1999, without increasing the operating risk facing the firm. In addition, Myers knew that FuzzyTronic's other pending capital projects, outlined in Table 3, weren't nearly as promising as the transmission software project. The 16 percent increase in sales would help boost the firm's market share, and more important, it would help feed the hungry shareholders' dividend appetite.

Looking at all the numbers, Myers still felt uncomfortable. The programmers lived in a world of bits and bytes, Xau lived in a world of numbers and formulas, and Myers lived in a world of dollars and cents. Could he locate the money in the firm's 1997 capital budget to make the programmers' dream a reality and keep FuzzyTronic's shareholders happy at the same time? He didn't really know the answer to this question as he fired-up his PC, loaded his spreadsheet software, and subconsciously noted the slight draft as the blower motor in his office ventilation system quietly sprang to life.

TABLE 1					
FuzzyTronic, Inc. *Statement of Revenue and Expense* December 31, xxxx ($000s)					
	Actual	**Forecast**			
	1996	**1997**	**1998**	**1999**	**2000**
Net sales revenue	$2,049	$2,151	$2,259	$2,372	$2,500
Cost of goods sold	(944)	(990)	(1,040)	(1,093)	(1,150)
Gross profit	$1,105	$1,161	$1,219	$1,279	$1,350
Selling and general expenses	(617)	(631)	(660)	(684)	(720)
Research and development expense	(147)	(153)	(162)	(158)	(160)
Depreciation expense	(54)	(77)	(80)	(105)	(110)
Net operating income	$287	$300	$317	$332	$360
Nonoperating revenue	40	45	45	45	45
Interest expense	(7)	(7)	(7)	(7)	(7)
Earnings before taxes	$320	$338	$355	$370	$398
Income taxes	(131)	(137)	(142)	(148)	(160)
Net income	$189	$201	$213	$222	$238
Shares outstanding (000s)	150	150	150	150	150
Dividends per share	$0.90	$1.00	$1.25	$1.50	$1.57

TABLE 2 FuzzyTronic, Inc. Statement of Financial Condition December 31, xxxx ($000s)					
	Actual	Forecast			
	1996	1997	1998	1999	2000
Assets					
Cash	$435	$450	$470	$500	$525
Accounts receivable (net)	312	330	345	361	379
Inventory	174	183	192	201	211
Current assets - other	85	60	65	53	56
Total current assets	$1,006	$1,023	$1,072	$1,115	$1,171
Property and equipment (net)	100	140	147	170	180
Other assets	31	31	35	35	35
Total assets	$1,137	$1,194	$1,254	$1,320	$1,386
Liabilities and Owners' Equity					
Accounts payable	$30	$34	$46	$69	$95
Income taxes payable	17	18	28	43	53
Accrued expenses	19	20	30	51	79
Current debt obligations	0	0	0	0	0
Current liabilities - other	16	16	19	29	29
Total current liabilities	$82	$88	$123	$192	$256
Long-term debt	55	55	55	55	55
Total liabilities	$137	$143	$178	$247	$311
Common stock	$422	$422	$422	$422	$422
Retained earnings	578	629	654	651	653
Total common equity	$1,000	$1,051	$1,076	$1,073	$1,075
Total liabilities and owners' equity	$1,137	$1,194	$1,254	$1,320	$1,386

TABLE 3		
FuzzyTronic, Inc. *1997 Investment Opportunity Set and Corporate Capital Cost*		
Pending Investment Opportunities	**Projected Rate of Return**	**Required Investment**
(A) Automotive transmission software project	16.0%	$175,000
(B) Office automation project	12.0	75,000
(C) New marketing plan	13.5	100,000
(D) Acquisition of materials supplier	10.0	375,000
(E) Laboratory expansion	13.0	150,000
(F) New release of current software product	11.0	50,000
Range of Total New Financing	**Weighted Average Capital Cost***	
$0 - $200,000	13.00%	
200,001 - 400,000	15.00	
400,001 - 600,000	16.00	
600,001 - 1,000,000	18.00	

Note: * Weighted average capital cost is based on a 7 percent after-tax cost of debt and a 14 percent cost of common equity at the optimal capital structure.

QUESTIONS

1. Examine the data shown in Table 2. Using this information, what is FuzzyTronic's optimal capital structure, and what is the firm's current weighted average cost of capital?

2. Given the information provided in Table 1, what is the total dividend expense that FuzzyTronic will face in 1997, 1998, 1999, and 2000?

3. The case reports that in 1996, FuzzyTronic operated with an optimal capital structure. If the firm desires to maintain this particular capital structure over the 1997–2000 period, is it possible to give shareholders the projected dividend payments you identified in Question 2? Why or why not?

4. Dividend payments represent a cash expense that FuzzyTronic must pay in each year of the 1997–2000 period. Based on an examination of the projected financial statement data shown in Table 2, how is the firm financing this expense? Do you think that this financing method is appropriate? Why or why not?

5. Given the information shown in Table 3, what is the optimal capital budget at FuzzyTronic for 1997?

6. Given the current projections concerning FuzzyTronic's dividend payments and financial condition over the 1997–2000 period, what is the market value of the firm's common stock? What is FuzzyTronic's market-to-book ratio and price-earnings ratio? Based on your answers to these questions, how does the market assess the quality of FuzzyTronic's earnings and growth prospects?

7. In considering the transmission software project, suppose David Myers uses the residual dividend model to establish FuzzyTronic's 1997 dividend payment, and then continues to use the projected financial statement data shown in Tables 1 and 2 to establish the firm's projected financial condition. Given these assumptions, *(a)* what dividend payment can FuzzyTronic offer its shareholders in 1997; and *(b)* how is the firm's stock price likely to change as a result of this modification in the firm's planned 1997 dividend payment?

8. Review your answer to Question 7. Is there any reason to suspect that this answer does not accurately reflect the change in (a) the 1997 dividend payment that FuzzyTronic will offer its shareholders, and (b) the firm's stock price if it accepts the transmission software project? In particular, what aspect of your application of the residual dividend model is flawed in Question 7? How should you change the assumptions used in this question?

9. Revise the pro forma financial statements shown in Tables 1 and 2 to reflect the impact of the transmission software project on FuzzyTronic's overall financial condition. In developing these revised financial statements, what important details about the project do you need to gather from the case?

10. Compare the pro forma balance sheet you developed to answer Question 9 with the pro forma statement shown in Table 2, and pay particular attention to the projected capital structure changes at FuzzyTronic in each year of the forecast. What is different about these two forecasts? In particular, why does the equity ratio deteriorate over the 1997–2000 forecast period in Table 2, while it remains relatively stable in your revised forecast?

11. Based on the revised pro forma financial statements you developed in Question 9, should FuzzyTronic accept or reject the transmission software project? Assume that the firm uses the residual dividend model to establish its 1997 dividend payment and identify *(a)* the specific benefits that this project offers the firm and *(b)* the drawbacks that FuzzyTronic faces in accepting the project.

PART VI

OTHER TOPICS IN FINANCIAL MANAGEMENT

Case 39

Corporate Strategy and Financial Performance

Performance Cycle, Inc.

Brian Hemple never really wanted a career in the family fruit-farm business, but then again, he didn't have many other choices. Growing up in rural California in the 1970s, he spent many long, hot summers picking and packing fruit in the family orchard to earn money for college. By the time he was old enough to go to college, however, Brian decided he didn't want that either.

It wasn't that Brian was a disagreeable sort of person—what he *really* wanted was to start his own business. From scratch. Now. Rather than entering college like the obedient and respectful fruit-farm heir his parents thought they had raised, Brian decided to invest his college savings in the bicycle business. His parents thought he'd been out in the sun picking fruit too long, but Brian simply wanted to transform his passion for pedaling into profits.

In 1983, the year Brian founded Performance Cycle, Inc. in an outbuilding on the fruit farm, bicycle technology was still at a level that Wilbur and Orville Wright might recognize. Brian's dream was to develop a mass-produced, aluminum frame bike capable of withstanding the rigors of off-road cycling—bringing modern technology to the bicycle business. In short, Brian wanted to build a mountain bike, before anyone else really knew just what a mountain bike was.

Now, it would make a nice story, and a good finance case, if Brian had been able to transform his dream into a successful business; but that's not how things worked out. Brian's age, education, and limited capital base prevented him from acquiring the high-tech manufacturing equipment he needed to build bicycles, and after all, the equipment he needed wasn't the kind of stuff you'd expect to find laying around a fruit farm. In order to survive as a businessman, Brian abandoned his hopes of building bicycles and concentrated on distributing other manufacturers' aftermarket bicycle paraphernalia. You know, stuff like nylon bicycle bags, bumper racks to haul bicycles on the back of cars, and performance parts to upgrade original-equipment seats, tires, and so forth.

Hey, it wasn't all that glamorous, but is was a living. Performance Cycle didn't exactly prosper in the 1980s, but it survived. Over the course of the decade, the business provided Brian with a steady income, as well as an on-the-job education in the ways of the business world. More importantly, it kept Brian out of the sun picking and packing fruit.

Trouble was, Brian wasn't exactly getting rich, and he was still putting in fifteen-hour days in the same outbuilding after ten years' work. By 1992, Brian had incorporated Performance Cycle, selling 5,000 shares of common stock to friends and family in order to expand the business. While it might have been logical for Performance Cycle to expand its inventory and spend more money on advertising, logical courses of action always seemed to escape Brian. Rather than spending money in a sensible way, Brian chose to invest some of the proceeds from the private sale of Performance Cycle's stock in research and development.

If you think it sounds a little crazy for a small retailer of bicycle parts to spend money on R&D, you should have heard what Brian's father—one of Performance Cycle's new shareholders—had to say. Fortunately for Brian, his father was a *minority* stockholder, and Brian wanted to tinker with some new ideas for manufacturing aftermarket bicycle parts.

By 1992, the market for bicycles and bicycle parts had changed dramatically since the founding days of Performance Cycle. Lightweight, composite metals; advanced frame designs; and a variety of high-tech gadgets were standard equipment on most high-performance mountain bikes. What's more, the bicycle market was now worth $3 billion a year, and mountain bikes comprised 60 percent of this market. Given Performance Cycle's 1992 financial statements shown in Tables 1 and 2, you don't need an MBA to figure out that Brian's share of this market was infinitesimal. That was good, because Brian didn't have an MBA.

But Brian did have an idea that he thought could change the size and stature of his business, and maybe even redeem his sullied business reputation within the Hemple household. Brian knew that the hottest new development in the high-performance bike market was the integration of active suspension pieces within a modern bicycle frame. The front suspension eased steering and smoothed the bicycle's ride, adjusting to various terrains with a simple twist of a frame-mounted knob. The rear suspension boosted rider comfort and control, softening bumps and allowing the rear wheel to maintain constant contact with the ground. Unfortunately, these new suspension components only worked on *new* bicycle designs—they couldn't be added as aftermarket replacement parts on existing bicycle frames.

Brian's R&D expenditures changed all that. In 1993, he devised a way to modify conventional bicycle frames that lacked front and rear shock absorbers to accommodate this suspension equipment. Rather than spending more than $3,500 to acquire a completely new bicycle, riders could modify their existing, fixed-frame bicycles using Brian's new suspension parts. Once again, however, Brian faced the same old problem that forced him to abandon the manufacturing business in 1983—he didn't have enough money to acquire the fixed assets he needed to begin a manufacturing operation.

But this time things were different. Brian was older and wiser, had ten years of business experience, and most importantly, had lots of new stock he could sell. He figured he'd need just $25,000 in new equipment to begin producing the new suspension parts on a trial basis, and he conservatively estimated that sales of the new equipment would boost Performance Cycle's after-tax income by $1,750 a year. Reasoning that this profitability estimate would provide a 7 percent return on invested capital, Brian was confident that adopting the project would not change the firm's operating risk level, and he was certain that he could convince investors to purchase new shares at 9 times Performance Cycle's current earnings.

After all, the 7 percent return on investment would exactly match the return on book value that current shareholders received in 1992 when they purchased equity in Performance Cycle at 9 times earnings. Since the existing shares were not traded, Brian felt that this figure provided a reasonable estimate of the stock's current market value. In spite of his logic, Brian knew he'd need his father's help, and his father wasn't exactly thrilled about the way Brian chose to invest the proceeds from the last sale of Performance Cycle's stock. Still, the aftermarket suspension idea looked like a clear winner, and Brian was sure his enthusiasm would convince his friends and family—even dear old Dad—to take the plunge and buy $25,000 of new stock issued by Performance Cycle. Maybe Brian wasn't always logical, but he was an optimistic kind of guy.

TABLE 1

Performance Cycle, Inc.
Statement of Revenue and Expense
December 31, 1992

Net sales revenue	$395,447
Less: Cost of goods sold	(257,041)
Gross profit	$138,406
Less: Selling expense	($63,272)
Research and development expense	(22,540)
Depreciation	(27,681)
Total operating costs	$113,493
Net operating income	$24,913
Less: Taxes	(7,007)
Net income	$17,906

TABLE 2

Performance Cycle, Inc.
Statement of Financial Condition
December 31, 1992

ASSETS		LIABILITIES AND SHAREHOLDERS' EQUITY	
Cash and marketable securities	$23,514	Accounts payable	$39,000
Accounts receivable	80,618	Notes payable	37,600
Inventory	57,105	Accrued wages and taxes	3,510
Other current assets	10,077	Total current liabilities	$80,110
Total current assets	$171,314		
		Long term debt	$0
Gross fixed assets	$191,469		
Accumulated depreciation	(26,873)	Shareholders' Equity	
Net fixed assets	$164,596	Common stock	$115,600
		Retained earnings	140,200
		Total liabilities and	
Total assets	$335,910	shareholders' equity	$335,910

QUESTIONS

1. Construct a table that contains the following financial data for Performance Cycle, Inc. using the firm's 1992 financial statements:

Total book value	Price per share
Number of shares outstanding	Total market value
Book value per share	Return on book value
Net income	Return on market value
Earnings per share	

2. Suppose that Brian can persuade his financial backers to provide new equity capital and finance the aftermarket suspension project without revealing the financial details of this project to investors. If Brian sells each new share at Performance Cycle's current market price, how many shares must he issue to finance the suspension project?

3. Suppose Brian is successful in selling new equity to finance the purchase of equipment he needs to produce the bicycle suspension parts. Immediately following the sale of stock and the purchase of new equipment, how will Performance Cycle's balance sheet appear?

4. Recalculate the financial data shown in Question 1, incorporating all changes that would occur if Brian issues new common stock at the current market price and undertakes the aftermarket suspension project.

5. Suppose Brian's financial objective is to maximize profit. Given this objective, should he undertake the bicycle suspension project? If his objective is to maximize corporate earnings per share, should he undertake the project? If his objective is to maximize the price of Performance Cycle's common stock, should he undertake the project? In each case, explain your answer.

6. Compare the profitability of Performance Cycle before and after the acceptance of the bicycle suspension project. Notice that net income _rises_ after the project is accepted, but earnings per share _falls_. Why do these two measures of corporate financial performance move in opposite directions in this situation?

7. Given the three different business objectives discussed in Question 5, which one should Brian select to guide his decision to accept or reject the bicycle suspension project? Why should he select this objective?

8. Given your answer to Question 7, should Brian accept or reject the bicycle suspension project? If he decides to accept the project, how will this decision affect the total market value of Performance Cycle's common equity? Based on this information, is it possible to calculate the project's net present value?

9. Excluding the cost of the bicycle suspension project from the total market value of Performance Cycle's common stock, what is the net market value of the firm *after* this project is undertaken?

10. Based on your answers to Questions 1 through 9, is it reasonable to assume that new investors would be willing to pay the current market price of Performance Cycle's shares to finance the aftermarket suspension project? What price do you think that new investors would pay for each new share, assuming they realize that Brian plans to use the proceeds from the sale of new stock to finance this project? Given your estimate of Performance Cycle's stock value, what rate of return will buyers of the firm's new common stock require?

11. If the aftermarket suspension project yields profits of $2,775 per year—rather than $1,750 per year as Brian estimates—would new equity investors be willing to pay the current market price for the firm's newly issued shares? Justify your answer by recalculating the financial data shown in Question 1, assuming that Performance Cycle is able to sell new shares at the current market price of the stock.

Case 40

Corporate Bankruptcy and Reorganization

Progressive Office Outfitters

Progressive Office Outfitters began operations in early 1988. Its business consists of retail sales of high-quality office furniture. The company serves a market that, heretofore, had experienced strong growth. In the period 1984 through 1991 the construction of new office space had proceeded at a compound rate of approximately 10 percent per year. The local economy had made the transition from a predominantly manufacturing and shipping environment to a financial and administrative economy. However, the more resilient segments of the manufacturing and shipping economy had remained and contributed significantly to the economy's strength.

The company sold office furnishings to businesses in a location that included a major urban center surrounded by a less populous area, which had experienced the relocation of several national and international companies. The firm operated from two showrooms located approximately 50 miles apart. The showrooms were approximately the same size; however, the one situated in the more urban area had 30 employees and the other showroom had 20 employees.

In essence, the company's sales associates offered their services to businesses on a consulting basis. If that part of the relationship were successful Progressive would likely be the office outfitter of choice for that commercial client. As the clients expanded their business or upgraded their office furnishings, Progressive would likely remain as the outfitter. The firm relied heavily on its skill and reputation as the complete office furnishings consultant and supplier to ensure the growth and strength of the business.

Progressive had enjoyed a dominant position in the region's economic growth. Almost from the beginning the firm's managers recognized the need for a larger, more luxurious showroom for its urban location. The firm catered to the "high end" of the office furnishings business, and management understood that it was necessary to project that image. The firm borrowed heavily for the renovation and expansion. Finding creditors to support the firm's plans was not difficult. The company's management was well known as a skilled and aggressive group. However, there were several factors that were combining to cloud the picture for the relatively well-run company. Having three consecutive years of losses, which in the first year had seemed anomalous, was now beginning to appear as a much more protracted and serious problem. Progressive had been caught off guard.

In the fall of 1992, the firm completed the expansion which in hindsight was ill advised. The northeastern U.S. city in which the company operated had experienced an oversupply of commercial rental property; as a result new construction had come to a virtual standstill. In addition to that set of circumstances, a competitor with a more regional reputation had established a retail presence in the same town in which Progressive had long held dominance. Progressive's president, Ted Francis, wondered about the survivability of his firm, which had gone public in 1990. The most recent balance sheet for Progressive is shown as Table 1.

TABLE 1

Progressive Office Outfitters
Balance Sheet
December 31, 1995
($000s)

Current assets	$ 3,000
Net fixed assets	9,000
Total assets	$12,000
Accounts payable	$ 500
Accrued wages and taxes	150
Notes payable	200
8% subordinated debt	8,500
Common stock ($2 par)	3,500
Capital surplus	1,000
Retained earnings	(1,850)
Total liabilities and capital	$12,000

It was clear to Francis that replacement sales would not provide sufficient revenue to remedy the firm's three consecutive years of a negative return on sales. In addition to the absence of a positive profit situation, the firm's creditors were starting to become impatient. It was a reasonable certainty, though, that the creditors — which consisted of a bank, several wholesale suppliers, and two different insurance companies, who held an approximate equal share of the 8 percent subordinated debt — had confidence in Francis's management skills. The firm's board of directors, which consisted of four local business practitioners and a finance professor, were also well known to the firm's creditors.

Francis took some small comfort in the fact that the creditors and the firm's directors were not total strangers. Perhaps this familiarity would serve the firm in some way as yet unknown to Francis. The fact remained, however, that the creditors had every right to think seriously about the safety of the funds that they had invested in Progressive. The company president decided that the time had come to have a meeting with the Board of Directors concerning the present situation and the future of the once-profitable firm. A meeting was scheduled for the following week.

At the end of the meeting with the board, Francis was saddened but relieved that a plan was finally in place. The assembled body had decided to file a petition with the bankruptcy court, thereby placing the firm in voluntary bankruptcy. The idea of "admitting defeat," as one director had characterized the situation, was not well received by the firm's management or its employees. Everyone involved wondered how the firm's strength had deteriorated so rapidly. In actuality, however, the firm's troubles had not been created overnight. The firm had planned expansion, with the accompanying debt increase, just as the local economy was entering a slowdown in its growth. It seemed as though a combination of factors had come together to cause the firm's present "insolvency."

Francis realized that now was not the time to ruminate on the past, but to direct his energies toward the most fair and equitable handling of the firm's assets and liabilities. It was imperative, Francis believed, to demonstrate to the firm's creditors that management was determined to act in good faith. At present his concern was that the bankruptcy court would not attempt to appoint a trustee to oversee the firm's reorganization but would recognize management's competence and leave that group to deal with the creditors.

In preparation for the days to follow, Francis wanted to be as familiar as possible with the details of bankruptcy. He requested the company's attorney to prepare a brief "tutorial" for him as soon as possible. Specifically, Francis wanted to be aware of not only what the firm would face immediately, relative to the voluntary bankruptcy filing, but what management's options were in this situation. Table 2 outlines the attorney's comments concerning the relevant aspects of filing for bankruptcy.

TABLE 2

Progressive Office Outfitters
Bankruptcy Memorandum

To: Ted Francis, President

From: Ella Thurow, Attorney at Law

Re: Relevant Issues on Bankruptcy

Date: February 5, 1996

Your voluntary filing of bankruptcy with the courts is under the Chapter 11 part of the Bankruptcy Reform Act of 1978. Chapter 11, one of several "chapters' under the Act each of which address the specific conditions that lead to a filing, addresses business reorganization.

Needless to say, this filing represents a serious state of affairs for Progressive. When I advised you and the board to take this step, however, I had in mind the benefits of Chapter 11 as well as its seriousness. Those benefits are outlined below.

1. The bankruptcy code permits an issuance of new debt. This situation is know as Debtor-in-Possession, or DIP. This feature of the code allows for the creation of liquidity in the near-term. As Progressive is a retail establishment, DIP may be useful if the inventory needs to be replenished during this period.

2. The interest on the debt that existed prior to the filing will stop accruing while the firm is in bankruptcy.

3. There is an "automatic stay" provision in Chapter 11. That means that creditors are not allowed to foreclose on the firm to collect their individual claims.

4. It is relatively easy to secure a reorganization plan in Chapter 11.

Beyond the foregoing, the main role of the bankruptcy court in a reorganization situation is to determine what is fair and feasible in the reorganization plan. Such determination revolves around estimating future sales and analyzing the firm's future operating conditions. The court will appoint a committee made up of the unsecured creditors. The role of that committee is to conduct negotiations with you and your management team concerning the nature of the reorganization plan. Please be aware that the laws governing bankruptcy are quite flexible. I believe that we will have no trouble convincing the court that current management is competent to negotiate a reorganization with the creditor committee. Beyond that, management must decide what specific items among the firm's liabilities need to be reorganized. I am prepared to discuss any of this in greater detail at your convenience.

Francis wondered about the details of Chapter 11 bankruptcy. He also wondered whether a voluntary settlement with the creditors would be more beneficial. It was likely that the shareholders would agree with the board's decision, in any case. Francis' primary concern was what to say to the creditors, the board, and the employees about the future of the firm. Moreover, he was interested in developing a firm idea of how the firm should "look" once it emerged from the reorganization plan which Francis hoped would be successful. Table 3 provides the firm's income statement for 1995.

TABLE 3

Progressive Office Outfitters
Income Statement
December 31,1995
($000s)

Sales	$27,000
Cost of goods sold	(22,140)
Gross profit	$4,860
Selling and general admin. expenses	(4,210)
EBIT	$650
Interest	(680)
EBT	($30)

The data in Table 3 presented a disheartening picture for Francis. He was aware that prior to 1992 the sales figure would have been 30 percent more than the 1995 figure, and the profit margin would have been at least 3 percent. The pre-1992 cost-of-goods sold figure relative to sales would have been no greater than 78 percent, with S&GA at 14 percent as a maximum.

As Francis reflected further on the company's present situation, his attention began to turn to the specific nature of what lay ahead, the reorganization of the firm over which he had presided since its inception. The firm's debt level would surely be the major focus of any reorganization effort. The $8.5 million of subordinated debt stood as an example of the firm's good reputation, the debt level included "new" debt and a rollover amount from previous borrowing — the cause of most of its present trouble. The debt level was burdensome, as is clearly demonstrated in Table 3.

It made sense, in Francis's view, to think of the bankruptcy and the upcoming meetings concerning trustee designation in "strategic" terms. The firm had been solvent and operating efficiently for quite some time. If sufficient time could be gained so that the firm's sales and profit could regain their previous levels in keeping with the company's approximate 10 percent compound growth rates, long-term viability was reasonably certain. Moreover, Francis had read recently of financial difficulties being experienced by the parent company of the competitor that had moved into Progressive's market area. The difficulty seemed to be of a level sufficient to warrant curtailment of business in the office furnishings segment, according to the article. Francis's research indicated that office furnishings was the least profitable segment of the conglomerate's businesses. He understood the vagaries of the business all too well.

The bankruptcy court met with the management of Progressive, the responsible parties from the insurance companies that held the firm's debt, members of Progressive's Board of Directors, and several attorneys. The meeting went well from Progressive's standpoint; company management was deemed competent by the presiding judge, and no trustee was placed in charge of the reorganization. In essence, the reorganization was in the hands of company management and the creditors. It would be a cordial process. In Francis's view, the future of the company was much brighter. The details of reorganization would likely end up being favorable to all parties concerned.

In return for suspending the interest due on the subordinated debt for one year, the interest rate would be nine percent when the interest payments resumed. In addition, the bank to which the $1.2 million was owed would provide additional short-term financing if such were needed for inventory purchases. Francis and the board planned no major changes at the firm because of the reorganization. The attention of company management was turned to two specific dictates of the bankruptcy court. Those were the forecasting of sales and free cash flow for the next two-year period.

QUESTIONS

1.   Discuss the meaning of Francis's view of the bankruptcy as a " strategic" measure.

2.   Of what likely relevance to Progressive during the bankruptcy negotiations is the following: the news received by Francis concerning the financial situation faced by the competition; the strong loyalty of Progressive's customers. Do these things matter once a firm has declared bankruptcy?

3.   What is the difference between a Chapter 11 filing versus a Chapter 7 filing?

4.   Discuss Progressive's debt level in view of an uninterrupted compound increase in sales and earnings of 10 percent. As a creditor of Progressive, would you be willing to give them time to regain profitability? Why or why not?

5.   Progressive is referred to as being "insolvent." How does insolvency differ from bankruptcy?

6.   What will Progressive's income statement look like in one year? (Assume sales and related items return to a level closer to what Francis believes is a normal level.) Use the following outline to calculate free cash flow.

   A.   Operating Cash Flow = EBIT plus depreciation minus current taxes, plus (minus) changes to net working capital.
   B.   Free Cash Flow = Operating cash flow minus capital spending, plus (minus) changes in cash flow from financing.

(Assume additions to net working capital is $50,000, and depreciation is $150,000, current tax rate is 30%, and there is no capital spending and no flows from financing.)

7.   What is the likely purpose of the "automatic stay" provision in the Chapter 11 bankruptcy code?

8.   In your opinion has Progressive's management acted ethically in its present situation? Why or why not? (Consider your answer to Question 1.)

9.   Is it reasonable that the laws governing bankruptcy are flexible? Why or why not?

10.   What might Progressive do in order to lessen the effect of commercial office construction on its sales level?

Case 41

Leasing Analysis and Internal Rate of Return

Xtronics Corporation

"The future belongs to you young folks! Yes, it sure does. This ole dog is lookin' forward to staying on the porch. I just can't run with you youngsters any more. In my day life was a lot simpler. Not so today. All these fancy financin' schemes sure do make life complicated. Yes sir. The future really does belong to you young folk. Now you take that young Walt Stephenson. Now there's a real comer! He sure is putting our Consumer Electronics Division on the corporate map. That was a smart thing I did to hire him after he got pushed out of American Photo Electronics when they were taken over. Yes sir. He's going far with this company. Just look at this proposal he's sent in. He's figured out how to do that new computerized costing system he wants without straining our capital budget. With interest rates going up to 9 percent last week, I don't want to borrow just now even though we could if we needed to. You take a look at Walt's proposal and see if you don't agree with me that Walt is a real innovator. Yes sir. Walt Stephenson sure can run with the big dogs!"

Bob Atwater had heard it before. So had everyone else in Corporate Financial Services. Jim Weston, Xtronics' chief financial officer, "Uncle Jim" to everyone, was one of the last of his breed. A courtly "gentleman of the old school," James T. Weston was a self-made man. "Uncle Jim" had never attended college. He had started with Xtronics as an eighteen-year-old office clerk. By hard work, attention to details, and some night school coursework, he had worked his way up in the organization: office boy, payroll clerk, accountant, cost supervisor, chief financial officer. Xtronics had been smaller in those early days. The company's accounting had been simpler, too. But Xtronics had grown steadily, and now was a large regional supplier of electronic components to several manufacturers. In addition to supplying parts to other manufacturers, Xtronics had its own line of consumer products. The Consumer Electronics Division, known throughout the organization as CED, had recently experienced very high growth because of the introduction of a new line of CD players. The division was growing so fast that its divisional accounting function was regularly adding people. At least it seemed that way. Walt Stephenson, the CED division controller, was rapidly building a reputation throughout Xtronics as a "mover and shaker."

Bob Atwater was a financial analyst in Corporate Financial Services. His job was to help consolidate capital spending proposals from the several divisions into an overall capital budget for Xtronics. Bob had come to work for Xtronics three years ago following his graduation from college. He was new to the capital budgeting assignment but was excited about being "in on" Xtronics' capital spending plans. He had met Walt Stephenson on several occasions and had been impressed with his "Go for it!; The ends justify the means!" approach. Even though Bob had heard some older employees express concern over Walt's methods, most everyone in Corporate Financial Services

This case was prepared by John E. Baber, The University of North Carolina - Charlotte, whose cooperation is acknowledged with appreciation.

expected Stephenson to be named CFO when "Uncle Jim" retired next Spring. Bob was curious about Walt Stephenson's proposal.

A copy of Walt Stephenson's proposal is shown in Table 1.

TABLE 1
XTRONICS CORPORATION
Capital Budget Proposal

To: Mr. James T. Weston

Subject: Computerized Costing System

From: Walter H. Stephenson

Your approval is requested for the installation of a computerized costing system in the Consumer Electronics Division. The proposed system will enable CED to extend its costing system to cover our rapidly expanding CD business. This is necessary in order for Divisional Financial Services to support the growth of CED.

The proposed project will involve the installation of an LAN network, which will tie all of our accounting functions together in one system. Each accountant will have access to all parts of our system from purchase order to receiving report to accounts payable, all the way through manufacturing, inventory, shipping, accounts receivable, to collection.

Equipment for the proposed system will be supplied by Continental Computer Systems. We have worked with them for several months on the design of the system. Software for the system will cost $30,000. The hardware will cost $100,000. We have worked out an arrangement with Central Capital Corporation to lease the equipment instead of buying it. Central Capital has offered us a five year lease at $25,000 per year. While this is a fixed term lease with cancellation penalties if we want out early, we have carefully drawn the lease contract so that it will not be classified as a financing lease. Thus, it will preserve our borrowing power for future uses. The lease also enables us to stay within this year's capital budget.

We expect the proposed system to enable us to meet CED's accounting needs without having to hire the new accountant authorized under Personnel Requisition 95-174. If this project is approved, that PR will be withdrawn. That will save us $40,000, counting salary and benefits.

The attached table summarizes the annual cash flows we expect from the project. As shown in the attached table, the proposed project achieves an IRR of more than 15 percent and has a positive net present value when cash flows are discounted at our 12 percent cost of capital.

Your approval is requested.

Walter H. Stephenson
Controller
Consumer Electronics Division

TABLE 1
(continued)

SUMMARY OF CASH FLOWS FROM *LAN* PROJECT

	Year 0	Year 1	Year 2	Year 3	Year 4	Year 5
Operating savings	$0	$40,000	$40,000	$40,000	$40,000	$40,000
Lease payments	25,000	25,000	25,000	25,000	25,000	
Software amortization	0	6,000	6,000	6,000	6,000	6,000
Increase in before-tax						
profit	(25,000)	9,000	9,000	9,000	9,000	34,000
Taxes at 40%	(10,000)	3,600	3,600	3,600	3,600	13,600
Increased profit after						
tax	(15,000)	5,400	5,400	5,400	5,400	20,400
Add back amortization	0	6,000	6,000	6,000	6,000	6,000
After tax cash flow	(15,000)	11,400	11,400	11,400	11,400	26,400
Software cost	30,000	0	0	0	0	0
Project cash flow	$(45,000)	$11,400	$11,400	$11,400	$11,400	$26,400

IRR   =   15.6%

NPV @ 12% = $4,606

Notes:
1. Software to be amorized strainght-line over five years.
2. Project life limited to five years because of rapid rate of change in this technology.
3. Tax rate of 40 percent includes applicable state tax in addition to federal tax.

QUESTIONS

1.   Is leasing the equipment better than borrowing from the bank at 9 percent?

2.   What would the project look like if the equipment were purchased rather than leased? (Assume the equipment would be depreciated using the 5-year ACRS method.)

3.   What are the implications of including the lease in the evaluation of the project?

4.   Suppose the lease turns out to be classified as a financial lease after all, how would this influence your perception of Walt Stephenson's proposal?

5.   Given that Walt Stephenson will in all likelihood become Bob Atwater's boss within a few months, what action should Atwater take?

6.   How should Atwater respond when "Uncle Jim" asks him what he thinks of Walt Stephenson's proposal?

Case 42

Evaluating the Lease versus Borrow (Buy) Decision

Harris Computers

The R. C. Harris Company designed and built personal computers for private branding by large, retail general merchandise chains. Private branding meant, simply, that Harris built the computers for sale to the chains which marketed them under their own brand names. Harris Computers was run by R. C. Harris, who had earned a bachelor's degree in engineering and a CPA certificate. Her focus was now upon maintaining profitability in a period when personal computer sales were not increasing. The data in Table 1 indicate revenue and profit after-tax for the firm's recent history

The company's capital investment decisions, including the treasurer's function, were handled by Betty Allen. At present, a major concern was the necessary replacement of a machine used in the fabrication of the primary internal circuitry for the personal computer.

The asset under consideration was offered by a firm which would accept a lease or a purchase arrangement for acquisition of the machine. The machine, known as a digital monitor, or DM, has the following characteristics relevant to the lease versus purchase option:

1. The machine would cost Harris $250,000, including installation and delivery.

2. Annual maintenance on the DM, if purchased, would cost Harris $50,000.

3. The funds necessary to purchase the machine would have an interest cost of 8 percent. The DM was in the five-year MACRS category. The loan would be amortized over six years.

4. The equipment could be leased for a period of six years at an annual lease payment of $70,000 per year. The lease payments would include maintenance expenses. The salvage value of the equipment, if purchased, would be $30,000. The company plans to purchase the machine at the end of the lease. Harris Company is in the 34 percent tax bracket. Assume that all cash flows occur at the end of the year.

While the foregoing was important to Harris and Allen, they both believed there were other issues to assess before a decision could be made to lease or purchase the DM. Among the concerns expressed by Allen were the following: (a) What was the likelihood that the salvage value would be as forecast by the lessor? The lessor's forecast of the salvage value was based upon industry data related to the market for such equipment. (b) How should the potential lease be classified—would it be a capital lease or an operating lease? (c) In the firm's capital budgeting activities the marginal weighted average cost of capital was used to discount cash flows. Was this discount rate relevant for the lease versus borrow analysis? (A corollary to that question is whether leasing is a capital budgeting decision or a financing decision; once decided, did it make a difference into which category the lease was placed?)

An important consideration for the company was its financial reputation, which included such aspects as its interest coverage, debt ratio, and the general ability to service its financial obligations in a timely manner. The company's most recent balance sheet is provided in Table 2.

In addition to the issues cited above, Allen wondered whether the decision to lease or buy would directly influence the company's debt capacity. That is, if the asset were leased instead of purchased, would the financial community view the lease payments as an additional debt burden? In addition to that concern, Allen had read recently that the duration of a lease relative to the useful life of the asset may vastly influence the decision to acquire the asset at all. In other words, if the cost of using the asset is reduced significantly through the lease, does that fact change the nature of the decision? Allen believed that each of the issues and concerns surrounding the lease versus purchase options needed to be clearly understood before the numerical analysis was begun.

TABLE 1		
Harris Computers *Recent Financial History*		
Year	Revenue (000s)	Profit After-Tax (000s)
1989	$154,324	$5,733
1990	167,744	8,687
1991	156,252	(557)
1992	149,200	200

TABLE 2			
R. C. Harris Company *Common Size Balance Sheet*			
Current assets	30%	Current liabilities	20%
Fixed assets	70	Long-term debt	35
		Common equity	45
		Total liabilities and	
Total assets	100%	equity*	100%

Note: * The company's marginal weighted average cost of capital is 9 percent, and the above capital structure is considered optimal.

QUESTIONS

1. Discuss each of the issues and concerns related to the decision.

2. Evaluate the financial alternatives associated with acquisition of the machine.

3. What influence should the revenue and profit situation in the industry have upon the decision?

4. Are there any other concerns related to the decision that Allen may have overlooked? If so, what are they?

5. In lease/buy (borrow) cash flow analysis discuss the role of depreciation and taxes.

6. In terms of financial versus operating leases, discuss the role of each as a substitute for borrowed funds.

7. How does the financial lease alternative relate to capital budgeting?

8. Recently, lessors and lessees have begun to work together to maintain equipment and to ensure a market for used equipment. What is the likely effect of this effort upon lease/buy analysis?

9. Is Harris' company too small to consider a complex alternative such as leasing? Why or why not?

10. Are some types of assets more suitable to lease? Discuss.

Case 43

Valuing Corporate Acquisitions

Print-to-Fit, Inc.

Ever since Sears announced plans to shut down its $3.3 billion catalog business in 1992, Theresa Dunsmore had been swallowing more and more Pepto Bismol. It's not that she liked the taste of the pink stuff, but as senior vice president in charge of in-store merchandising at C. J. Nickel's—the nation's fourth-largest department store retailer—Theresa developed stomach problems when Sears retired the Big Book. At first glance, you'd think that Sears' abrupt exit from mail-order retailing would cause celebration in the hallways at C. J. Nickel's. But remember, Theresa was responsible for Nickel's *in-store* retail operations—not the mail order business.

While Nickel's catalog sales rose by almost $200 million in 1993 as thousands of former Sears' customers started ordering from Nickel's, the in-store division of the giant retailer faced some major troubles. During the 1980s, Theresa worked hard to differentiate Nickel's merchandise lines from those offered by Sears. She dumped hardware items, garden supplies, and auto parts, in favor of trendier fashions and more upscale apparel items. She expanded in-store merchandise selection and incorporated pricier brand names into the product mix, and targeted the stores' merchandise mix toward affluent, sophisticated shoppers.

Then the 1989–91 recession hit, and consumer confidence plummeted. Conspicuous consumption was replaced by value-conscious shopping, and Theresa was stuck with a huge inventory of upscale, high-fashion junk. Nickel's managed to move its merchandise only through a big end-of-season markdown sale, and in the process, the retailer's annual earnings fell 36 percent from the previous year. If that wasn't bad enough, soon after the end of 1992 the catalog division at Nickel's started reporting record-breaking sales increases as former Sears' customers shifted their business to the Nickel's catalog.

Needless to say, the transparent "glass ceiling" that blocked Theresa's move into top management at Nickel's was rapidly turning into very visible concrete. Unless she improved the financial performance of the in-store retail division at the firm, her career in retailing would face an untimely and involuntary demise. Now, you might argue that Theresa was a victim of circumstance—in the wrong management job at the wrong time—but the handwriting she saw on the corporate wall was clear: Restore sales growth and profitability within Nickel's in-store division, or seek work elsewhere.

After twenty years in retail management, Theresa was tough enough and smart enough to accept the challenge. She quickly revised her division's merchandising strategy to emphasize consumer value—focusing on a combination of lower retail prices and higher product quality—to restore sales and profit growth. She moved product emphasis away from the stuff covered with little alligators and started stocking moderately-priced, private-label brands to boost her stores' gross margins. Finally, she slashed in-store operating expenses to boost Nickel's net operating margin.

All these changes suited Theresa's superiors fine and dandy, but like most bosses, they pressured her to do more. Nickel's still faced intense competition from several national retailers, and Theresa needed to gain market share from these firms to earn the respect of Nickel's top brass. In order to gain market share, she knew Nickel's must broaden its merchandise mix and become more flexible in offering new shoppers a wide assortment of product choices.

Unfortunately, expanded product selections meant an increased investment in floor inventory, and more inventory meant higher operating expenses and dwindling profit margins. After the dismal 1992 selling season, Theresa could scarcely risk the adverse financial consequences associated with expanding Nickel's product line.

There *had* to be another way—and with a little creative thinking and a little luck, Theresa thought she'd found it. Scanning an industry trade publication late one evening after work, Theresa noticed a brief article about a small, unknown firm in the retailing industry, Print-to-Fit, Inc. Unknown in retailing because the small firm wasn't a retailer, Print-to-Fit was a manufacturer of textile printers that modified Canon's color laser printing technology to print on fabric, rather than paper. Using its patented, bubble-jet transfer method, Print-to-Fit was able to squirt microfine droplets of yellow, cyan, magenta, and black ink on a variety of textile surfaces, creating colorful designs and patterns on ordinary, ready-to-wear fabrics.

While Print-to-Fit was a computer manufacturing company, Theresa immediately recognized that the firm's future was in retailing—not manufacturing. Using Print-to-Fit's printers connected to microcomputers in selected areas of Nickel's retail stores, customers could literally design their own clothing, preview various designs on the computer's screen, and print their favorite selections on blank apparel items stocked in Nickel's inventory.

Theresa envisioned almost unlimited potential for the new technology: customers in the menswear department could design their own neckties; in womenswear, shoppers could instantly change the color and pattern of mix-and-match separates; and even better, in the children's department kids could dress up dull, white tee-shirts with full-color pictures of their favorite cartoon characters and other images. From the shopper's viewpoint, this would be a different and fun way to shop. From Theresa's perspective, it would be an efficient and inexpensive way to move merchandise. Nickel's could offer, quite literally, an infinite array of merchandise, yet the firm's inventory could be reduced to a small set of pattern masters waiting to be printed.

After thinking quietly about the potential changes that Print-to-Fit might bring to Nickel's, Theresa had a frightening thought: If Nickel's could purchase textile printers from Print-to-Fit, why couldn't other retailers do the very same thing? Theresa answered her question almost as soon as it entered her mind—Print-to-Fit's technology was protected by patent, and if Nickel's bought the entire *firm*, rather than just its printers, she'd own the patents. Finally, Theresa had a new retail strategy, and the means to prevent her competitors from copying it.

Over the course of the next several weeks, Theresa negotiated with Print-to-Fit's managers and Board of Directors for the purchase of the small firm by Nickel's. As the income statement shown in Table 1 reports, Print-to-Fit's 1993 sales volume was a modest $9 million, which was dwarfed by Nickel's $17 billion in 1993 sales. Clearly, Nickel's could afford this small acquisition.

After extensive negotiation between Print-to-Fit's Board and her own finance people, Theresa was able to assemble the projected financial statements shown in Tables 1 and 2. These data conservatively estimated how Print-to-Fit would perform as a division of C. J. Nickel's over the 1994–97 period. While Theresa considered the projected statements reasonable, she made sure that they reflected the dramatic sales potential that Print-to-Fit's technology offered Nickel's retail stores.

In addition, Theresa prepared the estimate of Print-to-Fit's optimal capital structure shown in Table 3. Using the financial information shown in these three tables, she was ready to estimate Print-to-Fit's acquisition value to her employer. In previous conversations with Print-to-Fit's Board, she learned that the firm would probably be receptive to a stock-for-stock exchange. In addition, she felt that Print-to-Fit's shareholders would be willing to accept around 250,000 shares of C. J. Nickel's common stock, currently worth $81.32 per share, to tender their Print-to-Fit common stock—lock, stock, and bubble-jets—to Nickel's.

Now, it was up to Theresa to make a decision. Her intuition told her that Print-to-Fit was a good strategic acquisition for Nickel's, but at what price? It was obvious to her that the small firm's Board knew she was anxious to deal, and looking at the projected financials, she began to wonder if perhaps she was *too* anxious. After all, she was accountable to the shareholders at C. J. Nickel's, and the last thing she wanted to do was squander the shareholders' money by approving an ill-advised and over-priced acquisition. Then again, Print-to-Fit represented an excellent opportunity to offer Nickel's shoppers a novel retail experience, and Theresa needed just such a novelty to build in-store sales and market share within her division.

TABLE 1

Print-to-Fit, Inc.
Statement of Revenue and Expense
December 31, 1993
($000s)

	Actual	Projected			
	1993	1994	1995	1996	1997
Net sales revenue	$9,194.0	$13,892.0	$17,859.3	$18,220.9	$21,592.4
Less: Cost of goods sold	(5,184.2)	(8,107.0)	(11,145.8)	(10,680.2)	(12,778.7)
Gross profit	$4,009.8	$5,785.0	$6,713.5	$7,540.7	$8,813.7
Less: Operating expenses	($1,400.4)	($2,670.9)	($4,100.9)	($4,539.1)	($5,563.3)
Depreciation expense	(12.7)	(85.8)	(132.4)	(178.3)	(245.8)
Net operating income	$2,596.7	$3,028.3	$2,480.2	$2,823.3	$3,004.6
Plus: Nonoperating income	$44.7	$113.0	$52.8	$243.3	$147.5
Earnings before interest and taxes	$2,641.4	$3,141.3	$2,533.0	$3,066.6	$3,152.1
Less: Interest expense	($29.8)	($80.0)	($227.6)	($158.8)	($203.6)
Earnings before tax	$2,611.6	$3,061.3	$2,305.4	$2,907.8	$2,948.5
Less: Income tax expense:					
Current income tax expense	($1,338.0)	($1,535.0)	($987.2)	($1,197.7)	($1,112.8)
Deferred income tax expense	(47.8)	(125.7)	(51.6)	(39.9)	(42.5)
Total income tax expense	($1,385.8)	($1,660.7)	($1,038.8)	($1,237.6)	($1,155.3)
Net income	$1,225.8	$1,400.6	$1,266.6	$1,670.2	$1,793.2

	TABLE 2				

Print-to-Fit, Inc.
Statement of Financial Condition
December 31, 1993
($000s)

	Actual	----------------------Projected----------------------			
	1993	1994	1995	1996	1997
ASSETS					
Current assets:					
Cash and marketable securities	$660.8	$601.7	$993.5	$1,714.2	$2,271.4
Accounts receivable (net)	1,200.7	2,046.8	2,762.0	2,893.6	3,912.9
Inventory	1,225.2	2,409.0	3,019.2	2,769.1	3,672.3
Prepaid expenses	23.2	108.2	99.0	117.3	123.3
Current assets - other	55.9	195.3	262.9	348.4	316.7
Total current assets	$3,165.8	$5,361.0	$7,136.6	$7,842.6	$10,296.6
Long-term investments:					
Plant and equipment (gross)	$1,030.6	$2,661.7	$2,756.5	$2,764.7	$2,638.6
Less: Accumulated depreciation	(19.8)	(89.7)	(184.2)	(305.4)	(490.2)
Plant and equipment (net)	1,010.8	2,572.0	2,572.3	2,459.3	2,148.4
Other assets	227.0	750.6	925.5	1,367.8	1,601.3
Total long-term investments	1,237.8	$3,322.6	$3,497.8	$3,827.1	$3,749.7
Total assets	$4,403.6	$8,683.6	$10,634.4	$11,669.7	$14,046.3
LIABILITIES AND EQUITY					
Current liabilities:					
Accounts payable	$843.5	$1,750.7	$1,371.3	$1,483.6	$1,660.6
Income taxes payable	343.8	382.7	346.3	438.3	490.7
Accrued expenses	0.0	0.0	84.9	85.4	85.8
Current debt obligations	221.3	550.2	756.1	22.5	700.7
Total current liabilities	$1,408.6	$2,683.6	$2,558.6	$2,029.8	$2,937.8
Long-term liabilities:					
Nonconvertible debt	$0.0	$105.7	$1,112.6	$1,085.7	$1,051.8
Capitalized leases	6.6	20.4	14.0	23.3	19.8
Deferred tax liability	12.4	26.2	42.2	87.9	69.6
Total long-term liabilities	$19.0	$152.3	$1,168.8	$1,196.9	$1,141.2
Shareholders' equity:					
Common stock - par value	$5.3	$11.3	$11.3	$11.4	$11.4
Additional paid-in capital	1,194.3	2,659.4	2,452.1	2,317.8	2,171.9
Retained earnings	1,776.4	3,177.0	4,443.6	6,113.8	7,784.0
Total shareholders' equity	$2,976.0	$5,847.7	$6,907.0	$8,443.0	$9,967.3
Total liabilities and shareholders' equity	$4,403.6	$8,683.6	$10,634.4	$11,669.7	$14,046.3

	Short-Term Liabilities*	Long-Term Debt	Common Stock
TABLE 3			
Print-to-Fit, Inc.			
Capitalization Summary			
December 31, 1993			
Optimal capital structure	20%	10%	70%
Current capital cost (before-tax)	7%	10%	14%
Shares outstanding	----------	----------	50,000,000
Corporate tax rate	37%	37%	

Note: Short-term liabilities include accounts payable, income taxes payable, accrued expenses, and current debt obligations. Only 50 percent of total short-term liabilities—representing current debt obligations—carry an explicit financing charge.

QUESTIONS

1. In general terms, how should C. J. Nickels approach the problem of valuing Print-to-Fit, Inc.? How is this valuation problem similar to the way that analysts might value financial assets such as corporate bonds and common stock?

2. In evaluating corporate acquisitions, financial managers often use a variety of different techniques to estimate the projected cash flows from a potential acquisition. These techniques often include (a) projecting the total cash flows that the acquired firm will provide to owners of its debt and equity securities, and (b) projecting the cash flows that the acquired firm will provide to holders of its common stock. Briefly explain how each of these cash flow streams would be calculated.

3. In valuing debt and/or equity securities, analysts typically use a single estimate of future cash flows to forecast what holders of these financial assets can expect to receive from their investments in future years. In contrast, financial managers often use a variety of different cash flow estimates to value corporate acquisitions. Why is a single estimate of future cash flows appropriate for valuing financial assets, while business acquisitions normally require a number of different cash flow estimates?

4. What are Print-to-Fit's (a) weighted average cost of capital, and (b) required return on equity capital?

5. [Questions 5 through 9 deal with the return to total capital model of corporate valuation]. What are the total annual net cash flows that Print-to-Fit's debt and equity holders will receive from the firm over the 1994–97 period?

6. Based on the forecast book value of Print-to-Fit's total capitalization in 1997 (i.e., the total quantity of debt and equity funds invested in the firm), what is the projected terminal value of the firm in this year? Based on the perpetual value of Print-to-Fit's earnings stream available to the firm's debt and equity providers in 1997, what is the projected terminal value of the firm in that year?

7. Given your answers to Questions 5 and 6, what is the total acquisition value of Print-to-Fit?

8. Given your estimate of Print-to-Fit's aggregate acquisition value in Question 7, what is the value of this acquisition to the firm's stockholders?

9. Based on (a) the total capitalization of Print-to-Fit, Inc., and (b) the total income that providers of the firm's debt and equity capital will receive over the 1994–97 period, what is the total return on capital offered by the firm over the 1994–97 period?

10. [Questions 10 through 13 deal with the return to equity capital model of corporate valuation]. What are the annual net cash flows that Print-to-Fit's common equity holders will receive from their investment over the 1994–97 period?

11. Based on the forecast book value of shareholders' equity in 1997, what is the projected terminal value of Print-to-Fit in that year? Based on the perpetual value of the firm's earnings stream available to common stockholders in 1997, what is the projected terminal value of the firm in that year?

12. Combining the cash flows developed in Questions 10 and 11, what is the total acquisition value of Print-to-Fit?

13. Based on the shareholders' investment in Print-to-Fit and the annual income that these investors will receive over the 1994–97 period, what is the return on equity capital that the firm will provide over the 1994–97 period?

14. What is the total value that C.J. Nickel's plans to pay to acquire Print-to-Fit, Inc.? Given the range of corporate valuation estimates that you developed in Questions 4 through 13, should Nickel's proceed with this acquisition? Why or why not?

Case 44

Evaluating Leveraged Buyouts

Phoenix Corporation[*]

In November 1988, Dennis Leavitt was devising a plan to purchase Phoenix Corporation. He hoped to develop a plan that would enable the company to be purchased on a small equity base using a sizable amount of borrowed funds.

Phoenix Corporation was a major U.S. producer of paper clips and other fasteners for office use. The company had enjoyed profits every year since it was founded in 1948 by William Hutch. By 1988, the company had gained a 26 percent share of the small, yet stable paper fastener industry. Sales during fiscal year 1986 were $20.2 million. Its net profit was $2.1 million, reflecting an attractive profit margin of over 10 percent. Recent financial statements for the company are shown in Tables 1 and 2.

Sales of paper fasteners during each year were quite stable, with little seasonality. Thus, the company produced on a level production schedule. Since products in the paper fastener industry were relatively undifferentiated, the critical success factor of the industry was to be a low-cost producer.

Even though Phoenix Corporation's products were sold primarily on the basis of price, the company had several competitive advantages. The company enjoyed economies of scale that would make it difficult for potential competitors to compete on price alone. And, given the moderate growth prospects of the industry, it seemed questionable that another company would find entry into the market attractive.

Over 80 percent of Phoenix Corporation's sales consisted of replacement orders from existing customers. Because paper fasteners were low-ticket items, most of the company's customers had little to gain from shopping around. And, because paper fasteners were a necessary expense for most businesses, the company's sales were insensitive to economic cycles. Very few companies reduced expenses by cutting back on the purchase of paper clips.

Phoenix Corporation had been inherited by the founder's son, John Hutch, who currently served as the company's president and chairman. Mr. Hutch was nearing retirement and had decided to cash in and sell the company. His asking price was $25 million.

Dennis Leavitt represented a small group of investors who were quite interested in purchasing the company, if it could be purchased on a small equity base. In other words, the company would be purchased using a technique called a leveraged buyout. Leveraged buyouts (LBOs), which involve using sizable amounts of borrowed funds secured by the firm's assets as collateral, had become a popular means of financing acquisitions in the 1980s. This financing technique had been used for the management buyouts of R. H. Macy and Company

---

* This case was prepared by George W. Kester, Bucknell University, whose cooperation is acknowledged with appreciation.

44-1

and Viacom International, and the buyouts of Safeway Stores, Beatrice, and RJR Nabisco by the leveraged buyout specialist, Kohlberg, Kravis, and Roberts.

Leavitt was intrigued by the fact that, under both the founder and his son, Phoenix Corporation had consistently avoided the use of debt financing. The company's internally generated cash flows had always been sufficient to meet its moderate year-to-year capital investment requirements. Indeed, dividends usually exceeded 50 percent of earnings. Dennis Leavitt held equity in the firm in the amount of $5 million. Leavitt was also intrigued by the healthy liquidity position of the company, given that a cash balance of only $1 million would probably be required to meet the company's transactions needs. He wondered if the company had any significant disposable assets.

Because a substantial amount of debt would be used to finance the purchase, Leavitt believed that the debt would carry an interest rate of 15 percent. For purposes of his initial analysis, he decided to assume that repayment would be in 10 equal annual payments against principal.

Leavitt believed that the company's sales would increase at a rate of about 5 percent per year for the foreseeable future. This growth rate was consistent with the company's past growth record. Notwithstanding the fact that the company's profit margin had increased in recent years, Leavitt projected earnings before interest and taxes (EBIT) to be approximately 16 percent of sales with no further improvements. The company's income tax rate was 35 percent. For simplicity, Leavitt decided to assume that capital expenditures each year would be equal to the annual depreciation expense of $500,000. In addition, the net working capital investment had been approximately 11 percent of sales and was expected to continue at that rate.

TABLE 1

Phoenix Corporation
Income Statement
1986-1988
($ millions)

	1986	1987	1988
Sales	$17.7	$19.1	$20.2
Cost of goods sold	(12.7)	(14.1)	(14.2)
Gross profit	$5.0	$5.0	$6.0
Operating expenses	($1.4)	($1.5)	($1.8)
Profit before taxes	$3.6	$3.5	$4.2
Income taxes	($1.3)	($1.2)	($1.5)
Net profit	$2.3	$2.3	$2.7

TABLE 2	
Phoenix Corporation	
Balance Sheet	
December 31, 1987	
($ millions)	
Cash	$6.0
Accounts receivable	2.0
Inventories	1.2
Total current assets	$9.2
Net fixed assets	$6.3
Other assets	0.6
Total assets	$16.1
Accounts payable	$1.0
Accrued expenses	0.5
Other current liabilities	0.4
Total current liabilities	$1.9
Common stock ($1.00 par)	$1.5
Retained earnings	12.7
Shareholders' equity	14.2
Total liabilities and equity	$16.1

QUESTIONS

1. Is the $25 million asking price for Phoenix Corporation a fair price? (Assume that a minimum acceptable rate of return of 12 percent should be used to discount the company's net cash flows.)

2. How much debt will be required for a leveraged buyout of Phoenix Corporation by the group of investors represented by Dennis Leavitt?

3. Develop a pro forma balance sheet (based upon the December 31, 1987 balance sheet) reflecting the leveraged buyout. Assess the resulting level of debt relative to equity and total assets.

4. Estimate the company's ability to repay the required amount of debt.

5. Evaluate the opportunities and risks of a leveraged buyout of Phoenix Corporation.

Case 45

Multinational Financial Management

Carolina Furniture Company[*]

George Fishburn, President and CEO of Carolina Furniture Company, sat leisurely in his office on a Friday afternoon reviewing the German sales figures for the second quarter of 1991. He was very pleased with his firm's exporting activities. Two years ago his company had no foreign customers and today it had several big customers in Germany, Japan and Singapore. About 12 to 15 percent of the firm's revenues came from export sales. Although sales to Germany had dropped somewhat from the previous year, they would still amount to about two million dollars in 1991. As he reviewed the figures he noticed that in one instance, the German mark (DM) had declined in value from $0.6693/DM to $0.5824/DM, from the time the sale to the German customer was booked to the time the firm received payment. The decline in the value of DM resulted in a transaction loss of almost $26,000 on an invoice of $200,000. Because export sales had a margin of 15 percent, it still left the firm with a profit of $4,000; however, George wondered if the company could afford to lose this kind of money from the vagaries of financial markets.

His thoughts began to stray as he scrutinized the numbers. He had worked hard for the past 12 years and the business had prospered under his leadership. He remembered that fall day in 1979 when he received a call from his mother at his dormitory at the University of North Carolina - Chapel Hill informing him that his father had just had a stroke and the prognosis was rather dim. He had rushed back to the family home in High Point, North Carolina. Albert Fishburn died the following week, leaving the reins of the business to his son. George Fishburn did not return to college after that, and never became the foreign correspondent for *Time* magazine that he had always wanted to be.

The Carolina Furniture Company was formed in 1958 by Albert Fishburn and his army buddy Leroy Brown. Initially, the company manufactured early American furniture that emphasized simple styles and high quality. The economic growth of the 1960s and 1970s, accompanied by an increase in home ownership, helped the company grow by leaps and bounds. By 1973, sales had grown to 5 million dollars and total assets rose to almost 1.5 million dollars. On the average, the firm maintained a healthy profit margin of 7 percent of sales, making the two army buddies quite affluent in a short period of time. In 1974, Leroy Brown sold his share of the business to Albert Fishburn and moved to Florida.

The initial days after his father died were difficult for George; he had to learn the furniture business and deal with the recession. For the first time in its history, Carolina Furniture Company suffered a loss in the 1981–82 fiscal year. During the next three years George learned the business and instituted major changes in the company. First, he modernized

---

* This case was prepared by A. Qayyum Khan, The University of North Carolina at Charlotte, whose cooperation is acknowledged with appreciation.

the plant with new machines which reduced dependence on manual labor, improved productivity, and most importantly, achieved substantial cost savings. Equipment holdings were reviewed annually, and as much as possible, the firm tried to remain on top of new technology. Outdated or obsolete equipment was sold to smaller furniture manufacturers. The improved productivity increased the profit margin to 12 percent, the highest in the industry.

Second, he implemented an aggressive marketing strategy. In the past, Carolina Furniture Company had depended entirely on wholesale furniture distributors for orders. Under George's direction, the company opened its first display booth in the furniture mart at Hickory, North Carolina. This allowed the firm to be more responsive to customers and to achieve a greater market exposure. The booth was a great success. Within three years, major furniture outlets and retail chains (like J.C. Penney's) on the east coast carried the Carolina Furniture line. In 1985, another display booth was opened in the Merchandise Mart at Dallas, Texas. The third display booth was opened in 1987 in San Francisco, California. With three display booths, the company achieved national coverage, and by 1989, annual sales had grown to 42 million dollars.

The third major change that George instituted was the expansion of the product line. In addition to the Early-American styles, the company introduced several avant-garde lines that the baby boomer generation found attractive. An in-house design team was recruited that worked closely with the marketing personnel and salespeople at the three display booth locations. Every spring the new designs were introduced and displayed in the major furniture shows and at the display booths.

In spite of these successes, George always remembered the recession of the early eighties. He recognized that the furniture business was essentially a cyclical business, and the next recession could have an adverse consequence on his business unless he diversified to new markets in other countries. The accessibility of the factory to several seaports in North Carolina and South Carolina, along with the presence of several major banks in the area, offered Carolina Furniture many advantages that domestic furniture manufacturers elsewhere did not have. In late 1988, George embarked on an export strategy. After preliminary research and consultation with bankers and the export promotion office at the North Carolina Department of Commerce, George Fishburn and Lisa Hammonds, vice president of marketing, decided that export markets should be targeted in countries that had a trade surplus with the United States and were expected to experience a faster economic growth than the United States. In June 1989, George and Lisa traveled to Germany, Japan, and Singapore to explore export markets and seek customers in those countries.

The trip was a great success. Several German retailers expressed interest, and two major furniture outlets signed firm purchase contracts worth $250,000. However, the German customers insisted that the orders be invoiced in DM. George knew that it wasn't difficult to convert DM to dollars and he readily agreed. Given the prevailing exchange rate of $0.5122/DM, he signed the sales contract for DM488,091. Delivery and payment were scheduled for the third week of September, 1989. When payment was received in 1989 the DM had increased in value to $0.5353/DM, yielding an inflow of $261,275, a gain of $11,275. George was very pleased with this outcome. Economic forecasts indicated that the dollar was expected to remain weak against all major currencies. Therefore, Carolina Furniture adopted a policy of invoicing all its foreign customers in their respective currencies.

Now that the dollar had begun to strengthen, George thought the time might have come to change the denomination of the firm's export invoices. He called Lisa for her views, and she reminded him of the difficult negotiations they had experienced with Japanese and Singapore importers to agree on the denomination of the sale. A request for a change in terms, especially when the dollar was showing signs of strength, might not be acceptable to the importers and could result in a decline in orders. Lisa, therefore, felt that the denomination of the export sales should not be changed.

Allen Bradley, corporate treasurer and vice president of finance was looking forward to some rest and relaxation over the weekend when George Fishburn called him. George was very concerned about the transaction loss from the German sale and he wanted to meet with Allen on Monday to discuss the alternatives for hedging foreign exchange transactions. The firm's bank, Nationsbank, had earlier offered its services to Carolina Furniture Company for hedging foreign exchange risk. "It just may be the time to take Nationsbank up on its offer," said George as he hung up. After he got off the phone, R & R was the last thing on Allen's mind as he began to compile the necessary information.

As Allen checked the records, he found that Carolina Furniture Company had the following foreign exchange transactions under contract. Unless these transactions were hedged, the dollar cash flow from these transactions would depend on the spot rate of the foreign currency at the time payment was received.

Germany

A sale of DM2,000,000 to the Hamburg International Hotel which is opening for business in January 1992. Parts of this order have already been shipped. The last consignment will be shipped in the second week of October and payment will be received on November 14, 1991.

Japan

A payment of JY150,000,000,000 will be received from Sakado Enterprises, a large trading company in Tokyo, on September 18, 1991. The furniture against this order was shipped in the second week of August 1991.

Singapore

1.   Two hundred and fifty thousand Singapore dollars (S$) are due on November 23, 1991 from Patusan Brothers, a furniture retailer. The furniture against this invoice was shipped in the last week of July.

2.   Another S$250,000 would be due from Patusan Brothers on February 17, 1992. The shipment against this invoice will be made in the last week of December 1991.

Next, Allen began outlining the alternative hedging strategies. Basically, he had two alternatives. First, he could recommend the use of forward contracts which allow the purchase or sale of foreign currencies in future periods. International banks make forward markets in the major currencies. However, no forward contracts were available for the S$ in the United States. Forward contracts could be tailor-made with respect to amount and maturity. Typically, banks did not offer forward contracts to speculators, and preferred to deal with hedgers only. The transaction amount of forward contracts' size is usually large, a million dollars or more. If Carolina Furniture chose to use the forward market alternative, it would have to execute a short hedge (i.e., sell foreign currency forward) since it is expecting foreign currency inflows.

The second alternative would be a money market hedge. This technique is especially suitable for those currencies that do not have forward contracts. A short hedge in the money market involves borrowing the foreign currency with the same maturity as the expected inflow. The borrowed foreign currency is then converted in the spot market and usually invested in the domestic money market. Since the foreign currency loan and inflow have the same maturity, the loan is paid with the foreign currency inflow.

While reviewing this information, Allen realized that the same hedging instrument may not be suitable for all the foreign exchange transactions and a different hedging instrument may have to be used for each transaction. Therefore, the problem, as he saw it, was to find the appropriate hedging strategy for a given foreign exchange transaction.

TABLE 1

Carolina Furniture Company
Exchange Rates - U.S. $ Equivalent
Friday, August 16, 1991

	DM	JY	S$
Spot	$0.5824	$0.007474	$0.5748
30-day forward	0.5796	0.007470	N/A
90-day forward	0.5733	0.007454	N/A
180-day forward	0.5700	0.007435	N/A

TABLE 2

Carolina Furniture Company
Selected Interest Rates
Friday, August 16, 1991

	1-Month	3-Months	6-Months
United States			
Prime rate	5.70%	5.85%	5.95%
LIBOR (London)	5.55	5.70	5.80
Germany			
Prime rate	11.47	12.10	10.21
LIBOR (London)	11.32	11.95	10.06
Japan			
Prime rate	6.40	6.95	6.95
LIBOR (London)	6.19	6.75	6.75
Singapore			
Prime rate	4.67	5.23	5.58

QUESTIONS:

1. How do you think the hedge will accomplish Carolina Furniture Company's objective of protecting the value of its foreign currency cash flows?

2. What are the expected cash flows from the DM transaction if it is hedged in the forward market?

3. How would the DM inflows be hedged in the money market? If this transaction is hedged in the money market, what are the expected cash flows?

4. Given the answer to the two previous questions, which alternative would you choose to hedge the DM transaction?

5. What are the expected cash flows from the JY transaction if it is hedged in the forward market?

6. How would the JY inflows be hedged in the money market? If this transaction is hedged in the money market, what are the expected cash flows?

7. What should be done regarding the JY inflows? Why?

8. What would be the net cash flows to Carolina Furniture Company by hedging the S$ cash flows in the money market?

Case 46

International Capital Budgeting

Narodno Pivo d.d.

In early March 1995, Matej Joksimovic, Marketing Director of the brewer Narodno Pivo d.d. in Ljubljana, Slovenia had received an overseas telephone call from an American named Rich Shiu. Shiu, a recent MBA graduate of Indiana University, was forming a company to distribute beers from Eastern Europe, and he was interested in representing Narodno Pivo in the United States. At first, Matej had been skeptical, as it was not the first time he had been contacted by a foreigner who had a grand business scheme in mind. However, Shiu had sounded professional, intelligent, and sincere on the telephone, and he had provided the names of several professors at the University of Ljubljana as references, all of whom had said very nice things about him when Matej called them to check.

Although Shiu had never been to the region himself, he had spoken to numerous Indiana students who had had memorable experiences studying and traveling in Eastern Europe. It seemed as if many of those experiences involved the beer, and the students couldn't praise it highly enough. Checking the local stores, Shiu had found that none of the brands the students were most enthusiastic about were available and could not even be special-ordered. After doing more extensive research, he had concluded that there was a niche market for Eastern European beer in larger Midwestern cities in the immigrant communities from Eastern European countries and among young adults who were looking for different beers and whose interests had been piqued by the rush of news coverage Eastern Europe was receiving.

Originally, Shiu had planned to import beers from only four countries—Poland, the Czech Republic, Slovakia, and Hungary—but he was surprised at how many people he talked to suggested that he also consider Slovenia. He had never heard of it, but soon discovered that it had been one of the republics of ex-Yugoslavia and had gained its independence in 1991. Contrary to the common opinion that everywhere in that part of the world was dangerous, Shiu had learned that Slovenia was a peaceful, prosperous country, whose economy was outperforming that of all of the other countries with which he had planned to do business. More importantly, there were large Slovenian communities in the Midwest, especially in Cleveland, and Indiana University had a close relationship with the University of Ljubljana, which he was able to take advantage of for useful information, contacts, and references.

All of this had come out in that first telephone call. In subsequent conversations, Matej learned the details of Shiu's proposal. Initially, ten breweries in five countries would be represented. Each would contribute $40,000 up-front for the initial marketing campaign to retailers and bars specializing in exotic beers. On an on-going basis, 10% of Rich's sales would be committed to marketing, primarily on special promotions to the target markets, and another

This case was prepared by Elton McGoun, Bucknell Univeresity, and Edita K. Krajnovic, University of Ljubljana - Slovenia, whose cooperation is acknowleged with appreciation.

10% would cover domestic transportation, administrative expenses, and Rich's profit. Narodno would receive 80%, or $.75 on each half-liter bottle based upon Rich's selling price of $22.50 per 24-bottle case ($.9375 per bottle). Hopefully, it would be possible to begin the project before the end of the year

Shiu also had recommended that Matej change the name of the beer from Narodno, which sounded "too governmental"—it means "national" in Slovene—to something more exotic. Matej suggested Triglav (Three Heads), the name of the highest mountain in Slovenia, whose three peaks are represented on the Slovenian flag. This change would entail an initial charge of 500,000 tolars (the Slovenian currency unit) to design an English label with new artwork. The exchange rate as of June 30, 1995 was 113.7 tolars per dollar.

Overall, the project sounded attractive, and when Matej had casually mentioned it to his friends in government, they strongly suggested that he go ahead with it and hinted that the Ministry of Economic Relations and Development might be willing to contribute to the marketing campaign. A recently released report regarding economic strategy for Slovenia recommended assistance for those sectors that had the potential to be internationally competitive. Narodno was a highly respected firm with a distinguished heritage. With over 50% of the domestic market, it was one of the most likely Slovenian firms to become a successful exporter.

Word gets around quickly in the close-knit Slovenian business community, and even before he had begun to prepare his formal proposal, Matej was receiving calls from board members asking for details. Because of the high profile the project seemed to have acquired beyond its purely financial considerations, he knew that the proposal would have to be very thorough. Consequently, he "borrowed" Sonja Prasnikar, who was spending her first six months with Narodno training in the different departments of the company, to help him prepare it. Sonja, who was a recent graduate of the University of Ljubljana Full-Time MBA Program, was familiar with international capital budgeting.

The first question she asked was what sales would be. Matej had no idea. Rich had been using 2,000 cases in the first year, 5,000 in the second, and 8,000 each year after in his planning. If the idea were a success, these numbers could easily be 100% higher, but if they misjudged the market, they might only sell 25%. Then Sonja had asked about the cost of a bottle of beer. For this Matej called the production manager. Because U.S. sales would only be a very small fraction of total production, Matej and the production manager decided that only variable costs were relevant. These were about 45 tolars per bottle; however, this number might be 20% higher or lower, as both costs and the cost accounting system were changing very rapidly.

Sonja had also asked about international shipping, which in his enthusiasm had slipped Matej's mind. Upon checking, he not only found that it would cost 200 tolars per case, but that the excise tax levied at U.S. Customs was 40% of the brewer's price. This customs duty would reduce Narodno's $.75 net revenue per bottle (the brewer's price, from the customs point of view) to $.45. Finally, in answer to other questions Sonja had asked, the controller told Matej that Narodno's tax rate was usually around 25%. When Matej asked for the cost of capital, the controller just laughed and suggested that the after-tax long-term commercial lending rate was as good as anything. With volatile interest rates, a brand-new stock exchange, and capital markets heavily influenced by the one-time process of privatization, U.S. cost-of-capital models made little sense for Slovenia at this time. Matej also broached the subject of hedging, which he had heard about from Sonja, but the controllers said that the relatively small sums involved and the thin forward market for the tolar made hedging inappropriate for this project.

TABLE 1

Narodno Pivo d.d.
Slovenia Consumer Price Index - Seasonally Adjusted
(Source: Slovenia Institute for Statistics)

Month	1992	1993	1994	1995
January	69.6	119.6	143.9	169.8
February	77.0	121.3	145.7	171.3
March	85.7	122.4	146.5	171.3
April	91.5	125.1	151.3	173.0
May	97.8	127.4	153.4	174.4
June	104.1	130.9	157.5	177.4
July	108.5	134.7	162.4	
August	111.3	138.9	166.3	
September	113.8	140.6	168.2	
October	114.2	142.1	169.1	
November	116.1	142.3	169.3	
December	117.0	143.8	170.4	

The consumer price index may not be indicative of inflation in the beverage industry. For example, in 1994 consumer price inflation was 18.5%. The increase in the retail price of beverages was 42.2% and the increase in the wholesale price of beverages was 24.7%.

TABLE 2

Narodno Pivo d.d.
Slovenia Long-Term Commercial Bank Interest Rates
(Source: Bank of Slovenia Statistical Information)

Month	1993	1994	1995
January		18.6 (41.3)	17.3 (33.4)
February		18.2 (42.5)	17.2 (35.1)
March		17.6 (36.9)	16.7 (29.7)
April		17.1 (33.8)	15.3 (22.6)
May		17.0 (49.4)	15.4 (22.8)
June		17.1 (32.1)	15.2 (19.5)
July		17.2 (41.2)	
August	19.4 (31.1)	17.2 (33.3)	
September	19.4 (46.6)	17.1 (33.8)	
October	19.4 (45.7)	17.1 (39.5)	
November	19.3 (68.9)	17.0 (48.9)	
December	18.6 (42.9)	16.9 (39.3)	

Interest rates in Slovenia are revalued to compensate for inflation. The numbers in parentheses are the overall nominal rates. The numbers outside the parentheses are the real rates over revaluation. Revaluation is an adjustment using the previous month's inflation rate. The inflation rate used for revaluation is not based upon the seasonally-adjusted consumer price indices in Table 1.

<table>
<tr><td colspan="5" align="center">TABLE 3

Narodno Pivo d.d.
U.S. Consumer Price Index
(Source: U.S. Department of Labor CPI Detailed Report)</td></tr>
<tr><td>Month</td><td>1992</td><td>1993</td><td>1994</td><td>1995</td></tr>
<tr><td>January</td><td>136.0</td><td>140.3</td><td>143.6</td><td>147.8</td></tr>
<tr><td>February</td><td>136.4</td><td>140.7</td><td>144.0</td><td>148.3</td></tr>
<tr><td>March</td><td>137.0</td><td>141.1</td><td>144.4</td><td>148.7</td></tr>
<tr><td>April</td><td>137.3</td><td>141.6</td><td>144.7</td><td>149.3</td></tr>
<tr><td>May</td><td>137.6</td><td>141.9</td><td>144.9</td><td>149.6</td></tr>
<tr><td>June</td><td>138.1</td><td>142.0</td><td>145.4</td><td></td></tr>
<tr><td>July</td><td>138.4</td><td>142.1</td><td>145.8</td><td></td></tr>
<tr><td>August</td><td>138.8</td><td>142.4</td><td>146.5</td><td></td></tr>
<tr><td>September</td><td>139.1</td><td>142.6</td><td>146.6</td><td></td></tr>
<tr><td>October</td><td>139.6</td><td>143.3</td><td>147.0</td><td></td></tr>
<tr><td>November</td><td>139.8</td><td>143.4</td><td>147.3</td><td></td></tr>
<tr><td>December</td><td>139.8</td><td>143.3</td><td>147.2</td><td></td></tr>
</table>

Historical Consumer Price Index for Urban Wage Earners & Clerical Workers (CPI-W): U.S. City Average, all items.

TABLE 4

Narodno Pivo d.d.
U.S. Corporate Bond Rates
(Source: Federal Reserve Bulletin)

Month	1993	1994	1995
January	8.24	7.25	8.71
February	8.01	7.39	8.50
March	7.83	7.78	8.35
April	7.76	8.17	8.25
May	7.78	8.28	7.86
June	7.66	8.27	
July	7.50	8.42	
August	7.19	8.36	
September	6.98	8.60	
October	6.97	8.83	
November	7.26	8.94	
December	7.28	8.73	

Seasoned issues, all industries, Daily figures from Moody's Investors Service. Based on yields to maturity on selected long-term bonds.

TABLE 5

Narodno Pivo d.d.
SIT/USD Exchange Rates
(Source: Bank of Slovenia Statistical Information)

Month	1992	1993	1994	1995
January	58.8696	99.1190	133.8611	125.3941
February	74.4996	101.2868	134.6600	123.1200
March	82.2383	103.8113	132.4118	115.3551
April	83.7294	104.2541	133.7150	112.7375
May	83.4898	108.5463	131.5431	114.7272
June	80.6670	114.2431	129.9219	113.9983
July	76.0238	120.1222	125.2679	
August	77.8032	119.1226	124.7576	
September	82.0542	115.0601	124.3859	
October	85.5644	118.2042	122.5802	
November	94.3542	125.7651	124.5197	
December	96.1504	129.3676	128.0775	

The exchange rates in the table are monthly averages.

TABLE 6

Narodno Pivo d.d.

SIT/USD Forward Exchange Rates
(Source: Blagovno borza Ljubljana)

June 30, 1995	Spot Rate	113.65
	August, 1995	113.53
	September, 1995 113.57	
	December, 1995	115.27
	March, 1996	116.25
	June, 1996	119.30

QUESTIONS

1. The first step in capital budgeting is to specify the incremental cash flows. International capital budgeting is complicated by cash flows in different currencies. Specify all of the dollar (USD) and tolar (SIT) before-tax cash flows for the project for Narodno. At this point, ignore inflation.

2. The next step in capital budgeting is to discount the cash flows at the cost of capital. International capital budgeting offers two methods to do this. One is to discount all cash flows at a rate appropriate to the currency in which the cash flow occurs, and then convert all foreign currency present values to the home currency at the spot exchange rate. Another is to convert all cash flows to the home currency at expected future exchange rates and then discount at the home currency cost of capital. The choice of method depends upon whether discount rates or expected future exchange rates can be estimated more accurately.

    Assume that in this case it is better to estimate future exchange rates. This can be done in four ways using the information in the tables. The first is to use forward rates. The second is to use inflation rates. (The theory of purchasing power parity asserts that exchange rates will move according to relative inflation rates—this is intuitive, as you should expect to receive more of a currency which is losing its purchasing power.) The third is to use interest rates. (The theory of the international Fisher effect asserts that exchange rates will move according to relative interest rates—this is also intuitive, as you should expect to receive a higher interest rate on a currency that is depreciating.) To apply the theories of purchasing power parity or the international Fisher effect, multiply the spot rate by the ratio between U.S. and Slovenian inflation or interest. The fourth way is to project future exchange rates using exchange rate history.

    Obviously, estimating future exchange rates is a matter of judgment. Make your best estimates of the future SIT/USD exchange rate for 1, 2, and 3 years in the future in each of these four ways. Which, if any, do you trust?

3.   Assume that the USD/SIT exchange rate at the beginning of the project will be 114 and for the following three years will be 119, 125, and 131. What is the NPV of the project in SIT?

4.   Compute a best-case and a worst-case NPV. In the best case, sales are 100% higher each year and production costs are 20% lower. In the worst case, sales are 75% lower and production costs are 20% higher.

5.   As you can see from the best-case and worst-case scenarios, the project can look very good or somewhat bad. Of course, capital budgeting does not incorporate any intangible benefits for the company or the country that might be realized through increased visibility and/or knowledge of the U.S. market. How should Matej present the results of the capital budgeting analysis? If he uses the dozens of scenarios that are possible, it will probably overwhelm the board. If he only uses part, should he select the parts which make the project look good or bad? He knows that the board is generally excited about the project and will want it to look good, but should this matter?

Case 47

Commodity Swaps

Valley Quarry Incorporated

Ronald Lamb reflected upon the days when being in charge of finance for a growing corporation was a simpler task. Success was achieved by insuring coordination between the corporate plan and the firm's capital budget. That aspect of financial management was still a critical variable for success. But, that alone was not enough. The modern financial manager had to think in terms of the interrelationship among all of the firm's financial arrangements. That is, the view was toward management of all the components of the firm's financial statements.

It was that understanding and point of view that led to Lamb's consideration of Valley Quarry's advanced sales of its granite production for the coming year. Valley Quarry was founded in 1944 and over the years had been a major supplier of high-quality granite for the building industry and for specialty uses such as monuments and the like. The firm was known throughout the southeastern United States as a high quality producer of granite and marble. The company's customer base, though loyal, had their own best interests at heart. But, shipments could be forecast with a reasonable degree of confidence. While confidence concerning the level of shipments was relatively high, the stability of prices was not. This was due in large part to the ability of some quarries to mine both granite and other rock. As a result the overall supply of granite fluctuated in a less than predictable manner. Lamb wished to hedge against a price decrease that would settle at or below production costs.

Over the last 20 years or so the year-to-year shipments of granite and marble had shown more dramatic swings in demand. This was due, in large part, to a shift in the way buildings, beginning with the culture among architects, were designed and the resulting materials that went into them. The trend was toward a greater usage of synthetic materials. This trend was because of such concerns as weight, interior climate control considerations, and the current styles and designs related to the current trend of town center revitalizations which was the mode in many urban areas.

At present, Lamb was concerned with the relationship between the price received for stone not yet mined and processed and the cost of such mining production. In essence, the firm now sells at a spot price but would like to hedge against any significant drops in that price over the next 12 months. The cost of production is relatively fixed, which permits a reliable gauge of the minimum spot price necessary to make production feasible. The fluctuation in price, therefore, was a legitimate concern.

This situation caused Lamb to contact an acquaintance of his who was an experienced corporate finance executive at a large brokerage house and who had developed a specialty as an intermediary in commodity swaps. Stephanie Daniels had faced this situation before on behalf of her clients. She firmly believed that a hedge against spot price declines could be satisfactorily established for Valley Quarry.

She also believed that Valley Quarry did not need to make such an arrangement through a broker, such as herself. She was happy to offer Lamb advice on the matter, as a friend. Daniels explained that the company could enter into forward contracts with their customers if they preferred that arrangement. That arrangement would differ from a futures contract, for example, which can only be sold on an organized exchange. The choice depended somewhat upon the loyalty of the company's customers.

The basis for the swap, according to Lamb's thinking was the costs involved in production. Valley's cost of producing one ton of stone was $18, therefore it was against that price that the swap had to be arranged. Daniels believed there were at least two ways in which the swap arrangement could be constructed. The swap could be based on a forward contract for block granite or upon a more widely traded and more well known commodity. For example, there was a likely correlation between block granite prices and silica used in the production of glass, a common item in commercial building. In addition, if a major user of block granite could be found who was interested in a swap, the swap could then be better facilitated. As with most swaps as hedging arrangements, there was an element of speculation. This was certainly a part of the motivation for Valley Quarry. Moreover, such commodities were usually traded in the region in which Valley Quarry operated due to the significant presence of the rock mining industry and brokers' familiarity with the commodities and the industry.

Southern Builders, Incorporated wished to hedge the revenue from building contracts for the next 18 months by securing a forward contract for block granite. Finished block granite purchased at the spot price was a major building cost component faced by Southern Builders, Inc. Table 1 provides spot prices for block granite and silica for the past 12 months.

TABLE 1		
Spot Prices		
June 1995		
	*Granite	Silica
June 1994	$26	$30
July	27	31
August	28	31
September	25	31
October	25	30
November	24	28
December	23	28
January 1995	23	27
February	22	26
March	24	25
April	26	26
May	27	28
*Per-ton basis	Mean = $25.00	Mean = $28.42

QUESTIONS

1. Is the commodity swap, based on a one year payment date, as described in the case, a reasonable strategy for Valley Quarry to pursue? Is there a better alternative, if so what is it?

2. What is the cost or risk to Valley Quarry if block granite and silica prices are not perfectly correlated?

3. Discuss the effect upon the relative positions of the two companies if there is a movement, up or down, of the prices of block granite.

4. Assuming the broker uses the average spot price of the two commodities to set the price for each counterparty, what will be the net payment, positive or negative, to each? Due to a recent slowdown of price increases for certain building materials, which occurred since the swap arrangement was finalized the spot price for silica is now less than $30 per ton. Southern Builders had agreed to pay a fixed price of $30 per ton for silica. Valley Quarry will receive $28 per ton for block granite. How much will Valley Quarry pay for granite? How much will Southern Builders receive for silica? How much will it pay for granite?

5. Describe, without calculations, what is taking place in the swap arrangement. A diagram would be useful in this regard.

6. What is the importance of the more widely traded commodity, silica, being considered as the futures contract for Southern Builders, Inc.?

7. In your opinion, are commodity prices likely more volatile than other types of assets that may fit a swap arrangement, such as equities or financial assets? Why or why not?

Case 48

Hedging Interest Rate Risk with Financial Futures

Bay Street Bankcorp

Michael Wang, president of Bay Street Bankcorp, peered anxiously at the thick envelope sitting on his desk from the Federal National Mortgage Association. Michael realized the envelope contained Fannie Mae's response to his request that the agency invest $5 million in the fledgling bank over the next year to expand BSB's highly successful and innovative minority lending program. Taking a deep breath, Michael quickly tore open the envelope and scanned the cover letter. He read no further than the second paragraph to learn that the FNMA had approved his funding request. BSB would become only the seventh bank in the United States to receive equity capital from Fannie Mae; the bank now stood on the verge of an ambitious and innovative expansion plan.

The plan was full of risks. But Michael, and now Fannie Mae, felt it was the right thing to do. Bay Street Bankcorp was chartered in 1991 and opened for business in a large, Southwestern city with a substantial population of Asian, Hispanic, and African-American residents. In a hotly competitive banking market, BSB grew quickly and confidently by offering a unique product mix tailored to the needs of first-generation Asian immigrants. The majority of the bank's common stock was owned by Taiwanese immigrants, and BSB's management team understood its basic business strategy well.

As the bank gained experience in minority lending to small Vietnamese, Chinese, and Taiwanese entrepreneurs, it started to reach out in the community to other minority groups. BSB opened a second office in 1993 in the barrio to serve the needs of the Hispanic community, and now planned a third office in the inner city to gain entry into the African-American community.

Over the course of its brief history, BSB succeeded by doing the little things that the mega-banks in town neglected. The bank's main office manager was an American-born descendant of first-generation Chinese immigrants who was fluent in both Chinese and Vietnamese. The bank's counter literature was always available in four different languages -- English, Spanish, Vietnamese, and Chinese -- to meet the needs of its diverse customer groups. The bank's Hispanic office regularly hired a popular local mariachi band, making customers feel quite comfortable in the bank's brightly colored lobby.

More important, however, BSB understood the financial needs of its minority customers better than any bank in town. The tiny bank aggressively extended business and mortgage credit to newly-arrived immigrants who had virtually no credit references. BSB understood that immigrants lacked credit histories because they had limited access to financial institutions in their home countries -- not because they were poor credit risks. In fact, many first-generation immigrants arrived in the United States with large amounts of cash provided by extended family members and saved over many years abroad. The family nest egg represented a down payment on the American dream for the immigrant family, and the opportunity to gain economic freedom in America.

Unfortunately, the larger, well-established banks in town rejected many business loan applications from immigrant families because there was no established credit history available from these potential borrowers. Adept at understanding immigrant culture, BSB took the time to assess the character of its customers in other ways, and approved many loans its competitors rejected. The bank quickly acquired a reputation among Asian and later Hispanic immigrants, and BSB grew rapidly in the shadows of the big, chrome-and-glass office towers in the central business district.

By 1996, the bank's asset base had reached $150 million, and its penetration of the Asian and Hispanic markets was almost complete. Recognizing that the bank's unique approach in marketing financial services across various minority groups could be extended to the African-American community, the bank proposed the establishment of a third branch office in the inner city. At the same time, BSB developed an aggressive, $30 million lending plan offering long-term, fixed-rate mortgage financing to black-owned business ventures. The plan would be financed by an innovative savings deposit program, attracting immigrants' savings by offering one-year certificates of deposit at 50 basis points above prevailing market rates to qualifying families. BSB sought to raise $25 million from this program over the course of the year, and in combination with the bank's $5 million infusion of equity capital, BSB could fund its $30 million minority loan program over the course of the next year.

The plan looked excellent on paper. BSB was an SBA Preferred Lender, which meant the bank could originate SBA-guaranteed loans without the prior approval of SBA loan officers. The bank was also rated in the "outstanding" category under the Community Reinvestment Act, providing testimony to its exemplary record in minority lending within the local community. Finally, the bank was profitable, posting a respectable profit of $1.25 million against an asset base approaching 150 million.

On the downside, however, BSB was still a young, and very small, financial institution operating in a large and competitive marketplace. The institution was adequately capitalized with sufficient reserves for future credit losses, but Michael Wang understood that a few unexpected charge-offs might destroy the bank -- and the businesses of its customers. Standing on the verge of a 20 percent expansion plan targeted to occur in only a year's time, Michael was clearly nervous. The bank had little room for error if the intended expansion was to succeed. At the same time, the community depended on the bank to provide innovative and flexible loans where other banks simply refused to tread. There must be a way, Michael thought to himself, to contain the plan's risks and give it the best possible chance for success.

Michael realized that an unexpected change in market interest rates, coupled with the proposed commercial mortgage loan program, could destroy the projected profitability of the program. The bank's forecast called for stable interest rates over the next 12 months, and because of the small average size and unique features associated with individual credits to minority borrowers, securitizing the new commercial loans was out of the question. Each loan must be priced correctly for the bank to earn a profit. At the same time, each loan must carry a reasonable cost to give fledgling entrepreneurs the greatest opportunity to succeed.

It was a delicate balancing act, and Michael needed a novel way to tip the scales in BSB's favor. Remembering an article he recently read in the financial press, he began to wonder if the bank might limit its risk exposure by using financial futures contracts. At first, the very thought of buying and selling derivative financial instruments was appalling; after all, derivatives had received so much negative publicity that Michael rejected them out-of-hand for BSB. Now, however, he was forced to rethink his position. The bank desperately needed a tool to contain its interest rate risk. Flipping to the third section in *The Wall Street Journal*, Michael scanned prices of three popular, and widely traded, futures instruments that would be easy for BSB to acquire and understand: the Treasury bond futures contract traded on the Chicago Board of Trade, the Treasury bill future traded on the Chicago Mercantile Exchange, and the

Eurodollar future traded on the Chicago Mercantile Exchange.

Michael decided the time was right for a little research project. Scanning a few weeks of futures prices on the three instruments noted above, he compiled the information shown in Table 1 below. These futures contract price quotes represented contracts with an expiration date one year from the date of each published price. Given the bank's limited experience with hedging risk in the financial futures market, Michael decided to limit his initial hedging activity to this time frame.

The minority lending project would involve three separate components over the course of the coming year. First, BSB would receive $5 million in cash from Fannie Mae to cover the agency's equity investment in the bank. While these funds would eventually be invested in the minority loan program, the bank planned to invest the money temporarily in Treasury bills. Second, the bank would issue $25 million in new certificates of deposit within the next six months. Finally, the bank would originate $30 million in new commercial mortgage loans before the end of the 1996 fiscal year to complete the program.

At the time of his analysis, the spot rate on one-year Treasury securities was 5.10 percent, the spot rate on one-year bank certificates of deposit was 5.04 percent, and the bank's price for fixed rate commercial mortgage loans was 7.21 percent. Michael used these rates in forecasting the profitability of the minority loan program over the course of the 1996 fiscal year, but he realized that BSB faced some sort of risk if market interest rates shifted from their current position. Scanning the numbers shown in Table 1 Michael set out to determine just how these financial futures contracts might limit the bank's exposure to this risk, increasing the minority loan program's chances for success.

TABLE 1				
Selected Interest Rate and Price Data				
	Annualized Yields		**Futures Contract Prices**		
Date	**Bank CDs[1]**	**FNMA Yield[2]**	**Treasury Bonds[3]**	**Treasury Bills[4]**	**Eurodollar Deposits[5]**
July 7	5.28%	7.69%	115-01	94.01	94.60
July 14	5.19	7.54	114-15	94.96	94.53
July 21	5.22	8.00	110-23	94.73	94.28
July 28	5.24	7.96	110-30	94.78	94.32
August 4	5.24	7.98	109-31	94.71	94.24
August 11	5.24	7.97	109-21	94.75	94.26
August 18	5.25	8.07	109-19	94.57	94.07
August 25	5.23	8.03	110-24	94.72	94.22
September 1	5.24	7.82	112-24	94.81	94.28
September 8	5.20	7.67	113-10	94.82	94.27
September 15	5.19	7.60	114-24	94.94	94.40
September 22	5.14	7.74	113-10	94.86	94.29
September 29	5.21	7.82	112-31	94.72	94.17
October 6	5.23	7.64	115-00	94.89	94.24
October 13	5.29	7.65	115-23	94.89	94.23
October 20	5.24	7.58	116-31	94.93	94.35
October 27	5.28	7.62	115-30	94.99	94.37
November 3	5.23	7.48	117-25	95.08	94.47
November 10	5.20	7.53	117-09	95.06	94.44
November 17	5.20	7.52	117-00	95.05	94.57
November 24	5.16	7.58	117-04	95.01	94.61
December 1	5.18	7.37	119-05	95.10	94.68
December 8	5.05	7.37	120-00	95.07	94.65
December 15	5.11	7.29	119-29	95.00	94.58
December 22	5.04	7.30	118-30	95.04	94.62
December 29	5.04	7.21	121-04	95.13	94.66

TABLE 1
(Continued)

Selected Interest Rate and Price Data

Notes

1. Annualized yields on commercial certificates of deposit represent primary new issues of 1-year negotiable CDs at major New York banks on deposits of $100,000 or more.

2. FNMA yields represent posted yields on 30-year mortgage commitments (priced at par) for delivery in 30 days to the Federal National Mortgage Association.

3. Treasury bond futures prices are quoted in 1/32 increments of par. Thus, 115-01 represents a price of 115 and 1/32 percent of par value. Contract yields are standardized using a 15-year, $100,000 par value, 8 percent coupon bond. Each futures contract represents $100,000 in face value securities.

4. Treasury bill futures prices are quoted at a discount from face value in increments of 1/100th of 1 percent. Thus, 94.01 represents a price of 94 and 1/100 percent of face value. Contract yields are standardized using a 1-year, $1 million face value Treasury bill. Similarly, each futures contract represents $1 million in face value securities.

5. Eurodollar futures prices are quoted at a discount from face value in increments of 1/100 of 1 percent. Thus, 94.60 represents a price of 94 and 60/100 percent of face value. Contract yields are standardized using a 1-year, $1 million face value Eurodollar deposit. Similarly, each futures contract represents $1 million in face value Eurodollar deposits.

QUESTIONS

1. Identify the cash market risk exposure facing BSB in each particular phase of the minority lending project.

2. If BSB decides to hedge its market risk exposure in each phase of the minority lending project, what is the appropriate direction of the hedge (i.e., long or short position in the futures market) for each component of the project? How will the hedge position immunize the bank from loss if market interest rates rise or fall?

3. Given the three separate phases of the minority lending project and the information shown in Table 1, what is the best futures contract (i.e., the Treasury bond future, the Treasury bill future, or the Eurodollar future) that BSB should use to hedge interest rate risk related to each phase of the project?

4.   Given the magnitude of BSB's exposure to interest rate risk in the cash market at each phase of the minority lending project, what is the appropriate number of futures contracts the bank should buy or sell in order to immunize its exposure to interest rate risk?

5.   Suppose interest rates increase over the course of the next year, so that one year from today the one-year rate on bank certificates of deposit stands at 5.5 percent, the yield on FNMA securities is 8 percent, and the yield on one-year Treasury bills is 5.6 percent. Given this increase in interest rates, the prices of the financial futures contracts described in Table 1 are:

Treasury bond futures contract	119-24
Treasury bill futures contract	94.63
Eurodollar futures contract	93.05

    Given this interest rate scenario one year from today, what is BSB's net gain or loss on each of the three components of its minority lending program?

6.   Refer once again to your answer to Question 5. Did the bank's immunization strategy depend upon market interest rates rising over the course of the coming year, or is the bank's profit position protected from both increases and decreases in the level of market interest rates? Explain your answer by demonstrating the bank's net gain or loss on each of the three components of its minority lending program, assuming that market interest rates fall over the course of the coming year. In this case, assume that the following interest rates and futures contract prices are observed one year from today, and recalculate BSB's net gain or loss on each component of the minority lending program:

One-year Treasury security spot rate	4.3%
One-year bank certificate of deposit rate	4.0%
FNMA yield	5.5%
Treasury bond futures contract price	124-03
Treasury bill futures contract price	95.93
Eurodollar futures contract price	97.91

7.   The case mentions that BSB seeks to eliminate its exposure to risk by buying and/or selling financial futures contracts. In using these derivative financial securities, does the bank eliminate all of its exposure to risk, or just a portion of the total risk the firm faces? Does the introduction of financial futures within the bank create any additional risks for management to consider? If so, identify and explain these risks.

8.   Examine the hedging strategy you developed for BSB in Questions 2 through 4. Does this particular strategy represent a static or dynamic hedge? Given your answer to this question, comment on the risk that BSB faces in executing this strategy, and describe how the bank's hedging technique might be improved to immunize the bank more effectively against changes in the level of market interest rates.